Caryn Franklin h... for sixteen years. She was fashio... editor of *i-D Magazine*, and researched and presented for a variety of TV fashion programmes including *The Clothes Show*. She is co-chair of the campaign Fashion Targets Breast Cancer, editor of the *Breast Health Handbook*, a committed ambassador for Oxfam as part of their Clothes Code Campaign, and a patron of the Eating Disorders Association. Inspired by her sister's battle with anorexia, she spends time visiting schools and talking about the fashion industry's preoccupation with thinness. She has written about the fashion industry in *Franklin on Fashion*, but this is her first novel. She has one daughter and lives in East London.

'*Woman in the Mirror* is a brilliant book, it describes the real lives beating below the surface of the fashion world, and the struggle all of us face to accept and celebrate ourselves for who we are'

ANITA RODDICK,
Founder of the Body Shop International

'The perfect read. Caryn Franklin is an accomplished storyteller, fusing comical and light-hearted delivery with a serious message'

OLLIE PICTON JONES, *Mirror*

'A warts-and-all account of the fashion industry. All you need to know is here.'

SARAH WALTER, *Marie Claire*

CARYN FRANKLIN

Woman
in the
Mirror

HarperCollins*Publishers*

This novel is entirely a work of fiction. The names, characters and incidents portrayed in it are the work of the author's imagination. Any resemblance to actual persons, living or dead, events or localities is entirely coincidental.

HarperCollins*Publishers*
77–85 Fulham Palace Road,
Hammersmith, London W6 8JB

This paperback edition 1999

1 3 5 7 9 8 6 4 2

Copyright © Caryn Franklin 1999

Caryn Franklin asserts the moral right to
be identified as the author of this work

A catalogue record for this book
is available from the British Library

ISBN 0 00 651110 4

Set in Sabon by
Rowland Phototypesetting Ltd,
Bury St Edmunds, Suffolk

Printed and bound in Great Britain by
Caledonian International Book Manufacturing Ltd, Glasgow

To Mateda – six, going on sixteen

ACKNOWLEDGEMENTS

Woman in the Mirror came about when a previous editor, Belinda Budge at Pandora, asked me to consider a novel. At first I was incredulous – lack of confidence would surely prohibit such a bold move – but the more I thought about the questions I am asked by students in schools and women in shopping malls concerning the fashion industry, the more I considered her suggestion with intent. It is because of Belinda and her encouragement that this novel about women and image has come to be.

Next I turned to my close friend and co-editor Georgina Goodman. Having worked together on two books previously, I wondered what she thought. She responded by offering her research services instantly, and much of the knowledge I have accrued about heroin is thanks to her and her excellent contact Mark Lee – but more about him later.

Rachel Hore and her then editor Lucy Ferguson gave me all the encouragement I needed to begin – and, in the early days of learning, to 'show' not 'tell' as all journalists must. I was grateful for their input and teaching.

My sisters Rayne, Suzanne and Lindsey have been an enormous help. Rayne and Suzanne for acting as early readers, and Lindsey for sharing with me her hellish teens when an eating disorder compromised her health. (My sister's story is not told here.) My brother Howard has remained interested and supportive via e-mail from across the other side of the world, and my parents Pam and Brian – who have always encouraged my endeavours – were there in all the ways that loving parents are.

Designer Helen Storey, now a professor but a friend since college days, generously instructed me in blow-by-blow detail of a designer's timetable. She relayed her own experiences and saw to it that my understanding of her world was as authentic as possible. At this point I would like to explain that I have knowingly accelerated the experiences of some of my characters as the correct time-frame of two months in the run-up to a designer's catwalk show does not allow for the development of an eating disorder or indeed the rapid decline of another character into heroin addiction. For the purposes of the story, however, it was necessary to allow things to run their course.

Mark Lee at Barnardo's has taken time and effort to explain to me the nature of chemical dependency, and as a small thank you I agreed to publish details of the following agencies: the National Drugs Helpline, freephone 0800 77 66 00; Release – for help with legal problems – 0171 729

9904: Turning Point 0171 702 2300; and Narcotics Anonymous 0171 730 0009.

Nicky Bryant, Chief Executive of the Eating Disorders Association, has also given me much needed encouragement and has overseen the information I relay about the culture of an eating disorder. To thank her, and because I know from my experiences as a patron of the E.D.A. that eating disorders and anxieties around body image are on the increase, I am donating a percentage of my royalties to the Eating Disorders Association.

One of the shero's I've yet to mention is Anne O'Brien at HarperCollins, who stoically waded through three drafts, never once allowing irritation to surface when I meditated out loud upon the business of image. Nor did she snort with derision when I got a sudden attack of Enid Blyton syndrome near the end of the book in an earlier draft. This final result, with her help, is something I'm proud of. And at this stage, because book cover designers rarely get mentioned in acknowledgements, and because I trained as a graphic designer myself, I would like to say 'nice one' to Becky Glibbery – the minute I saw it I loved it.

I have two agents: Rosemary Sandberg, my publishing agent, has always been a calm and supportive influence. Her way of ringing at just the right moment with encouraging words is uncanny. Sally Judd, my TV agent, has exhibited patience beyond the call as I have ignored her messages and turned down . . . oh, loads of things – just to get this book done on time. I have, however, made an effort to wash my hair and get dressed now, and Sally, if you're still out there . . .

Personal thanks go to Suzie Macleod, who told me a small and rather beautiful story, which I hope I have done justice to. To my friends – thanks for believing I could do it. And Ian – my monogamous love spar, as we non-marrieds say – I am now prepared to let you off for prioritizing the making of a lengthy and celebrity-packed documentary over being my novel slave, but you won't get away with it next time! And, of course, enormous gratitude is due to Debbie, who keeps my daughter Mateda safe and loved when I am slaving over a hot keyboard.

In closure, I would like to say thank you to each and every one of my modelling friends who have told me their stories over the years, and indeed I send my encouragment and support to those who constantly have to fight a system that defines femininity so rigidly.

Finally, thank you to those whose words head the first page of each chapter. In particular, a big thank you to Alison Lurie, whose seminal book *Language of Clothes* (from which the quote on p265 is taken) is one of my favourite reads. Thank you also to the young women students whose thoughts begin chapters 17 and 20; these were samples taken from anonymous questionnaires.

Grateful acknowledgement is made to Bloomsbury Publishing for lines from *The Language of Clothes* by Alison Lurie.

PROLOGUE

CHARLOTTE looks at herself in the mirror whenever she can. It's not simply a question of checking her appearance. She thinks she might find something. What, she doesn't know, but she has a feeling that if she can catch herself off-guard as she moves from one room to another she might make some sort of discovery.

There are mirrors in every room. Some merely allow for a head-and-shoulders kind of moment, framing her like a hairdresser's press shot, others, like the one in the hall outside her bedroom, are a walk-in wardrobe experience. A head-to-toe confrontation. This is the mirror she uses most.

She has developed a mirror procedure over the years –

well, who hasn't? – and after garnishing herself with various clothing favourites, begins a strict set of manoeuvres. Hands on hips ... two ... three, and down ... two ... three, profile left ... two ... three, profile right, and turn ... two ... three; then rework the whole routine from the side, and follow with freestyle fussing and preening. This usually involves repeated smoothing down of skirt, jeans or hair, and much locating of imaginary dust specks. After the essential brushing and flicking gestures, there is the final composure-regained position, hold ... two ... three and finish.

Any new item of clothing requires fresh choreography and considerably more time in front of the glass doorway. She never tries things on in the shop. Changing-room mirrors are rarely big enough in cupboard-sized cubicles, and when they are – great walls of reflective heaven, like the ones that span the back of trendy shops – others can watch. This is fundamentally inhibitive, not because the watchers intrude upon her performance with their casual interest, but because she cannot watch for them watching her and concentrate on herself at the same time. Back home, the private presentation can begin.

Other times Charlotte uses her mirror to mark time. This is me today; tomorrow, I will be different. Lately she has found herself staring into the glass without reason. Sometimes, trance-like, she will lock eyes with the woman on the other side and stay that way until her opponent seems to give in and move, disturbing the silent communication. She has taken up position and tried many times to encourage the person before her to respond. Like a statue measuring time, she waits patiently. The woman in the other world will not speak.

1

'everything in your closet should have an
expiration date on it, the way that milk and bread
and magazines do.' ANDY WARHOL

'MADDY, can you get a fan in here, I can't cope
with this heat.' Elle Cartwrite – or 'The Crow' as she was
affectionately called, though certainly not to her face –
had had her feathers ruffled. Italy had been on the phone,
warning of a possible delay. 'God, I can't believe it!'
she tutted, thumping a leather-bound book down on her
desk. 'Why can't anything arrive when it's supposed to?'
Timing during the run-up to any catwalk show was crucial;
and with Fashion Week less than two months away, there
was a tightrope of time-management to be trodden. Con-
currently, Elle must oversee delivery of last season's
autumn collection, completion of the samples for next
spring, and – as if that wasn't enough – preparation for

the following season had to be got under way. If fabric delivery didn't happen on the nail, it threw everything else out.

'Maddy,' chivvied Elle, more urgently now, her voice taking on a shrill squawk and carrying out of her glass-partitioned office and into the large open-plan studio beyond, 'I'm burning up in here. And call Lucy again, will you –' she was beginning to lose patience – 'we must have a meeting this week. Tell her I'm not interested in postnatal fallout, just PR.' Elle glared at her assistant. There was no time to waste, but Maddy was moving in slow motion. Elle was on a roll. 'I also want a list of all outstanding payments for last season. If that nasty little store in Bath – or is it Bristol? – hasn't paid for spring stock yet, she's off the book and Harold can send something legal through the post.

'And, Maddy,' she added testily, 'don't let anything go without a spot check. Ask Alicia to open a few boxes this time.'

Elle Cartwrite had been in the clothing business for long enough to avoid elementary mistakes and merchandise needed to be checked before being sent on its way. On a crowded wall space between fabric swatches and line drawings of figures, Elle displayed her favourite Bette Davis quote for all to see: 'If you want something done well, get a couple of old broads to do it.'

At fifty-seven, Elle liked to think of herself as an old broad and did not, as was the norm in her industry, pretend to be younger. She'd had it with all those tight, pinching clothes of her youth and celebrated the chance to appear streamlined, pared down and elegant. She wore Esteem – her own label – and plumped for black and navy trouser suits, occasionally ringing the changes with a little some-

4

thing by the German minimalist Jil Sander. She accessorized sparingly. Definitely no flashy jewellery, fussy shoes, or nasty menopausal scarves. Too many women her age piled it all on and ended up looking like a Christmas tree with flashing lights.

'What you see is what you get,' Elle was fond of saying. 'I look like a hatchet-faced virago because I am one!'

This was not true. For a woman in her autumn years, Elle was striking. But there was a strictness in her dress which appeared to border on a pathological fear of frivolity. On first impression, she let presentation speak for itself; like a treacherous governess stalking a candlelit hallway in swishing skirts and starched collar and cuffs, she could effortlessly traumatize a work-experience student. Even the simple act of setting her handbag down on the desk of a minion would send waves of panic throughout the junior end of the office. It was a favourite move – but, like all strategists, Elle Cartwrite was careful not to over use it.

Those who knew her better interpreted her dress sense as a natural reaction to a traditional fifties upbringing. Little Elsa Crabtree – Elle renamed herself in 1975 upon the launch of Esteem – had refused to emulate her mother bogged down by six children, housework and a husband, and made a commitment to herself. She was where she was now because of a sensible refusal to pour herself into somebody else's life. It seemed to her no coincidence that married women had a shorter life span than single women, and, more tellingly, that married men lived longer than bachelors.

Age had softened the flesh around Elle's angular cheekbones and jaw, but not her resolve. Life was to be lived without masculine interference at all times; as far as was possible, she surrounded herself with women. Over the

5

years generations of wide-eyed students had filed through her studio. Some managed only a few months, but those who survived her fiery outbursts and keen eye for perfection had learned their trade well, eventually leaving to become respected designers in their own right. It pleased Elle that out of fifty top British design names due to show this September, three had begun life in her pattern-cutting department. Then there were others – Elle let out a sigh – who had sabotaged their talents. Babies were such a waste of a good woman.

One of the two phones on her neat desk trilled. 'It's Yvonne from Advantage,' explained Maddy in her transatlantic drawl. As Elle's personal assistant it was her job to take all the calls and block 75 per cent of them. 'She's wondering why you haven't asked for any of her girls to attend the casting tomorrow.'

'Because the agency is crap, Maddy,' snapped Elle. 'Could you get her off the line and come in here?'

'But, Elle, I can't tell her that. What about Soraya? She's in *Harper's* this week.' Maddy spoke as though she was recommending a friend, but that was fashion folk for you. Everyone appeared to be on intimate terms. Co-workers insisted on addressing each other as 'Angel'. Models kept it deliberately simple with cute call-me-soon appellations. Names like Tawny, Tilly and Twinkie were employed by sophisticated women without the slightest trace of humour. Designers had no say in the matter: it was 'Betty', 'Katharine', 'Vivienne' – because everyone who was anyone on Planet Fashion was required to know the Mesdames Jackson, Hamnett and Westwood personally.

'Check out the coverage, Maddy,' said Elle dismissively, flicking through a pile of magazines in front of her. 'She's in readers' offers, for God's sake! I'm only looking at top agencies for this job. Tell Yvonne I'm not working with her again. The last batch of models she sent were dogs. Then come into my office, I need to talk to you.'

Normally Madeline Montgomery would have handled any kind of unsolicited call with a devastatingly polite brush-off, but these days Elle's unutterably cool assistant was in a hot sweat over most things. 'Betrothal doesn't suit everyone,' muttered Elle as she reached for a tissue to wipe the perspiration from the back of her neck. Oh, the frustration of having to stand by helplessly as her number one right-hand woman metamorphosed from Executive-Ice-Maiden to Pink-and-Fluffy-Girl before her very eyes. And in August, which was always such a stressful month. Summer might be in full swing, but those in the fashion world lived in the future. Next season's autumn/winter orders were lined up downstairs, ready to be freighted to Japan, Europe and North America. And with London Fashion Week round the corner, next year's spring/summer collection needed launching.

Elle watched the flaxen-haired woman flirting outrageously down the line, and knew she'd lost her office wife to another. 'Maddy!' she bellowed.

'I've got to go, Tom,' said Maddy hastily to her fiancé, turning to wave in the direction of the angry noise. 'I'll call you back later.' She replaced the phone lovingly in its cradle and in one balletic motion arrived, with portable fan in hand, at the door of her employer's office. 'The casting will start at 2 p.m. tomorrow,' she said crisply, watching Elle for telltale signs of an impending demerit mark. 'Everything is under control. Trena has called most of these in – have a look,' she instructed, handing over an assortment of black-and-white A5 photographs.

Elle had come to trust Trena's instincts. Her no-nonsense

approach had won her the respect of many within the industry. Still a long way from thirty, Trena Golding was reckoned to be one of the best show producers in the business. Perhaps her penchant for other women had helped refine an already erudite understanding of the women's ready-to-wear market; this, added to a wicked sense of humour, ensured that her diary would always be bulging with work. Unusually, she had expanded her role within Elle's business over the years, prioritizing the smooth running of Esteem over the work of other clients. It was customary to leave it much later before casting for the catwalk show, but this season, with the Esteem label no longer doing as well as it once had, urgent change was needed. Elle was gambling all of her profits on a risky re-entry into the marketplace with an expensive make-or-break advertising campaign and a top model needed to be found.

But how can one woman say everything about Esteem? worried Elle as she thumbed anxiously through the photographic sheets now vying for her attention. Some contained one large head-and-shoulders shot, while others offered a variety of poses and locations. Each sheet bore a shopping list of vital statistics including hair and eye colour. A crowd of pleasing and ready-to-please faces filled her view. It was like trying to pick a lottery number.

'I need more time,' she said, throwing the pile on the desk and running her hands through her hair. 'After twenty-five years in the business I'm not going to risk it all by rushing into a decision I might regret. The yen might be weak, and Japanese customers are editing their expenditure, but I'm not going to panic.' Elle smoothed the jacket of her suit. Satisfied that calm had been restored, she spoke carefully: 'The model that I choose to be the face of Esteem has got to be right.'

'You don't have to choose now,' soothed Maddy, leaping at the chance to recover some points. 'You can meet all the models in person tomorrow . . . you know, watch them move. And Trena will be there with Alicia and Petra.'

Ah yes, thought Elle, feeling the tension disappear momentarily. As a top photographer, Petra Mayhew worked with models every day and her eye would be invaluable. She was one of the few women photographers to be working in the higher echelons of image manufacture and had acquired a reputation for feisty, sparky, reportage-style images. Petra liked her women to party all night and then pull on a few designer togs for an impromptu shoot. She and Elle had met in the early days and Elle had put some work her way when no one else was interested. Until recently, Petra had mostly worked for British publications, but then came a bit of a career breakthrough. She had taken the models, the hairdresser, and the stylist and make-up artist clubbing, and completed the shoot at the end of the night – or morning, to be precise. At about 3 a.m., in crumpled splendour, the mannequins mooched in padded coves with practised ease. Hair and make-up perfect, clothes not so. The magazine had printed the story over six pages and sniffed loudly at the bill for expenses, which included a large amount of specialist dry-cleaning.

That might have ended her association with that particular colour supplement, but shortly after publication Petra had been summoned by an American clothing giant to inject a little designer sleaze into his forthcoming campaign. Then, after a few shoots for American *Vogue* – the big one for all those who work in pictures – the phone began to ring with confirmation of her newly acquired celebrity status.

The reputation of Petra Mayhew ensured that top make-up and hair people would be happy to collaborate on the Esteem campaign. Well-known models and stylists would also relish the chance to work on such a shoot and from the outside the results would look like a quality job from head to toe. Elle couldn't have afforded Petra and her entourage, but no one else would know that.

'What I mean, Maddy,' snapped the Crow, 'is that I need a couple of weeks to get this one right. I'm sick of having to sandwich creative decisions between meetings with accountants, bank managers and agents. I've had more discussions about dodgy pro forma payments and shipping agreements this month than anything else. I didn't sign up for accountancy with just a little dress design, for God's sake.' Elle began to re-tidy things into piles on her desk as if to control the chaos that hovered close by. 'Do you know,' she burst, getting up to stalk the room like a caged animal, 'I can't think of the last time I spent the day quietly drawing, uninterrupted. Or, even stranger, looking for a little inspiration . . . you know, feeding the soul.'

'Ah, creative juices,' quipped Alicia as she popped her head round the door. 'Loaded with calories, surely!'

'Oh, good,' said Elle gesturing for Alicia to enter whilst reaching for a bottle of water on the filing cabinet. It was empty. 'Maddy –' she waved the bottle and then binned it – 'would you be a love? I'm parched.'

As Maddy floated out of the room, lean limbs and long blonde hair in tow, Elle turned to her design assistant. 'Now, Lissy,' she said in market-research mode, 'these women all look the same to me. Tell me who you like.'

Alicia jumped at the chance to insert herself between the designer and her secretary. Maddy had a strong bond with Elle, she had already served three years with the company before Alicia joined. But the Crow had been immediately impressed with her new recruit. Alicia Fraser had completed work experience with the likes of Moschino and Valentino, and seemed to display a compelling confidence. She was also more classically inclined than the average starry-eyed art school graduate, with strong pattern-cutting and drawing skills. Added to that, this college leaver could answer the phone and make good coffee like ordinary human beings!

The coffee queen sifted through the pile of pictures and set to work with customary self-assurance. With a faint trace of a Scottish accent she pronounced judgement. 'Hate her, love her, she's dull, she's too strong. She's gorgeous ... too gorgeous, though.' Elle sat back and watched. Alicia was so very different from Maddy. Brown straight hair. Big blue eyes and a stunningly curvaceous body. She was a beauty, all right, but no one would photograph her lavish curves for a magazine cover. This was a world where hips were exclusively infinitesimal and linear frontage *de rigueur*. Sadly, Alicia herself was always trying to trim off a few pounds. But then, who could blame her, surrounded as she was by images of obsessively svelte mannequins twenty-four hours a day.

Elle pushed her reading glasses up her nose and snatched a card from the desk. 'She's got something – what do you think?'

'Nah, too tarty,' pronounced Alicia. She perched on the arm of a chair and continued her search.

Elle sucked on the frames of her designer specs. Alicia really did have the most glorious thighs. And Esteem was in the business of making clothes for women ... women like Alicia, with delicious bodies. Or Kirsty, Esteem's receptionist: she had the lushest cleavage on the block and at five foot nothing would pass for a miniature Brigitte Bardot. Then there was Maddy: tall, tanned, athletic. Women

11

were individuals and Esteem needed to reflect that. Suddenly Elle knew what was needed. Watching Alicia had given her sweet inspiration . . . at last.

'One won't be enough,' she said excitedly, leaping from her chair and liberating a model called Clementine from the pile on the desk. She propped her up against a column of books. 'One won't say everything. I want women to see themselves – there has to be more than one. Two or three maybe.' She selected two friends for Clementine and arranged them either side of the cardboard lovely. 'I don't want big names or big personalities, and definitely no big egos.' Elle stepped back to survey her choices. 'I want women,' she continued with more certainty, 'who look like their lights are on. I want some savvy, some nous.' It was becoming clearer to Elle by the second. 'There'll be no dim-witted pretties pouting their pants off round here.'

'Three models means three times the price,' said Alicia, selecting a well-known model and scanning her credentials. 'We're talking serious handbag here. Are you sure we can afford it?'

Elle grunted dismissively. 'My mind is made up,' she said, resolving to speak to Harold. She would do whatever was needed to get her accountant's backing on this one.

For the umpteenth time that day, the phone rang.

'Elle, it's a journalist from the *Post* about the latest bomb threat from Global Defence,' said Maddy. 'He's collecting quotes from designers and wants to know if you're scared.'

'Maddy, I'm right in the middle of something now,' squawked Elle. She watched Alicia seize upon a card featuring a woman with a skeletal frame. 'Medical emergency,' mouthed her assistant gravely before tossing the lifeless invalid into the bin. Elle nodded. 'I can't talk. Get him to ring back later. Oh, on second thoughts, tell him to ring the British Fashion Council for something official. We've all left statements with them. And then tell him that London Fashion Week will still go ahead, as far as I'm concerned. I'm not giving in. I've got a business to run and wages to pay, not to mention a new campaign to launch.' Elle replaced the receiver triumphantly and turned to survey the outside world. From her window she studied the sticky city scene below. Esteem was not a major-league player and therefore unlikely to be a target, but everyone was on edge. And the papers for their part were enjoying the chance to sensationalize the fashion industry once again.

It had all started in the early spring. At first there had been no clue as to who was behind the bombing of offices and factories owned by a well-known and highly influential German fabric manufacturer. No one had been hurt in the blasts, but top designers around the world had experienced shock waves as fabric stocks and orders were destroyed in the flames. Then Parisian shopping hot spots Faubourg St Honoré and Avenue Montaigne had also had bomb scares. There followed a graffiti campaign – billboards in New York were daubed with the words 'FASHION STINKS'. At first none of the popular newspapers in Britain displayed any interest. Fashion to them was a scantily clad nymphet and a write-up about her boyfriend. But all that changed dramatically when a celebrated British designer with a gilded establishment in New Bond Street became the latest victim as fire gutted the premises. The tabloids proclaimed the scoop of the week and there was frenzied speculation as to who would be next. As the metropolis dozed in sleepy urban heat, the fashion world waited uneasily.

'Alicia,' urged Elle conspiratorially. Her assistant looked

13

up. She had amassed a large pile of rejects and held half a dozen hopefuls in her hand. 'I know this sounds silly, but keep your eyes open.' She lowered her voice. 'You know, what with this Global Defence mob on the warpath, we can't afford to be careless.' Elle looked out into the open-plan studio and watched her staff pottering away. 'I want everyone to walk out of this building with body parts intact at the end of the day,' she said, then muttered under her breath, 'even if they are a bunch of slackers.' She looked at Alicia seriously. 'Tell Kirsty to be careful who she lets into the building. I want her to keep an eye out for strange parcels – strange anything.'

'OK,' said Alicia, smiling. She placed the remaining contenders in front of her employer and turned to leave the room. 'I'll tell her to get an angle on strange.'

'Don't joke, Lissy. I'm serious,' scolded Elle as the screams of police sirens filled the room from the street below. Elle craned her neck to watch as cars and vans mounted pavements. The roads were choked with traffic and the noise was deafening.

'I need a holiday,' she told herself as she cleared a space on her desk. 'But,' the Crow raised her voice slightly, 'I've got staff a-plenty who are vacationing for England just now.' She picked up the photo of Clementine. 'To add injury to insult,' she complained to the sultry brunette, 'the whole country has also elected the month of August as a good time to slack off. And it's my busiest time.'

From her vantage point, Elle could see the studio notice board packed with brightly coloured postcards bearing exotic postage stamps – a reminder of a national tendency to find a faraway place and send home regular bulletins about weather and sunstroke progress.

'And is it my imagination,' quizzed the fashion designer

14

as she half-heartedly flicked through a glossy magazine while the paper woman listened patiently, 'or does travel take twice as long in a city that is supposedly empty? Have public transportation systems shut down entirely?' Elle looked at Clementine and raised an eyebrow, then returned to her journal. 'Or are the excessively casual arrival times' – she thumbed a few more pages – 'employed by the remainder of my staff, an indication of a work force in need of a bollocking?'

The Crow came to a halt, her eyes narrowing hawk-like as she scrutinized the colour spread in front of her. Leafing through subsequent and previous pages she searched for something in particular. And did not find it. 'Maddy,' bellowed Elle as she reached the door that separated employer from employees, 'get that damn PR on the phone – now.'

Maddy looked to her for an explanation before obeying.

Elle Cartwrite strode out into the studio, bearing down on her assistant with the magazine in her hand. 'I can't believe it! That stupid woman has two sets of samples in her office, yet do I see any of the midnight blue silk georgette dresses in this story?' She shook the offending publication under her assistant's nose, daring her to answer the obvious. 'And last month,' she said, gathering speed, 'I saw two beach stories and neither of those *fashion directors*' – she spat the words through gritted teeth: fashion directors were the same animal as fashion editors, only on a higher wage – 'had taken our swimwear. Nicole Farhi had three whole pages to herself. What the hell do I pay a press officer for?

'Mad, she's having a meeting with me,' instructed Elle as she raced back to her desk to collect her bag, 'whether she likes it or not. Get her on the phone and tell her I'm on my way now.'

'Elle, wait!' implored Maddy, launching herself towards her employer. 'You know you'll say something you'll regret. It's only been five weeks since she gave birth and . . . well, things are probably a bit difficult. You had great coverage on last season's range. Let me ring her in the morning and speak to her. It's not worth upsetting her . . .'

'I'm not going to upset her, but I am going to put a rocket up her arse,' barked the battle-axe to a now silent studio. 'So she's had a baby – does that mean I've got to have sleepless nights? Those sarongs and one-piece swim-suits were hot and they were *supposed*,' Elle emphasized the word, aware that she now had an audience, 'to go to the Caribbean with a top photographer and a few nubile super beauties. They were *supposed* to appear in a top magazine with prices and stockists helpfully written in the credits. Then, customers are *supposed* to make a day trip to Harvey Nicks and, before a visit to the food hall for some overpriced pasta, they will try on and buy one of my pieces. Then I'm *supposed* to pay all of your wages' – she made a sweeping gesture, taking in the entire room – 'while we work out how to finish the production on what they'll be wearing when it gets colder. Is that the way it's supposed to fucking well work, or have I got it wrong?'

Elle, having concluded matters verbal, observed her trusty sidekick sharpening a lead pencil. This was a move Maddy always carried out when upset or under pressure. Perhaps it helped her to brandish a deadly point. Perhaps she was thinking about stabbing Elle with it right now.

'Maddy, I'm sorry,' said Elle. What a cow she could be at times. 'I'm feeling the tension, what with the new cam-paign and this heat. Look, it's five o'clock, why don't you have an early finish? I won't speak to Lucy until tomorrow – you're right, of course.' Hopefully that would do it. Maddy smiled thinly and Elle turned and bolted for her desk.

God, what a summer this was turning out to be. Hose-pipe bans since late June. Grass everywhere scorched and scratchy. Parched flowerbeds and wilting petunias, open-air swimming pools dry as a bone, broken down air-cooling systems, sticky melting ice-lollies attached to hot and flustered children. And as if the smoky and grime-ridden roads, clogged with quick-tempered motorists and sweaty leather-clad bikers, didn't make life out there dangerous enough, now there was a bunch of loony frock-objectors waiting for the chance to add a bit more spice to the mix.

She noticed Clementine on the floor, having been blown from the desk by the draught from the fan. From her new post, the sultry maiden stared straight into the designer's eyes.

'Ah, yes, Clementine,' said Elle brightening. 'Dear Clementine. Let's see now.' She bent down and scooped up the lonesome lovely. 'What I need,' confided the designer, walking over to the window, 'is the campaign of the century, and for that I need three women. Yes –' she placed the paper woman gently on the table – 'three women with amazing personalities, laughter in their eyes, hope in their hearts and excellent dentistry. The problem I have,' she explained, 'is finding them tomorrow.'

As if hoping for some guidance, Elle looked hard at Clementine's perfect face. The exquisite beauty pouted some more.

'No one said fashion was easy,' she seemed to say.

2

'time is a dressmaker, specializing in alterations.'
FAITH BALDWIN

CHARLOTTE could not sleep. 'I'm no good at it,' she moaned. 'What is it about sleep that is so unnaturally hard? Is there some kind of method I've yet to learn? And why,' she demanded, turning to Rick, 'is it that some people can be asleep instantly – the minute, in fact, that their head hits the pillow?' After the silence she added resentfully, 'And why don't they go out with their own kind?'

Rick snored rhythmically; blissfully unaware of the life Charlotte lived beside him each night. She knew him so well when he was sleeping. With his breathing calm and slow, eyes and mouth very slightly open, he rested flat on his back for the first half hour or so and then after turning to face the wall he would take one large breath and sink into deep sleep. Sometimes, just before the business of

19

settling with his face slightly puffy and his hair unattractively dishevelled, he would lift his head for a fleeting glance at his surroundings. Catching sight of her, he would return to his world, satisfied that everything was as it should be. In the early days, she had found it all rather sweet, but now it only added to her sense of isolation. His body was next to her, they were together, but he was gone, having left the room and quite possibly the physical world for an astral party that didn't include her.

'It's all right for you,' she said to the corpse by her side. 'I hate the night before a casting.'

'You should have some weed,' Rick had said earlier as he rolled his second joint of the evening before he himself had sunk into a carefree stupor, fully clothed. 'You'll conk out in no time, trust me.'

Charlotte didn't like the hangover she got the next morning and she didn't like weed either. It gave her the munchies, and any unscheduled snacking was to be avoided at all costs. An early night would have been the best thing all round, but it wasn't to be.

'Twelve years I've been in this game,' she said out loud as she got off the bed and walked up to the bedroom mirror. Rick wouldn't be woken by a brass band. 'And the night before a casting still feels awful. But this is the last time. If I don't get the job then that's it. I'm calling it a day.'

She examined the face in the mirror, illuminated by the glow from the television, and beheld a small, straight nose cushioned by well-defined cheekbones, full lips and strong white teeth. The green-eyed beauty shook her raven hair restlessly and watched as it fell about her shoulders.

'Models are called "girls" –' Sally Murphy paced the bleached wood offices of Everywoman Modelling Agency, attempting to rationalize an industry that did not care for women – 'it's not just some patronizing term that everyone has agreed to use, it's the truth about this world. Beautiful women can only work as long as they agree to be girls, or girls dressing up as women. Femininity is prized only if it conforms to certain criteria – and getting old is a sackable offence. It's not right that all the fantastic models I've had on my books have been written off at twenty-six. Written off, for God's sake!' This agent was indignant. 'At a time when they're beginning to look interesting. Clients – I can't stand them. They don't know what they want, so they employ some nasty little ad-agency oik in a Helmut Lang suit to tell them. They're all out there,' Sally ranted, wildly gesticulating in the direction of Sloane Street, 'on a mission to wallpaper the world in teenagers with pert breasts.'

Charlotte had been at the top once. She had in fact enjoyed considerable success, but now it was over. At twenty-nine there were few photographic offers coming her way. Maybe she could eke out another year on the catwalk – it was a kinder environment for older mannequins; the cameras weren't so close or the resulting prints so large.

'Look, I've got to meet a client for lunch,' Sally had apologized, getting up to leave, 'but it's a casual arrangement. Come with me.'

Charlotte declined. Deep in thought, she left the building with her agent. Modelling was all she had known. She had seen models re-invent themselves by losing weight. Trimming off half a stone would not be hard; she was used to watching what she ate. And maybe, just maybe, it would buy her some extra time.

As they kissed and said goodbye, Sally was unaware of the fresh challenge one of her older models had set for herself that day.

In her bedroom, Charlotte stood watching the tiny lines on her face as she moved her mouth. 'It wasn't so difficult,' she said with satisfaction to the woman in front of her. 'All it took was a little self-control. And in this business you've got to have plenty.' She jabbed at her head in pursuit of a single grey hair. 'Gross.'

A life-long devotion to restrictive eating practices had served her well and Charlotte experienced a noble pleasure when exercising such saintly control. In this industry your only worth was measured in centimetres. IQs could be large but bodily dimensions must remain small.

In the loft there were boxes of old magazine spreads featuring a green-eyed beauty. If all the glossy images were laid side to side, it would be hard for the casual observer to pinpoint tangible changes. Charlotte, on the other hand, could see everything. Each fresh picture, colour transparency or tear sheet would provide yet another chance for examination. Her eyes would dance from hips, stomach and thighs to upper arms, lips and cheekbones, as she searched the flawless exterior of the woman in the glossy facsimile.

Scrutiny would eventually pay off. There was always something. A blouse tucked into a skirt, bagged inconspicuously at the waistband. A tiny, carefree disruption to line, but enough to distort the silhouette. Satisfied then that the lumpen gargoyle in the photograph was indeed her, Charlotte could yield to a familiar and reassuring disgust, banishing the sheet to her collection at the top of the house.

'Perfection is what counts in this business,' explained Charlotte to her reflection. 'And to survive you have to have very high standards.'

As usual, the woman in the mirror said nothing. The woman in the mirror was not her but someone Charlotte had grown up with. Every time Charlotte came to the mirror she was there . . . watching. Charlotte spoke to her most days. When she stood in front of the mirror, she would pull and poke at her flesh or home in on a minute blemish. Must do better, she would say, and the woman in the mirror would silently agree.

In the kitchen the kettle steamed. Gently Charlotte unwound the string and label from the dainty bag of dried flowers. She poured hot water into a white mug and inhaled the camomile fragrance. She had learned to drink herbal teas without honey, but a cigarette would stave off hunger pangs.

'Have you seen them?' Charlotte quizzed the dark-haired woman to her left. 'Ah, here they are. Typical – only two left.' Rick had helpfully disposed of at least three before turning in. She lit one and watched the blue smoke rise. 'He always makes a fuss about these air fags,' she said, blowing out the smoke loudly. 'He thinks smoking is all about being man enough to take in lungfuls of nicotine and other cancerous tars.' After a few exaggerated draws on her brand Rick would crush them into the floor or ashtray with contempt. He still smoked them, though.

'I know acting is an option,' said Charlotte, reviewing the situation with her glassy companion, who now watched her from a neat plastic frame on the fridge. 'Rick has been saying I should do it for ages. I haven't told him that I can't. I mean, it's a different thing entirely, isn't it? More competition, more rejection – apart from unflattering camera angles and no beauty lighting.' Charlotte laughed emptily. 'I'd be a total failure.'

But the pressure was on to maintain the lifestyle she and Rick had come to know. They'd had it all in the early days. He, the dashing entrepreneurial type, and she a top model. They were perfectly matched, he'd said so the day they met at the opening of a bar in Soho. She had already spotted the tall, broad-shouldered and handsome stranger with an Elvis Presley hairline and was prepared to overlook any cheesy overtures for the sake of progress.

She had said yes immediately and by the time he dropped her home at 3 a.m. Charlotte had seen no need to disguise her approval. Rick, for his part, had been unable to conceal his delight at her postal district, or indeed her location right by Battersea Bridge, and anyone watching the young lovers would have noticed him appreciatively checking over the outside of her quarters with undisguised satisfaction.

He had moved in shortly after, and for a year or so it was bliss. Then Rick received a letter from the Customs and Excise demanding to know why VAT hadn't been paid on technical equipment he and his partner had acquired for the studio. They'd made the mistake of putting a large amount of knock-off gear through the books and a full-blown investigation revealed that they now owed a considerable amount of money to Her Majesty's Treasury for a series of twilight transactions and undeclared jobs.

Rick had taken a blow, and not only because of the slightly humiliating business blunder: shortly after, his partner pulled out, leaving him with all the debts. If he wanted to carry on he had to make provision for repayment. An agreement was struck between parties and, as long as regular amounts were posted, the bailiffs agreed to hang fire.

Rick had been aggrieved ever since. As an art director of a production company, he had once been a name to watch. Cocky and charming, he knew how to seduce a client into letting him hire the best people to work with. It had been all too easy to blame past accountancy discrepancies for the bad patch he seemed to be stuck in now, and Rick would do so regularly, then he would pressure Charlotte to help him.

'If you say you won't work with anyone else,' he'd plead, 'then they have to use me. Stop trying to be so perfect and rock the boat a little. Are you scared that no one will like you if you pipe up?' Charlotte hated seeing the desperation on his face. 'I need your help here,' he would whine. 'I can make better results than half those arseholes out there.'

This went on until Rick grasped the fact that he wasn't going to get an introduction through Charlotte. That hadn't stopped him from coming to pick her up at the studio to squeeze a few of her contacts. Once in the door he would be Mr Advertising himself, talking to the client, the camera operator; ignoring her in favour of the art director or set designer.

'Who was that eighties reject?' asked one photographer when he next saw Charlotte. She resolved then and there never again to tell Rick about studio days and to lie about the wrap time.

Gradually Charlotte's high-profile advertising jobs dried up, and with them went the invites to film premieres, parties, shop launches and art exhibitions. Rick wasn't happy.

'Did you get invited to the opening of the new Conran

restaurant?' he had asked that morning during a rare appearance before midday. 'Only, I know some people who are going, and I should be there, Charts. Can't you get that agent of yours to get her finger out and do the job she's supposed to do here?'

Charlotte was beginning to feel the strain keenly. Rick didn't pay any rent or bills as it was, and – strangely for someone who was not fully employed – he managed to be out of the house for long hours. Never did she come home to pasta on the stove, or a pile of washing ironed.

'Rick, I don't know –'

'Look,' he had cut in, 'I've been thinking: your agent is beginning to take you for granted, babe. You gotta strike while the iron's hot. You can't sit around. There are new girls out there, and they're taking over your turf. You gotta move on to the next big thing. What about television presenting? You've got the looks and you'd be sensational in a bikini on the front cover of a men's magazine. They're all doing it now.'

'It doesn't appeal, Rick. Really, I . . .'

'Don't dismiss it, Charts,' he said crossly. 'What, had a hard life? Too taxing, is it? All you've ever had to do is look gorgeous, and you got given that in your Christmas stocking. You don't appreciate what you've got; you can't throw it away and say, "Actually, I'd like to balloon out now and make bread." Jeez, if I had your chances, I'd be out there hustling. Nobody gave me anything; I gotta make it all happen from nothing. How do you think that feels? You've got to get off your arse, Charlotte,' he had shouted spitefully as he stormed out of the house.

It was midnight now and Charlotte was still hurt. She had been working on herself for weeks, only Rick hadn't been around to notice it. She'd drunk enough mineral water to fill a swimming pool, and her skin, flushed of all impurities, gleamed like porcelain. She had watched her body each day and revelled in its ability to diminish. This was the only part of her life that Charlotte felt able to control. Fortunately, she was well aware of the tricks a fleshy torso could play on its owner and paid no heed to cries of protest from her stomach.

'Yes,' said Charlotte as she stubbed out her last cigarette and switched off the kitchen light, 'an advertising campaign with a British designer would be a quality piece of work to have in my book.'

Anyway, she'd set herself more than one challenge on the day she left her agent's office. She had fulfilled one of her goals and dropped eight pounds. Tomorrow, if she did not get this job, she would fulfil the other and jack it in.

What to do in a world without airy studios and cat-walks? She'd think about that tomorrow.

Charlotte felt a growling in the pit of her stomach and walked out into the hall to find her favourite place. For now at least, she'd refer all questions to the mirror.

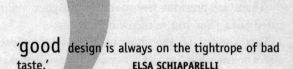

3

'good design is always on the tightrope of bad taste.'   **ELSA SCHIAPARELLI**

'*I* was standing there in a G-string and he came in. Three times, I'm telling you. I asked him to wait until I was changed, then I told him to stop gawping. He said I'd got nothing he hadn't seen before. I said, "Push off, Specky." That's all I said. If he hadn't been in the changing room in the first place ... Sara, if I'm changing, I'm doing it without styling suggestions from some sweaty little photographer. I don't care if he is Boy Wonder.'

Tessa Collins had just risen and was not in the mood to placate her agent, Sara Avery.

'You've got to be careful, Tess,' said Sara in weary tones. 'He works on top campaigns. If he likes a model, he will request her again. Someone like him can be very useful. He shot that whole story in *Vanity Fair* and next thing you know the girl he used is doing the new Gucci perfume. Why don't you try keeping your mouth shut occasionally and think of it as a career move?'

Tess grunted. In old faded jeans she lounged across the chair cradling her coffee. Her blue-black curly hair was secured with a red, gold and green band, and her rich and creamy brown skin contrasted with her faded white T-shirt, emblazoned with the words 'One Love'.

'I wasn't rude to him, Sara,' protested Tess as she curled the telephone cord round her fingers. She pulled at it as if to straighten the rebellious plastic ringlet. It reminded her of her own hair.

'There are precious few models with your ability,' lectured Sara, 'but you're throwing it away.'

Tess kneeled on the chair to get a better view of the street below while Sara let off steam. Everyone was stripped down to the bare essentials. Boys showed off tattooed Celtic armbands, and girls in long skirts and bikini tops riffled through rails of second-hand clothes at the market on the corner. It was the hottest August on record, but yesterday Tess had been sweltering in tailored leather suits with boots, gloves and overcoats.

That was the fashion world for you. Summer was already over for fashion editors. Most magazines were shooting autumn/winter clothing for their October and November issues. Dripping heat and stifling, scratchy wool jumpers, fur-trimmed coats, sheepskin accessories. And then swimwear in winter. Sure, there were the trips abroad to find sun and lighting conditions, but a lot went on in Britain. In the early days she had faked holiday frolics on windy Dorset beaches, pretending it was Africa and she was happy. 'It's all you're paid to do,' cautioned one stylist when Tess had asked to come out of the icy waves. The photographer had not finished his shots and the light was fading, she would have to continue. Modelling was one way of paying the rent, she supposed.

'Look, someone ought to complain about him for a change. I get fed up when I'm treated like a piece of meat, and that idiot wasn't even on the same shoot as me. I think he wants to work for *Playboy* or something.' Tess knew things could be worse. One top photographer routinely abused his models, calling them slags and whores. The agencies all turned a blind eye, and even the women themselves tolerated the great man's pathetic expletives for the sake of kudos.

Sara wasn't listening. 'Tess, you've got too much attitude. I don't want to go over this ground again. You are a model, not a feminist professor.'

'Oh, and by the way,' added Tess – this would really tick Sara off – 'I said no to the last shot.'

'For goodness sake, Tess! What was so un-PC about it *this* time?'

'Well, I thought we were working on a quality supplement, but I was being asked to wear a push-up bra and hold a leather whip, and the heels were so high and I could hardly walk ... I'm standing out in the sun in a leather jacket open to the waist, trousers, and a coat draped over my shoulders. I was sweltering. The make-up artist keeps putting powder on my cleavage to stop it from shining, and he says, "No, let's get it really hot and sweaty." So then she's spraying water down my front, and I swear he decides he's got to do a separate light reading for the bazookas.'

'Really, Tess, it doesn't sound that bad ...'

'For the final outfit,' complained Tess, 'the stylist gets out this suit and the trousers are loose. He says they're "no good – not sexy enough" and I can't wear them. He wanted me to step out into the street wearing only thigh-high boots and a jacket. I'm telling you, it was nasty.'

Sara Avery was having her say. 'You're too picky,' she chided. 'And you've got a reputation for being hard to get on with, Tess. He's a top name – you should be grateful.'

Tess slumped into the cool brown leather. 'All I'm asking is that you have a word with Captain Sleaze, or get your agent to have a word with his agent, you know,' instructed Tess, 'whatever it is that these people understand.' It was always the same. Male photographers with large lenses thinking they were on a promise because they'd got some beauty right where they wanted her.

'It's going to get to the point where no one will work with you,' persisted Sara. 'You're twenty-five and you should know better than to give someone like that a hard time. All the top magazines love him. He doesn't have a spare day for months. I know agents who are on their knees trying to get him to work with their girls. You get given the chance and you don't do anything with it.'

Sara took a breath. She allowed a small silence before continuing: 'Anyway, there's more. I did speak to his agent this morning . . . He liked you, Tess. He liked you a lot, but he said you were carrying far too much weight. There's a job he'd like you for if . . .'

'I'm not losing weight for anyone,' interrupted Tess. 'Sara, I'm five foot ten and I need some flesh on my bones.'

'It could be one of the last opportunities you get to work with a big name. What do you think you're going to do after this?' Sara's voice softened. 'You've got to get some money behind you, at least. You're an intelligent woman; you've got to come out of this business with a bit of cash to set yourself up in the next one. Tess,' said Sara as carefully as she could, 'you *are* larger than most of the models out there. OK, you may be the smallest size on *our* books, but this is a plus-sizes agency. You're competing with teenage waifs for the same jobs. Losing a bit of extra from your thighs might mean the chance of some prestige work. Think about it.'

Tess did, all the time. Modelling wasn't such a bad way of making money most days, but there was too much bad attitude going on and this model wasn't going to swallow it.

'Now, this afternoon is a solid job,' continued her agent down the line. 'If you get it, you'll be working with Petra Mayhew. That's if your reputation hasn't preceded you. She'll be good for your book ... And, Tess, think about what I've said.'

Tess put the phone down and slurped on the rest of the coffee. The sun entered through the open glass and warmed an extended bare foot. She never wore shoes indoors. It was a chance for her toes to uncurl and enjoy some spread. Most of the models she knew had corns, bunions and ingrown toenails. Because everyone in fashion worked a season ahead, shoes came only in sample sizes of six or seven, sometimes eight. Her modelling friends ranged from five foot nine to six foot, and many took a size eight or nine shoe.

'Yeouch,' Tess grimaced as she pulled at some unsightly skin on her heel.

Catwalk shows were the worst: walking briskly in shoes that pinched and rubbed, even tore soft skin, was excruciating. The trick was to fake comfort. It was no wonder many models turned to acting after the modelling work dried up – they had to do it all the time on that damn catwalk. Yesterday's footwear had all been a size too small and by the end of the job her feet were throbbing. She had felt humiliated and 'Leather Boy' was winding her up. It was a struggle to deliver a smouldering pout straight into his Nikon when all she wanted to do was land a swift kick into his . . . Well, it would even things up if they were both in pain.

'Leather Boy, get a life,' said Tess to herself as she reached over for a Polaroid from yesterday's shoot. 'We are on to you, and you are a sad person.'

She studied the photograph. True, the effect was great; the lecherous lensman had created a dark brooding sky-scape which gave the clothes in the foreground a murky malice. What she hadn't liked was his inability to look her in the eye when he was talking to her. His field of vision seemed to centre on her breasts.

'I'm wondering whether my head will be in those pictures at all,' she said with resignation, slipping the miniature prints between the pages of her portfolio.

This afternoon she would smile sweetly like Sara wanted. How difficult could it be? And Petra Mayhew, she was good. Tess would enjoy working with someone like her. If, of course, she got the chance. At size fourteen she was noticeably larger than her modelling contemporaries, so her book must have been specially requested. She could be sure of polite interest at least. At some castings – the ones where her book hadn't been called for – she frequently endured the most basic of critiques. Too fat, too heavy, too much: these were the judgements that followed Tess everywhere in fashion land. In the end though, it was all right-time-right-place stuff. She knew that. That's why it was hard to focus on modelling work. There never seemed to be any evaluation of the person or their particular skills. It didn't matter whether Tess wanted that job like her life depended on it, or couldn't care less. If the client liked the way she looked on the day, they would pick her. If not, well . . .

'I'll keep my mouth shut. Mmm Mmm Mmmm.' Tess levered herself from the chair in the direction of the music. 'But right now, Bob, you and I have some business together.' She guided a CD into position and turned up the volume to enjoy the satisfying introductory thud of the anthem she knew so well.

'Exodus,' she chorused unselfconsciously, swinging her body rhythmically around the airy room, 'Movement of Jah People.' The world below moved to a different beat across pavements sticky with grime. But for a moment, as the music wafted into the street, West London's Ladbroke Grove looked like one big dance floor. She swayed towards the open window and belted out the words.

'Exe . . . eeeeee . . . dusss, Movement of Jah People. Oh yeah.' No one looked up to the third-floor window for the impromptu performance given by the beautiful brown-eyed woman, but Tessa Collins put her heart into it all the same.

4

'*T*HAT looks really disgusting,' declared Becks.

Her friend Marcia was now standing in front of her. 'It fucking hurt, you know. I couldn't stand it any longer. He's still got a bit more to do to the design and then I'm gonna choose some colours, but I've gotta wait until the scabs drop off.'

Becks looked closely at the tattooist's artwork, which was raised slightly away from the skin. Marcia kept dabbing at the viper's mouth, where two fangs gleamed. More ink and pinpricks had gone into the detailing around the markings on its head, and the flesh wept tiny droplets of blood.

'It'll have dried out by tomorrow,' said Marcia, already the proud owner of a winged unicorn and two love hearts joined by blank scroll and dripping blood. 'The scabs don't last that long. But you can't pick 'em, otherwise you'll muck about with the line of the drawing underneath. Come back with me next week and get one yourself.'

'I didn't realize it looked so rough afterwards,' squirmed Becks. 'I don't think I fancy that. Anyway, it's not a good career move. Big names can get away with it – you know, some of the supers have got them . . . little ones. But they don't like it at the agency.'

'Who's gonna notice?' said Marcia as she inspected potential sites on her body for further decoration.

'Well, anyone who wants me to strip off,' retorted Becks. 'You know, swimwear clients, underwear people. It's all right if they've drawn something on, like a fake rosebud or something, but they don't go for the real thing.'

'What a job,' said Marcia unimpressed: 'standing around in your pants while people look at yer arse.'

'I know girls who've had moles removed,' said Becks, self-consciously rubbing at the scar – a present from her mother – on her forehead. She was flouting existing standards as it was. 'One of the girls came in with a sleeper in her eyebrow the other day; the rest of us got threatened with dismissal. Not that I'd fancy piercing, after what happened to Lal.'

'Yeuch, that turned into a real mess!' agreed Marcia, turning up her nose at the memory. It had been an impulse piercing at Glastonbury. The stranger had pocketed a fiver and then unceremoniously punctured Lal's brow with an old ear-piercing gun, almost stapling the flesh together before moving on. After being drilled full of cheap metal and germs, Lal had filled himself with Woodpecker to deaden the pain, but an infection had set in. The doctor said he was lucky not to have contracted hepatitis B or worse, and to expect some kind of scar. The rings slowly worked themselves out of the brow but, undeterred, Lal had selected another site for perforation and was currently sporting a jaunty silver labret in his bottom lip.

'Why are you suddenly concerned about modelling success?' questioned Marcia as she dabbed at her arm with fingers smothered in silver rings. Her room smelt of incense and there was a hand-painted astrological mural on the wall. 'You're always complaining about not being chosen for work.'

'Well,' began Becks, 'I've been a new face for over six months now. I don't know how much longer they'll keep me on. Anyway, I want to get a job. I want my mum to see me in a picture one day and know I'm all right. I want to make something of myself.' She began to use her fingers to count out the reasons.

'Don't get a tattoo then,' said Marcia flatly. She made small movements with her head; any unchoreographed motion agitated the beads in her braided hair. 'But do something to make yourself look a bit more . . . well, older. You know, like you'd been around a bit.'

It was true. Alongside Marcia's gothic smoulder, Becks was the human equivalent of a Labrador puppy. Her strawberry-blonde hair, wide blue eyes, skin so soft and pink that she could have been the original model for one of Botticelli's angels, made Becks look like an extremely tall child. This outward vision was not helped by the way she shuffled along the street, head down and shoulders hunched.

Becks' modelling career had begun one morning the previous winter. Nothing could have been further from her mind as she'd made her way home on the tube after an all-night bender. She was nursing a blinding headache and wanted nothing more than to be under her duvet. When: 'Hello,' piped a breezy redhead, 'I'm sorry to wake you, but I'm getting off here and I want to give you my card.'

Becks had found this first contact with the fashion world brutal and deafening. She would have preferred to pocket the card in silence, but there was a question to be answered: 'I'm eighteen,' she replied crossly. Satisfied with the answer, the agency scout eventually exited through the sliding double doors, and the sleeper had returned to her tranquil post.

When Becks arrived at the W1 offices for an appointment some weeks later, the redhead introduced herself as Tallulah Bell. 'Call me Lulu,' she said, leading the way to a small office and fetching two cups of tea from a vending machine. 'If you're up to it, I'll organize a few grooming sessions with a hairdresser and make-up artist to establish a look, and then book some test shots. You've got potential, you know. Hasn't anyone ever approached you before?'

'No,' said Becks. 'I've only just arrived in London.'

'We need to think about a name for you,' said Lulu unexpectedly. 'We've already got a Rebecca on the books. She's got romance covered – you know the look: long hair and eyelashes all over the place. You've got a fresher quality ... You need something snappy, something short, maybe. Have you got any nicknames, or do you want to make something up?'

'My friends call me Becks,' volunteered the lanky blonde, unsure about the suitability of such a name.

'Love it,' said Lulu, pleased. 'Becks will look good on your card. It suits you, and it's individual enough to be memorable. Good.' Lulu pencilled in a few more notes, underlining her new conscript's name in her jotter.

The most enticing offer of the day had come when Becks mentioned her lack of a permanent address. She had been sleeping on floors, and occasionally, on warmer nights, under the stars. There was an agency flat for the new recruits, right in the middle of town. The agency itself would pay the rent, charging a nominal service fee for the first three months. Becks was, of course, delighted to become a new face.

Her shoulder-length hair was shortened to a more boyish cut and her eyebrows were plucked into shape. Grooming included deportment, skin-care advice, and coded messages about weight maintenance. Becks had never concerned herself with such a thing before and was grateful not to receive a humiliating once-weekly lecture about flabby thighs. During the test photo shoots, Becks used her new-found posture to make graceful shapes and discovered that, with make-up and well-cut clothes, she could affect the presence of a woman years older. Throughout her initiation period of a hundred days, she learned that 'Go Sees' – the new model's daily grind – were hard graft.

'But, Lulu,' complained Becks after the umpteenth visit to a photographer's studio, 'surely I've met everyone in this business now. They've all looked at my book.'

Becks hadn't picked up much work: just a few freakish photographs in a cult magazine. When her hundred days were up, she moved into a bedsit further out of town and met Marcia and Lal – they lived across the road and used the same launderette. She paid the rent with part-time bar work and did her very best to charm anyone who might be offering employment of a more aspirational nature.

'It will happen,' said Lulu with conviction. 'Trust me, Becks. People in fashion aren't as imaginative as they like to think, you know. They're all waiting to see you in one big campaign before they move in. I've seen it so many times.'

Becks dutifully passed her days in the stylishly minimal offices of advertising agencies, show producers, magazine editors and designers. Often one of many in a queue, she would smile professionally as clients stared absent-mindedly in her direction, glancing over her pictures before handing back the portfolio in silence. Becks lived in hope she'd find some enlightened life form with enough basic social skills to enter into conversation. Asking about the job usually engendered a series of primitive grunts – that was as good as it got.

Back in her bedsit, apart from her new friends, there was no one to share her day with. She had left home without leaving a forwarding address. Fashion people were her family now. Fickle, flighty and out to lunch they might be, but at least there was no compulsory religious worship. Or if there was, it usually centred around an overpriced pair of shoes.

'Anyway, today's the day,' pronounced Becks optimistically to her friend. 'I've got a casting this afternoon. A really big one. My book has been specially requested.'

The agency had been excited. Apart from the forthcoming catwalk show during London Fashion Week, the job with Esteem offered the chance to appear in a cinema campaign and billboard posters.

'This could be my big break, Marcia, it really could,' said Becks excitedly.

'So I suppose you won't want to be wandering about aimlessly with your mates any more,' lamented Marcia. 'If you hit the big time, you'll move into some swanky flat in the centre of town and call everybody darling.'

'If I hit the big time,' laughed Becks, 'you can come and live with me!'

'A woman who doesn't wear perfume has no future.'
PAUL VALÉRY

ELLE Cartwrite was in her office early. The sun outside, still watery and fresh, poked through each window illuminating a corridor of dust particles at regular intervals along the studio wall. A gentle breeze entered as she opened the first window of the day.

In the warehouse she had converted before the housing boom of the late eighties all was quiet. Layout paper, Pantone markers and 2B pencils rested on workstations, and a tailor's dummy swathed in coarse cream calico waited patiently for the fitting to continue. In an hour or so the Islington offices and showrooms of Esteem would be chock-full of employees and Elle would again assume the mantle of employer. But for now, she savoured the time in which she could be herself, walking the length of the studio and lingering in sunspots that warmed the polished wooden floors.

A great deal rested on today. In her office the interviewees greeted her. They remained where she had left them the night before. Laid out in ordered rows, waiting expectantly.

'I've got to bring younger women into the picture, but I've got to do it without alienating my older customers,' Elle had explained to Petra the night before as they sat in a stylish Moroccan eatery. 'So I don't want girls leaping about like they're doing a Pepsi commercial.'

Elle tore up pieces of pitta bread and dunked them in a small container of aromatic oil. 'How is it you never see older women in ad campaigns? They're the ones with the cash. Women don't stop being beautiful when they get older, they just stop being young.'

'You've been working in the business all this time and you only thought of that now!' said Petra incredulously as she devoured a dish of lentils. 'Don't you ever get sick of being invisible?'

'But I'm not,' protested Elle.

'OK, let's go for a reality check here. When was the last time you saw a woman your age selling a skin-care range? It's all over the place, Elle. Watch a Hollywood film and see Clint Eastwood get the girl – who happens to be young enough to be his granddaughter. Plenty of parts for older men – still shooting guns and mouths off for big bucks – but what about the girls? When they become old enough to look like women, someone somewhere decides that they've passed their sell-by date.'

'I've got to increase my customer base and reel in younger trade,' said Elle. 'Sure, I want to secure brand loyalty from women in their twenties, maybe even late teens – they are our future customers. But –' she jabbed her finger in the air – 'they don't spend like women in their thirties and forties, and I don't want to alienate women in their fifties. I'm here because of them.'

'Well, let's start by working out what you want your advertising campaign to say,' said Petra. She had sat in on endless committees where social trends, brand-marketing strategies and mission statements were analysed for months before anything actually happened. Millions of pounds would be set aside to promote a product through a progression of stages in the scheme of brand hierarchy. From concept brand to brand religion, the Americans had perfected global colonization of taste.

Elle thought for a minute. 'I want it to capitalize on what I stand for: confidence and self-esteem. I want women out there to stop giving their power away to petulant boyfriends, overbearing husbands, demanding children, exacting bosses, or hard-to-please fathers. I want women to please themselves. I want women to enjoy themselves and their lives, and I want them to do it in my clothes.'

'There you have it,' said Petra. 'That's an attitude you're talking about, and that's what marks you out from the rest. You've got to create that look in the pictures you do. The women you choose to front your campaign are crucial.'

Elle downed the last of her Rioja and handed her Access card to a heroically moustached waiter of middling years, while Petra networked the next table.

'Ah, Petra,' welcomed a man of generous girth, 'nice to see you in town! Loved those Italian *Vogue* pictures. Come to my office while you're here and we can talk.'

Elle turned to apply her signature to the credit slip and smiled. 'Thank you,' she beamed.

The waiter stonily returned her card with a perfunctory nod.

She poked at her hair self-consciously. If she had been forty years younger, he would have managed a bit more interest, no doubt.

The low lighting provided a genteel glow like sunlight at dusk and while she waited for her friend, Elle cast an eye over the restaurant's clientele. A lavishly proportioned African woman in migraine-inducing textiles was holding court over in the corner; she had exquisite cheekbones. At another table two city women with understated court shoes and matching executive briefcases discussed office politics. One had a shock of red hair, freckled skin, and the grace of a ballerina. She had attempted to subdue her flame-coloured tresses by clamping the unruly tendrils to the side of her head.

On another table a woman whispered conspiratorially with her lover. In the candlelight she looked like a Navajo woman. She flicked back her long, dark hair and laughed to reveal straight white teeth. This, thought Elle as she swept the room, was real life. And real life was beautiful.

She and Petra continued to ponder life and marvellous bone structure as they scoured the street for a cab.

'So what's wrong with real?'

'There's nothing wrong with it, but it won't sell,' cautioned Petra. 'Reality is mundane, uninspiring and often disappointing. It's ordinary. We already have plenty of ordinary in our lives. Women won't buy something they already have. When they look at your poster they need to see something they want. That's where fantasy comes in. Ask any woman what she wants, and after she's requested world peace and an end to starvation and poverty, she'll ask for personal fulfilment and happiness. *Possibly* –' Petra made a seesaw gesture with her hands as if to say maybe, maybe not – 'possibly romance. Ask yourself how you can deliver that in a campaign.'

'Taxi!' yelled Elle. 'Go on, I'm listening.'

'Personal contentment,' said Petra, 'enlightenment – these are states we aspire to, but what do they look like? Look at the culture of femininity for a moment. A lifetime of fairy stories setting passive beauties against ingenious but old and ugly witches teaches us from an early age that beauty and youth is in itself some kind of virtue, and knowledge and age is sinister. We've been taught to see our bodies and appearance as either advantageous when it comes to achieving happiness, or obstructive.'

'So teenage models satisfy a historical tendency to worship innocence and purity?' said Elle, raising her eyebrows. 'I think that's taking it too far.'

'Fashion advertising is a modern-day equivalent of the fairy story,' said Petra. 'It all ends happily ever after in photographs, doesn't it? And who do we see when we look at a poster or a billboard? We see a happy and fulfilled woman. And why,' said Petra, turning to look at Elle, 'is she like that? Because she's young and beautiful, she's wearing a stunning gown and there's usually a handsome prince lurking in the back of the shot.'

Elle and Petra climbed into the cab. 'You have to create a world that your customers want to be part of. Nobody ever did that with ordinary. I'm not saying it's right, Elle. God knows, I've photographed enough beautiful women with smack habits and personality disorders. They've got bodies and faces made in heaven, an apartment in each of the fashion capitals and money coming out of their ears.

That doesn't mean they know happiness. A boyfriend walks out and they're overdosing just to relieve the boredom. But the picture tells a different story.'

Petra's words stayed with Elle. Later that night, surrounded by the stately elegance of her home in Highgate, she had sat in the dark as the clock ticked on the marble mantelpiece. If real life was about anything, it was the passing and marking of time. This the fashion industry celebrated with enthusiasm. Seasons, times, moods – all of these things flitted by, lingering long enough to be documented, yet passing quickly enough to create opportunity for another collection.

The beginning of a season or an idea was always alive with potential. Change, new ideas and new beginnings: it was what everyone lived for. Excitement gave way to composure, and as the 'new' became the 'now' there was stillness for a brief while. Then 'now' would become 'old' and everyone would start looking for the start of 'new' once again. A deliciously frivolous way of measuring time, and one that required the correct attire at any given moment. If the need for change was not encouraged, fashion houses would be nonexistent! Elle sipped at her brandy.

But why should the fashion world be so frightened of the effects of time on a woman's face and body? Was it the appearance of wrinkles, or perhaps confirmation of something deeper? When women reached an age of contemplation and wisdom, the masculine world lost its free reservoir of feminine effort dedicated to male achievement. Women in their thirties – creative, resourceful, and energetic – focused on themselves. Older women hadn't stopped being beautiful; they had started becoming powerful.

The fashion world loved words like fragile, waifish, and delicate. If girlish women were beautiful flowers, designed to embellish even the darkest corner for a fleeting moment, then older women were great towering oaks, capable of giving shelter and shade. People needed oak trees to be close by, but they didn't want them in vases around the house. An older model would not reach the younger clientele Elle was so desperate to attract – young women did not want to look like their mothers – but there must be some compromise she could reach.

'I don't want girls. I want women,' declared Elle. Clementine and her friends listened attentively in the empty office. 'The Esteem women will have beautiful yet ordinary faces, eyes that shine with optimism and joy, yet tell a story of life with all its struggles. Their bodies will be strong and supple, their shoulders solid and square – not too square like Amazonian athletes ... No, they'll be fleshier, more ordinary. I want bodies that have soft round bits like breasts and hips and stomachs – why doesn't the curve of a beautiful belly ever find its way into commercial pictures?'

Elle watched Alicia arrive at her desk. Alicia gestured with a coffee cup and Elle nodded then returned to thinking aloud.

'The Esteem women will have round stomachs. They'll have physical personalities. They'll have bodies that look lived in and faces that combine a timeless beauty with the wisdom only someone over their first crush can convey.

They will have travelled . . . with stories to tell not simply about their own experiences but of life itself. They could be daughters, sisters, friends, mothers, or business colleagues. They will be whatever women want them to be.'

'Excuse me?' enquired Maddy as she breezed into Elle's office. 'Hope I'm not interrupting anything.' She smiled. 'I've got Tiger Lil's delivering chicken coriander and noodles at midday. I'm going out now while things are quiet to get bottled water and some white wine. Any other requests?'

'Yes please, Mad: stop off for a hand-tied bouquet. Something classy. We can have it on the side over there.'

As the office started to fill up, Elle turned to gaze once again at the faces on her desk. More easily now she could look into the eyes of those before her and search for something bigger than beauty. She was still doing it when the fragrant aroma of fresh coriander and lightly battered poultry dipped in garlic, ginger and soy sauce, signalled lunch.

'Hey, we've got a model infestation out there!' joked Trena as she blazed into the studio, past the pine screens temporarily erected to divide the studio into casting office. 'Sorry I'm late, everyone. I had a hosiery launch this morning. You know, tights and major styling. Well, it ran on for ever. But, hey, hosiery ain't what it used to be. Graduated compression is what you get these days – control panels to tone leg profile and special control-top construction. In my day,' she snorted, 'we just had baggy crotches. Did you know you can buy tights with a deodorized gusset now? I couldn't believe it. They'll last even through six machine washes. Course, I had to have a few vol-au-vents with the suits and talk about the future of support tights. They don't say tights now, they say legwear.' Trena surveyed the food. 'Can I have some of those noodles? I'm desperate for an eating moment here. Have you finished, Elle?' She licked her lips.

Trena, in between mouthfuls, was still incredulous. '"Legwear innovations that blur the boundaries between lingerie and hosiery," my arse! I can remember when they brought out edible tights. You should have seen those company directors trying to get a look at models with no clothes on. Strange how they all needed to be backstage when the girls were changing. Bunch of perverts. They'd have to be to come up with deodorized gussets.' Trena put down her lunch. 'What is it about women's bodies that upsets masculine sensibilities? I mean, intimate deodorants, scented panty-liners. Nobody suggests that a man might like to wear perfumed Y-fronts to freshen up the workspace, do they?'

Trena, a wiry presence in oversized tracksuit pants, Adidas old school trainers, and dark heavy-framed glasses, leaned back against the chair and devoured all edible material in front of her. She was a stylish woman with a survival manifesto that did not allow for masculine sabotage. Trena had made her mind up long ago that heterosexuality would not be good for her mental health and, judging by the experiences of some of her straight friends, she had chosen wisely.

'Let's crack on,' announced Elle. She was sitting in the middle of a large trestle table, nursing a mineral water. 'Trena, I've just been briefing the others about what I think the company needs . . .' she paused for a moment, gathering her thoughts. 'Women!' she said decisively. 'Three women. Not girls.' Elle looked over her glasses at Trena. 'It's not

an age thing – I don't want to alienate my existing customers. It's a –'

'It's a spirit,' interrupted Petra. 'The models we choose
have got to have something ... something more than
pretty.'

On the other side of the screen, Charlotte's empty stomach
was complaining loudly about the lack of lunch. She lit a
cigarette to help quell the pangs. She had watched the
woman in the glasses pass by about ten minutes ago and
could smell the food they were enjoying. She had been one
of the first to arrive and had not anticipated waiting so
long. The room – tastefully decorated in cream and pine
– was filling up.

There weren't many 29-year-olds left in her field of work,
and over the years Charlotte had watched most of her
modelling friends give up and return to the real world.
She unconsciously tucked herself into a corner while two
teenagers – one sporting a miniskirt that could have passed
for a belt – eyed her suspiciously. Charlotte squirmed in
her chair. Recent castings had yielded a strange unease
which seemed to involve an unspoken disapproval of her
presence. Was she paranoid or did everyone here think she
was past it? And if they didn't, what were they staring at?
A fleeting memory rushed her thoughts. Hailed as the new
face and at the height of her sudden fame, Charlotte had
been thrown together with an older model for a high-profile
campaign. During a break, she had stumbled upon the
fashion editor and photographer discussing the demise of
the elder woman. They had acknowledged Charlotte and
continued; the hurtful words did not apply to their new

young star, so why should they exercise tact or sensitivity? Charlotte had listened intently as she feigned disinterest by making a lightweight phone call to a girlfriend. She recalled how she had enjoyed the confirmation of her own superiority by implication, and continued to work the remainder of the day with a smugness she saw no need to hide.

Now, a decade later, the conversation returned in its entirety to haunt her. They would be saying the same thing about her. She smiled warmly at the young women in front of her – it was a gesture of solidarity she wished she had shown back then. They were all in the same boat, after all. Her spontaneous display of sisterhood was lost on the Barbie lookalikes. Union activity had yet to penetrate Planet Handbag. Charlotte shifted her gaze to a small mark on the floor and pondered the nature of her own being. She was used to attention, hers was a life that had been spent in performance of one kind or another and long before she'd ever thought of modelling as a career, she had learned that it was her job to look pretty. Presentable, her mother had called it.

By the time Charlotte was three or four, she knew that everyone was looking. It didn't matter what she did, as long as she remembered to do it in pretty clothes. Her mother always gave her an extra hug when she was clean and white. 'Now you've got to stay that way,' she would caution. 'Don't play with Paul or Michael in the dirt.'

Charlotte watched out for dirt carefully. Her mother would stand her in front of the mirror and say, 'There now, there's a good girl, all clean and pretty. Look how pretty you are today, Charlotte, with your shiny shoes and your pretty dress. Won't Daddy be proud when he comes home and sees his little girl all dressed up and waiting to give him a kiss?'

Charlotte would stare into the mirror, switching from herself to her mother and back. In the mirror everything was right. In front of her was a world that looked like one she wanted to be part of. Her mother was smiling at her, hugging her. If she could stay as clean and pretty as the girl standing before her, she would be being good. Her mother would stay pleased. She fixed her eyes on the person she saw, and then went out to play. Later, she would come back to check that everything was all right; the mirror would tell her. She took to checking herself with frequency. Mrs Davis liked and approved of this. Charlotte was becoming a fastidious little thing.

As she grew, Charlotte continued watching herself carefully, but it wasn't until she was ten or thereabouts that she first noticed her body as something separate that existed under clothes. She was lying on the floor at the time, propped on her elbows reading, and as she shifted position a strange fire exploded in one side of her chest. Up until now her experience of bodies and pain was a toe-stubbing, knee-grazing thing. A plaster was a cure-all and, wrapped round a small portion of body, effective. She'd never had discomfort this high up before, and thinking that if any kind of twinge reached neck or head height, death would follow, she said goodbye to all her dolls.

But nothing did happen. The mirror revealed no mark. There was nothing out of the ordinary to see, though she looked for a long time. She knew girls became women with breasts and then they could have babies, but she had assumed that there was some choice involved, like putting on high-heeled shoes. In Charlotte's mind, the two were intertwined. You put on high heels and a bra, and then you got married. Only when you'd worn a big white dress like a princess and kissed a man could you have babies. If she didn't want a baby, would she have to grow breasts or could she stay the way she was? She hoped so. A few months later, more fire, this time the other side of her chest. The presence of the slight thudding ache on both sides of her body was vaguely reassuring in a symmetrical kind of way. Such strange feelings on the inside but nothing (except a growing swelling) to see on the outside. Nothing to put a plaster on. In her room she watched her chest in the mirror for any symptoms needing a medicated dressing. If anyone did come up the stairs, she would hurriedly button her pyjamas and leap back into bed.

She lost interest in her girlish physique for a while, but then one day, on a dull grey morning remarkably similar to the many that had passed since that month, she couldn't get out of bed. Too much reading under the bedclothes with the bicycle lamp and not enough sleep, she supposed. This would be the only answer, since hungry bodies needed food and tired bodies needed sleep. Life was still that simple. She whiled away the morning drawing felt-tip bras on her Sindy dolls, but by lunch-time fever gripped her body. She was drifting in and out of consciousness and at some point later in the day the stairs creaked with the sound of a different shoe.

The doctor made his way to her bed, followed by her mother, who tutted loudly at the clutter covering the floor. Mrs Davis parked her feet in the middle of a doll disco and, unseen by her daughter, shifted various dancers roughly to the side of the dance floor with the toe of one foot in a dismissive 'party's over' kind of move. The doctor sat on the bed and in the distance Charlotte heard the medical man arrange his utensils. The warmth of her duvet nest was disturbed by the insertion of a cold metal creature that rested on her chest and warmed itself. She heard words that had no meaning and prepared to drift slowly off now that the chill had disappeared. But something odd was happening to the stranger at her side. The doctor had undone more of her pyjamas to access her feverish skin with his stethoscope but was now rooted to the spot. Though ailing and groggy, she registered his tension and watched his face change. Her mother, who was looking over his shoulder, repeated the expression and then they both retreated to the door for hushed discussion. Thinking that her body was now covered in, at the very least, a purple and pink rash, she lifted her arm to her face and then, exhausted, allowed the leaden limb to flop down. Several attempts at focusing and refocusing had revealed nothing. The grown-up contingent, however, had definitely found something and was locked in conversation. Charlotte's mother had her arms tightly folded across her chest all the while, but snapped into action to help her daughter pull her pyjamas together and drag the cover back over the offending body.

Charlotte learned that she was fighting a virulent flu bug. She needed plenty of fluids, bed for at least twenty-four hours, and a bra. Her mother was still struggling with disbelief at the sight of her ten-year-old daughter's well-developed breasts. She, too, took to her bed with plenty of fluids secured from the apothecary known as the King's Head off-licence.

After that, life wasn't simple for Charlotte any more. A visit to the local haberdashers, for instance, where a stern-faced matron measured her up, was just one of the ways in which life had changed. Never before had she experienced a tape measure stretched under her ribcage, the measurement rounded up to the nearest even number and two inches added on. This was vaguely bearable and reassuringly like the arithmetic lessons she tolerated on a Thursday with Mrs Price. Talk of cup sizes, however, induced waves of humiliation. Her mother and the noticeably large-breasted sales official carried on discussing her body measurements, oblivious to the fact that the ground had not opened up and sucked her under, despite the prayers that had been offered.

Friends slowly stopped being friends. Girls she had grown up with were not grown-up enough and passed her in the school corridors, blank and expressionless, silent only until they passed – then the whispering would begin. Playtime was often spent alone or in the sick bay, waiting for the bell to ring. She still wanted to play and wished her body were covered in a purple and pink rash that would fade and eventually vanish, leaving her free to resume childhood.

Boys were easier to work out. Alternating between cavalier and bashful, they were happy to talk about protuberances – theirs as well as hers. They seemed to find her bewitching. Suspicious of their new interest, she became withdrawn in their presence. This seemed to act as a signal of submission, and the boldest amongst the gang began to trail her during the lunch hour. Harassed and hungry, she stopped queuing for school dinners and waited a week before asking for packed lunches.

Mrs Davis seemed unaware of the confusion her daughter was experiencing. Charlotte watched her mother keenly. Did growing breasts mean you lost interest in netball and going out to play? As far as she could see, it did. Her mother didn't do either. Instead she spent her time getting ready for various grown-up activities and gathering clothes from the wardrobe. Charlotte would watch through the gap in the bedroom door as, in her underwear and tights, Mrs Davis tried on various combinations of clothes. She would hold a dress to her body and shift her balance from foot to foot, turning slightly, tilting her head from side to side. Then, in a flurry of tutting and inaudible words, she would dismiss the vision in the mirror and start again with another outfit. Charlotte's mother seemed to spend a lot of time examining her body from the side and the back. Her bottom was not to her liking. Sometimes, when Charlotte was sitting on the bed talking to her mother about nothing in particular, there would be a lapse in attention from the older woman. She would stare at the reflection of her rear end and begin smoothing it away with her hands. 'I *must* lose weight,' she would say, as if she wanted to add: 'I must lose weight or I will be struck down dead,' or 'I must lose weight because my child's life depends on it.'

Finally, an outfit would be selected, and then there followed the ritual of finding matching earrings and other items of adornment – gold on, gold off; chunky silver bangles on and off; a brooch, a pendant, small earrings, drop earrings, no earrings, a charm bracelet . . . maybe. Or should it be the pretend pearl earrings? Yes.

Once these were fixed to the lobes, the make-up could begin. It was a rare treat for Charlotte to be allowed to watch from the bed. Often Mrs Davis would be shooed out of the house and into the car to apply her face paint because the getting-ready period had run into overtime. Charlotte, sitting in the back seat, strapped in and patiently waiting for lift-off, would anxiously marvel at her mother's nonchalant skill. As the car spluttered into life and rolled out of the driveway, the steady hand that could apply sticky brown paint so close to the eye without wounding its owner, worked meticulously over the face. Potholes, stops and starts, even shoddy gear changes – none of these events could ruffle the steely determination of the woman in the front seat with the lipstick and visor mirror.

As a woman, Charlotte still practised much of what her mother had taught her and was reviewing her skin-care routine when a tall American woman popped her head round the corner and introduced herself as Maddy. 'Who's first?' she asked. Several of the younger models impatiently volunteered and so were ushered one by one into the studio beyond the screens.

'How long will this casting take?' asked another. 'Only I've got to phone my agent. Can I use your phone? My battery is down.'

Charlotte watched a stunning creature in her mid-twenties make her way to the phone. She didn't look like a standard model. A bit on the large side, with velvety brown skin and thick blue-black hair that upon closer inspection was a mass of tight curls. They bobbed around her face, never leaping in front of her eyes. She picked up the phone and turned to look at Charlotte as she waited for the call to connect. They exchanged smiles.

I could have had breakfast, thought Charlotte.

'Yeah, Sara, I've been here ten minutes and I'm looking at the other women . . . I don't think I'm in the right place. This isn't my kind of job. We're talking court shoes and natural nail polish. And I don't see any other "big girls".' Compared to her friends, Tess was anything but large – in fact, she was the envy of them all – but in fashion industry terms, 'big' was the tag that applied to her.

They talked some more, but Charlotte couldn't make out what was being said. She envied the beautiful woman with the polished brown skin, slightly flushed in places where she had obviously been sunbathing in the park. Charlotte wouldn't even go to Sainsbury's without lashings of factor 25. Dark hair, white skin – it looked good in the studio, but in real life it wasn't that practical. Sun worship, however, was not cause for her envy right now. Whatever was being said on the phone seemed to placate this model. She returned to the group a little sheepishly and fished out a paperback from her rubber rucksack. No, Charlotte envied the woman because she didn't need this job. Or maybe she needed it but, even better, she didn't want it. Charlotte didn't know which was worse, wanting or needing a job. She wanted it because she didn't want to come away from a casting having failed to secure the thing she'd worked for all this time. She needed it because it would be the job to set her back on track. She needed it because she didn't know what she would do if she didn't get it.

The models were disappearing thick and fast round the screens now. The people on the other side weren't taking very long to look over the goods. Charlotte watched a few girls chat together without feeling any inclination to join in. All wore trainers and impossibly short skirts. Two models were going through each other's books.

'Did you hear about Naomi?' one said to the other.

Charlotte switched off. Model chat did her head in. She noticed that the woman with the beautiful skin and ringlets wasn't listening either. She was wrapped up in her book. 'What are you reading?' enquired Charlotte, motioning to the book in Ebony Woman's hand.

The brown eyes looked up to take in Charlotte, and she answered lazily: 'Oh, a few notes on cryogenics. You know how it is, I've gotta brush up on my techniques.' The eyes twinkled. 'No, that was stupid of me, it's a novel. I'll read anything,' she laughed. 'I get so mind-numbingly fed up in these places, don't you?'

Charlotte was about to answer when the assistant beckoned her into the room behind the screens.

'Hey,' said the bookish belle, 'good luck.'

'Thanks,' said Charlotte.

Once on the other side, she felt a little better. As she walked over to the long table she observed each of the women seated behind it.

'Hello,' she said confidently, 'my name is Charlotte, I'm with Everywoman. Who shall I pass my book to first?'

Over the years, she had seen her fair share of designers, art directors and stylists, and it was a cinch to pick out who each person was without the aid of an introduction. The designer herself was wearing an elegant trouser suit in shiny navy fabric with a jacket that zipped up to her throat. She had a big silver ring on the middle finger of her right hand and wrote with her left hand.

Charlotte thought about her own mother, now in her fifties. The designer looked powerful, stylish, serene and confident. Her mother, on the other hand, had a knack for appearing overdressed, fussy, uncomfortable, even girlie at times. In contrast to her more stylish contemporary, Mrs Davis seemed to favour a pile-it-all-on-and-fuss-about-with-it-for-the-rest-of-the-day approach. Her favourite necklace would dive between her bosoms and need fishing out at regular intervals. Her close-fitting jackets or sweaters would seem to ride up around the waistline, requiring a specific set of manoeuvres to yank them back down.

'Ah, I see you've worked with Jean Luc,' said the navy-suited woman. 'How did you find him?'

Well, he was a complete tosser who didn't know what he wanted. He was rude and arrogant, and on the last shoot I did with him the hairdresser burst into tears because he made me have my hair changed completely three times before he was happy with the Polaroid. Charlotte would have liked to tell the truth. Instead she lied: 'I learned a lot from him.' That one always went down well. 'We've worked together on quite a few occasions in the past. I did that series for Revlon.' Everyone nodded appreciatively.

The portfolio was handed across to a younger woman called Alicia. While this new player directed her attention to the 2D pictures in the book, the others around the table concentrated on the 3D version.

'Could you walk?' said the woman with librarian's spectacles. Charlotte took up position at one corner of the room and delivered the catwalk promenade with practised ease, swinging her hips in an exaggerated way and leaning back as she did so. Apart from one current favourite who trotted down the runway like a dressage pony, female models were expected to glide, while their male counterparts stalked the boards like swarthy security men. Female models were required to smile or look demure as they fluttered by. For male models there was the compulsory grimace; some ground their teeth to pad out jaw muscles, others – neurotic boy-outsider types – sulked. Was that a case of art imitating life, or was life mimicking grossly exaggerated gender tendencies? When Charlotte reached a certain point she made a 360-degree turn, leisurely and gracefully, without the drama or showiness that a pirouetting dancer might inject. She took stock of the whole room and continued walking without missing a beat.

'OK, thanks,' said the bespectacled one – definitely a show producer type. She leaned over to whisper to her companion, using her hand to shield her words.

The assistant designer had finished working the book and now turned her attention to the real thing. 'How long have you been modelling, Charlotte?' she enquired as she passed Charlotte's portfolio on.

'About ten years in all,' Charlotte lied again. Twelve years would make her seem ancient. 'I started out with Prestige, but for quite a while now I've been with Everywoman,' she offered helpfully. 'Well, for about eight years, in fact,' she continued. It was hard to make conversation with these people when it was all one way.

'Could you tell me a bit more about the job today?' she ventured.

'Well,' took up the designer, 'I'm Elle Cartwrite and Esteem is my company. I always have a twice-yearly catwalk show, but this year we're looking for more than that and will be making a campaign to promote Esteem to a younger audience. I am looking for more than one model – for a cinema commercial as well as a billboard campaign.'

Charlotte's heart sank. Younger women – that ruled her out. She had thought because of the company's profile she would be in with a good chance. But not now. God, this was awful. They must be desperate for her to go, so why didn't they give her back her book and let her leave?

The designer leaned forward at that very moment to hand over the offending item and she looked her straight in the eye. Holding Charlotte's gaze momentarily longer than was necessary, she asked, 'Who should we speak to?'

'Sally. Sally Murphy,' said Charlotte, uncertain whether this woman was going to issue a complaint for sending someone so clearly ill-suited and over the hill.

'OK,' said the designer. 'Thank you for coming.'

On her way out of the studio, Charlotte exchanged glances with the beautiful brown-skinned bookworm. 'Your turn. I hope you do better than I did.'

Ebony Woman smiled as she strode into the interrogation room.

6

'life becomes a work of art ... All of us, actors and spectators alike, live surrounded by mirrors.'
CHRISTOPHER LASCH

ANGER, panic, humiliation. Ears humming, throat dry like a desert. The rush to get outside was so intense that Charlotte ran down three flights of stairs (she never used lifts) and hit the sunshine. The glare was solid, like running into a brick wall; lifting ice-cold hands to her sweating brow, she held her head.

'Are you all right?' asked a strawberry blonde. 'Have you come from the Esteem casting?' She looked at the building. 'Is it in there? Only I've forgotten my diary and my agent will kill me if I cock this one up.'

Charlotte managed a smile. 'I'm fine, really. A bit hot, that's all.' She motioned with her eyes. 'It's up there.' She straightened herself.

'Thanks,' said the blonde, removing an enormous piece of gum from her mouth and fixing it to the wall. 'Are you sure you're OK?'

'Yes,' called Charlotte over her shoulder as she turned away. 'I'm fine.'

The blonde smiled again and disappeared into the dark shadows and up the stairs.

She was thirsty, so hot and thirsty. Car fumes entered her mouth and lungs. Every way Charlotte turned she could see shimmering heat. Her legs almost melted beneath her as she pointed her body homewards; heat and lack of food were making her feel nauseous. The cool shade of a café with blue awnings beckoned and she headed towards it.

She had wanted this job so badly. This was to have been the answer. It was her fault Rick was losing interest. It was her fault that the party invitations had dried up. It was her fault no one wanted to employ her. It was all ... her ... fault. Yet she had worked so hard, spent her whole life trying to be what others wanted her to be.

Her mother had never actually outlined any kind of demands, opting instead to imply what was desired by means of a subtle reward and punishment scheme. 'I need you to be a good girl, a happy girl, a clean girl.' After a while Charlotte hardly noticed the difference. She had set herself a challenge that day when she saw the reflection of mother and daughter happy. Like a beautiful photograph of the best day in the world, the image occupied a special place in her heart. Now Charlotte would live by the rules of the mirror. There and only there would she find the life she wanted – pleasing, smiling, peaceful people – like the ones in books, magazines and television. She had given her mother everything, and the bulging picture albums that rested on the coffee table ready to impress the neighbours comprised Charlotte's first portfolio. She had been working the camera long before she'd even know what modelling was.

Charlotte chose a chair by the window, well away from the attentions of a waiter who polished glasses at the bar with a soft cotton cloth. She could feel the perspiration trickle down her back as she stared miserably out of the window. This was it then. Modelling career over. 'They hated me,' she said quietly to herself. With her elbows on the table, she rested her head on her hands and observed her lap. Her thighs spread sedately on the chair, below her rounded stomach. Charlotte straightened up quickly and the tiny mound disappeared. 'They hated this,' she said with a weariness that was as old as a sepia memory of childhood.

She always blamed her body. At ten her newly acquired womanly curves had ruined an orderly existence, and life had never been the same since. If Jennifer Davis mourned the death of her child's prepubescent form, then she hid it well. But things had definitely changed between them and as a result Charlotte learned that women's bodies were trouble – and not simply because they could no longer be done up in layers of pink ribbon or teddy bear print. They were messy and fleshy. They never stopped growing and swelling. Or bursting out of clothes and getting in the way.

After the doctor's departure, there had been no more confidential, whispered revelations between layers of pretty clothes. Gone were the gentle stroking and grooming moments that were so everyday and yet so intimate. These were the times when Charlotte had thought she understood true happiness, losing herself in the joy of a sweet-smelling, skin-on-skin relationship that was more important than anything she'd ever known. Being held and cuddled was like the moment just before sleep arrives, when all earthly sensations cease as the drifter yields to heavenly travel nestled in the softest satin duvet. Charlotte loved her mother's body and longed to wrap it round her once again.

The frills, ruffles and flowery prints that Charlotte used to wear were powerful and magical mascots of a time when everything was under control. At the mirror she would close her eyes and hug the lacy cloth to her chest, luxuriating in the smell of her mother's perfume. Occasionally she would cram her body into one of her favourite dresses, and wait patiently in front of the glass doorway for the world she once knew to return. How awkward those party frocks looked as the fabric warped across her body. She was a freak. The contrast of childish garb and grown-up physique mocked her. What good was a pretty dress if it couldn't mask the ugly reality of the body inside?

'They all hated me,' she chanted like some whispered mantra.

Everyone at the casting had seen beyond the fragile layer of niceness and got right through to the rotten core. Nasty, ugly, Charlotte. No doubt they had glimpsed the festering fury within. Frightened perhaps that a foul and disgusting thing straining at its membranous covering would leap out of her body and pollute everything it touched, the panel of jurors had wisely saved themselves from further contact. Maybe someone had realized that there would never be a way to quell the monstrous savage that lived within the pretty little girl.

The waiter was standing beside her. 'What can I get you?' he asked pleasantly.

Charlotte was shocked to hear a voice, her voice: 'I'll have a plate of chips and two eggs and toast – and bacon, please. And a black tea.' A drink was all she had intended to allow herself, but the body insisted on food, and she had not eaten since yesterday. Charlotte had lowered her guard for only a few moments, but that was enough it seemed for the insatiable beast to beat her.

'Excuse me . . .'

The waiter turned. 'Yes,' he said expectantly, stopping by a couple as they shared an impossibly large yet swiftly diminishing ice-cream dish. He waited for instructions.

She was angry, but in her belly lived a rage bigger than anything she had known. Her stomach released a menacing growl. 'And lemon, please,' said Charlotte weakly. 'Black tea and lemon.' She had intended to cancel the order; instead she had given in. Charlotte examined her hips, resolving to chain the demon tighter to its post. It needed teaching a lesson.

At home she raided the bathroom cabinet for something to ease the heaviness in her body. How many laxative tablets would it take to purge the fury from her insides?

Charlotte had eaten every last crumb from her plate, but not before proving to herself that she could contain the rapidly growing tumour that consumed everything in its path. For forty minutes, while the meal cooled in front of her, she had read the menu, then her diary, making pretend notes, all the while refusing to allow the food past her lips as the hunger reached its peak. Strengthened by this restraint, Charlotte slowly forked a sliver of pork on to her tongue. She would hold the food in her mouth before chewing, to check again that the control remained with her. There was so little that she could actually master. Her body, however, would always do her bidding.

She was still pondering a future without the camera when Rick returned.

'Knocked off early today,' he announced happily as he breezed into the house. 'I'm starving,' he said as he opened the fridge door and sorted through the contents. 'How did today go, Charts? Did you knock 'em dead?'

'It was awful.' Charlotte heard her voice falter. 'I don't know why I bothered. They were obviously looking for a younger model. I felt so humiliated, Rick. One of them even asked how old I was. I'm sure she did it to make me squirm. I wish I hadn't gone. I really want to finish this stupid life now. I'm going to call Sally tomorrow and . . .'

'Oh, great. So you're going to throw it in, just like that.' Rick slammed the remains of a large pizza on to the table. 'No talking it over; that's it. I was counting on you getting this job, Charts. I'm going through a bit of a patch myself.' Rick suppressed the irritation in his voice and tried his best at reasonable. 'It's . . . well . . . maybe you're pitching wrong,' he said carefully. 'There will be other jobs. You do really well with catalogue stuff. Haven't you got any trips coming up soon?' He removed his meal from its cardboard box and tucked in. 'What is that agent of yours doing out there?' he said through a mouthful of pepperoni.

'Rick, I didn't get asked on the last trip. You know, the catalogue shoot I always do. The same crowd went – to Gambia, I think – but I wasn't asked this time. They've all gone without me.' Charlotte turned to look in the mirror on the fridge. 'I've got to face up to things,' she said matter-of-factly, talking to her reflection. 'I'm not out there any more, and I don't want to be some sad old has-been that crops up in thermal underwear catalogues.'

With a withering look, Rick opened his mouth to speak, but Charlotte was firm. 'I've got dignity, you know,' she said.

'Hold on a minute,' challenged Rick as he reached for a bottle from the cupboard and jabbed at the open cutlery drawer for a corkscrew. He strained with the effort of wrenching out the cork. 'Are you saying you can't be bothered to go out there and earn a buck?' There was faint mockery in his voice. 'What are you going to do? Jobs don't just pop through the letterbox, you know. You can't do anything else except look pretty. So how are you gonna make money, Charts?'

Rick slammed the bottle on the counter. 'Jeez, I don't need this.' He put his hands to his head. 'Do you know, I've been out there hustling today, trying to get something together, not for me – for *us*. I want us to have a good life. I want what everyone else out there has.' Rick reached for a glass. 'How are we gonna get anywhere if you can't stick out a rough patch? Get a grip, Charlotte. OK, they asked how old you are – so what?' More tenderly he joked, 'Hey, you might be getting on a bit, but you're still beautiful and you're still all mine.'

Rick poured the red wine for himself. A glass of the old Ribena and a Marlboro, those were his comforters. Tutting, he scrunched up the empty red pack and reached inside her bag for the Silk Cut. He lit his nicotine fix in silence, then, sucking with deep commitment, he spoke.

'The thing is, Charts, I think I'm in with someone at Sassoon's.' Jets of smoke escaped with his words. 'This is a major contract if it happens. They could put loads of work my way. I've got to get a few proposals together and meet some people, you know, and I don't wanna look like I'm not up to it. This could be big time.'

Rick allowed a meaningful pause. 'Anyway, I'm gonna need a bit of cash. I was thinking that you could lend me some to tide me over. You know, until I get the go-ahead.' He dropped the cigarette into an old coffee cup and returned to the pizza. 'Want some?'

'No, I had a huge lunch,' confessed Charlotte. She held her stomach and turned sideways to stare into the glass oven door. 'I feel really bloated now. I don't want anything.' She was about to walk away.

'That's the thing I love about you,' said Rick, seizing the moment. 'You're a fighter. You keep at it. I can think of loads of women your age who've let it all go. You just get better and better. I love the way you look after yourself, but you've gotta get over this career thing. What was today, anyhow? Some tacky little designer poster? You're better than that. Tell Sally she's not to send you for crap jobs. I could manage you better myself, you know.'

Charlotte chose not to reply. Rick's words were empty. She watched him slurp and chew, like some kind of eating machine. In between mouthfuls of gluey cheese he would lift the wine glass to his mouth and gulp. Without conversation, the sound of mastication was amplified until the intensity of it disgusted her. Charlotte was not like this gluttonous creature before her and, as if to prove it to herself, she reached for two more laxatives from the packet on the fridge. The first lot was taking a long time to work and she felt swollen and sluggish.

Later, in front of the TV, Rick brought up the subject of money again. 'I'm gonna need a couple of grand, Charts.' In his voice she detected an assumption that capitulation would be forthcoming and it irked her.

'I don't have it,' she said crossly, remembering all the times he had borrowed money – a few hundred here and there. It was rarely, if ever, paid back. And he was forever helping himself to a twenty-pound note out of her purse, or a fiver, even coins. 'I need a bit of spare for the taxi,' he would say as he went out of the door.

'I need that money for myself right now,' she said.

'Charts,' Rick coaxed, slipping his arm round her shoulder, 'I'm only talking about a few weeks here. I'm not just doing this for me, you know. If you want to give up modelling you need to have some breathing space to look around. If I can get this job, I can keep things ticking over nicely. You'll get your cash back.' He was distracted by a loud noise from the screen.

'Look –' began Charlotte forcefully. When he wasn't looking at her it was somehow easier.

Rick turned his attention back to Charlotte, his face strangely unfamiliar.

Anxiously, she fought for her savings. 'It's money that I've put away for myself; I don't want to hand it over. How do I know it's all going to work out?' Charlotte thought for a moment. 'For all I know, this deal might . . . well . . .'

Rick pulled his arm from her shoulder. 'I don't believe I'm hearing this!' he thundered. 'I thought we were a team here.' He got up and paced the room. 'What happened to "Charlotte and Rick together forever"? What happened to "What's yours is mine and what's mine is yours"? What's changed?

'I'll tell you what's changed,' he said, warming to his rant and gesticulating wildly. 'You're becoming selfish in your old age.' He turned to face her and, with hands on hips, he completed his verdict: 'You're getting old and frightened. You're too afraid to take risks. I really thought I knew you, Charts,' he said shaking his head with an exaggerated tsk-tsk kind of move, 'but I don't know if I do any more.'

Charlotte remained on the sofa and attempted to explain. 'All I'm saying –'

'What you're saying is that you don't trust me,' Rick finished, returning to the sofa. 'Or maybe you're trying to say I'm not up to it. Is that it?' He sat back down and shifted position a couple of times. 'Well, I've got to hand it to you for being so snide. How long have you been walking around thinking "Rick's a loser," Miss Superior? Hmm? Tell me that.'

'Well,' said Charlotte, trapped but unsure how, 'you never pay back money you borrow. You take money all the time. I don't know what's my own any more. Anyway, this is a difficult time for me, Rick.'

'Oh, and don't we know it,' jeered Rick. 'And while we're on the subject, I haven't taken anything from you. I'm not the one who creams 20 per cent plus VAT from each pay cheque yet does nothing to earn it.' Rick stood up and walked over to the door. 'I'm the one who comes up with a plan for the future. I'm the one who sits across the table from you every day listening to you go on and on.' He reached for his jacket. 'I'm the one who cares about your career – which is more than I can say for that crappy agent of yours.'

Rick picked up his keys and turned. 'I'm going out for cigarettes,' he spat. 'Don't wait up.'

Charlotte heard the door slam and listened to the silence after the tempest. The tightness in her stomach was beginning to give way to cramps and she turned her full attention to her belly. It was hard and bloated and she was beginning to feel dull thudding pains at her temple. The day raced past her like a film on fast forward. This morning she had started out with so much hope for things to come and now, only twelve hours later, it was all over. Dark was falling on this muggy summer's eve and her life was spinning out of control. Charlotte thought of Ebony Woman. What was the betting that a woman like that wouldn't care one way or the other whether she landed the Esteem contract?

7

'YOU may have three halfpence in your pocket and not a prospect in the world . . . but in your new clothes, you can stand on the street corner, indulging in a private daydream of yourself as Clark Gable or Greta Garbo.' **GEORGE ORWELL**

EBONY Woman sat on a chrome barstool over the other side of town and drank from a beer bottle. It had arrived with a lime sticking out of the top. As she savoured the added citrus, Tess thought about the casting.

'How did it go today?' asked her flatmate, Belle, lifting a gin and tonic to her mouth.

'I don't know,' replied Tess honestly. 'And in about two beers' time I won't care either. Let's get a takeaway on the way home and stop off at Blockbuster.'

'I can't,' groaned Belle. 'I've got to do a bit of overtime. It's a cruise-wear launch.'

'Ah, free beers,' said Tess, perking up. 'Let's go now.'

'Champagne, yes. Smoked salmon, yes. Things on sticks, yes. Beer – no,' lamented Belle.

'OK, let's go, have one drink and move on,' said Tess encouragingly. 'It's only just off Regent Street. It'll be a laugh. We can grab a taxi, zip straight in and stay for twenty minutes – that's all you need, isn't it?' Tess downed her drink and thumped the bottle on the bar. The barman looked over, ever attentive to the needs of the deliciously proportioned drinker at his watering hole, and waited for instructions. Tess stretched out her long legs and in an instant was out of the door – much to the disappointment of her admirer.

'Just sign your name in the book, chat to the PR, and check out the clothes,' she advised as they hailed a cab. 'There's bound to be a bit of something on a cracker and we can nip into the tandoori on the way home. I'd quite like to see that Spike Lee film. I'll get that while you order the food and we can meet up at the flat.'

Belle allowed herself to be propelled towards the taxi. She remembered how pleased she'd been when she got the job, and how she'd rushed home to present her mum with the free bottle of Chanel perfume she'd collected after attending the first of many promotional events. 'Did Mr Chanel give you this himself?' her mother had asked, thrilled, in the way that only someone who thought St Michael qualified as a designer label could.

These days though, there were times when another shop, clothing collection or fragrance launch just wasn't at the top of her list.

Tess and Belle walked up to the double doors where a distinguished pensioner in pseudo military costume asked to see the cruise-wear invitations. 'She's with me,' said Belle.

'Sign here,' said the septuagenarian, nudging a leather-bound visitors' book towards Belle.

Inside the shop, empty of consumers and sales assistants, they were offered buck's fizz by uniformed catering staff. Each helpfully removed a glass from the silver tray in front of her. All around the shop, fashion types snacked on trays of overstyled biscuits and shrimp paste. The conversation was of circulation figures, failed editorships, and sexual misconduct, the goal being to feign interest in the clothes – if pressured by an earnest press officer – and cross-pollinate industry gossip. Belle made sure she was seen to be paying attention. Some clothes hung from rails while others paraded the room courtesy of silent tall thin women.

'When will the samples be ready for studio?' Belle enquired, much to the pleasure of a preppy blonde in a promotional suit. Together they eyed two models appreciatively and watched them roam aimlessly through the crowd of unconcerned reporters. The decorative women occupied a strange twilight zone between performance and nonchalance – hanging around in immaculately pressed linen separates, talking to no one was an everyday thing for them. They walked a little and posed, careful not to catch the eye of anyone in particular. They used the shop's columns and alcoves as props. One – a rangy Black woman – parked herself in a spot by a marble statue and surveyed the crowd. Tess looked up and saw her.

'Sasha!' she said. 'How you doing, girl?'

'Tess,' responded the mannequin. Her dark brown skin was highlighted with a dusting of gold at her temples, cheekbones and collarbones. 'What are you up to?'

'I'm hanging out with Belle, my flatmate. She's gotta write about this or something. We're going soon, though. How long have you got to stay?'

'Oh, about three more outfits' worth, you know. We've done a couple, just gotta keep changing and coming back out. God, I hate these things, don't you? At least when it's catwalk they're a bit more interested. Did you speak to Kisha recently?'

'No,' said Tess as she liberated a few skewered delicacies from a bed of rose radishes. 'Want one?'

'Better not,' said Sasha. 'I'm on duty. You should ring Kisha – she'd like to speak to you. It's no big deal; she's just had enough. She walked out the other day. Her agent hasn't bothered to ring her. Said she was trouble. I think that hurt her.'

'So, what now?' said Tess. She already knew why Kisha would have quit. There weren't that many Black models on the circuit and most knew each other's business.

'I don't know, man,' said Sasha. 'She said she's glad she did it. I dunno, if it was me I wouldn't have said anything. She got fed up with it, y'know. Some White guy was being an arsehole. Ignorant. Like, she's going for some commercial casting and they want a Black woman. But he says, to her face, "You're too dark."

'So she says to him something like, "At this casting for this job in this room I'm too Black, but last week for some other White boy, I wasn't Black enough. I don't hear any of the White girls here being told they aren't White enough. I don't hear anyone with a problem around White models. You White boys wanna make your mind up, cha." Then she walks out.'

Sasha looked around as she spoke. Seeing no one in authority who might prevent her from socializing further, she carried on. 'I'm telling you, man,' she whispered conspiratorially, 'I couldn't believe it. "Whaa, you said that?" I told her. "Good! Stupid White boy." Thing is, he was probably on the phone to her agent straight away. She hasn't had a phone call from anyone, but she heard from one of the others at the same agency that the woman said Kisha is trouble and she doesn't want her on the book any more.' Sasha began to move off. 'She's sad, you know, but she's glad she said it. Look, I gotta go now. I'm supposed to be working. Catch you later.'

'Yeah, speak soon,' said Tess, turning to exchange an empty glass for a freshly poured champagne cocktail. Sipping it, she thought about her own experience earlier in the day. The casting at the Esteem offices had not been a particular success. There was no real reason she could find to explain her unease. No one had said anything much. They seemed to like her pictures. It was hard to tell. She wished she could just come away from something thinking, 'They didn't think I was right,' instead of 'They didn't think the colour of my skin was right.'

Her dad had written something once. He used to send her postcards in the early days after he left Britain. He'd said, 'In Trinidad, when a policeman knocks on your door to tell you your music is too loud, you know your music is too loud.' This was lost on Tess at the time, but it sure meant something to her now. Having been to plenty of parties where the house would be full of young Black people having a good time, she had sometimes felt that the arrival of the police was not wholly to do with noise pollution – especially if the party was taking place in a White neighbourhood.

Belle broke into her thoughts. 'Let's go home,' she said.

'I'm done here. Who was that model you were talking to? She was nice.'

'Her name's Sasha,' explained Tess as they stepped out into the street to hail a cab. 'She was telling me about a friend who just quit modelling. She couldn't deal with the attitude any more. That would be a good story, you know. Never mind about the latest hemline report, what about a bit of reality? What about exposing the magazines who refuse to photograph Black women for their covers? There are enough of them.'

'Henrietta wouldn't want a story like that, Tess.' Henrietta Hargrieves was Belle's editor. Widely tipped as the next Brit to cross the pond and take charge of an American magazine, Henrietta lived and breathed glamour. Belle shook her head. It didn't interest her either. 'She doesn't report about real life, She lives in La-La Land. Everything in her realm has to smell as sweet as a fragrance launch at Harrods.' A cab spotted her and waited for the lights to change. 'I couldn't get that one by her in a million years,' Belle laughed.

'Well, maybe you lot aren't so cutting edge as you like to think,' said Tess as the taxi pulled alongside. 'I can't see anyone being particularly innovative in the fashion world. You like fashion as long as it's about being on Planet Gorgeous. As long as the labels are happening and the parties are hot. You should try it from our side of the fence sometimes, Belle. I mean, you have to turn up at a champagne reception and eat shrimp-and-pepper kebabs and you got a problem with that. Come September, you'll be complaining loudly about what hard work it is having to go to Paris, Milan and New York. Hello,' mocked Tess, 'Earth to Belle . . .'

'Yeah, yeah,' said Belle as she flopped on the large divan

seat. 'Ladbroke Grove, please – and don't take any notice of my friend here, she's off on one.'

6

Maddy had her going-home face on. 'It's late, Elle,' she said. 'I think the choices you've made are good. And Petra and Trena were unanimous – that says something, doesn't it? You feel the same, don't you?'

Elle looked thoughtful. For the umpteenth time she looked at the faces on her desk. 'It's so much more competitive out there, Maddy. When I first started, I was in it because I loved finely made clothes. I was a seamstress who had a little business.' She smiled wistfully. 'I used to sew. I used to do personal fittings with clients. Now all I do is attend meetings about licensing and financing.'

'Elle, you're tired,' cautioned Maddy. 'You've really been overdoing it recently. I know it's an important time right now, and we're all behind you, but you've got to think about letting up once in a while.' Gathering her bag she moved towards Elle. 'Sitting there staring at those photographs isn't going to do anything. Why don't you go home? There's still plenty of evening left.' Maddy picked up the phone. 'I'll call you a cab before I go, shall I?'

'What for? I'm only going to sit and stare at home,' protested Elle sullenly.

'Why don't you come out with us, then?' cajoled Maddy. 'Tom and I are going to grab something to eat . . .' Maddy corrected herself: 'I mean, "have some supper",' she laughed at her fake English accent. 'Nothing fancy, maybe the Dome. Come on, Tom would love to meet you. I've told him so much about you.'

'No thanks, Mad,' said Elle. 'I don't feel like it. You're

right, though. I'll finish up here and then go. And, Mad –'

'Yes?' said Maddy flicking her flaxen hair out of her face.

'Thanks.' She suddenly felt a rush of affection for Maddy. Was it some misplaced maternal yearning? Maddy was more than an assistant. She had crashed through the boundaries of professional fondness long ago. Elle didn't want to lose Maddy, but she had begun to accept the inevitable. Over the years some of her favourite assistants had moved on, promising to keep in touch, only to vanish into thin air.

Maddy closed various windows around the studio and as a final gesture removed the fresh bouquet from the table and placed it squarely on the front desk at reception. She turned the vase until she was happy with the angle of the blooms, then, calling 'Goodbye' over her shoulder, she let herself out.

Elle returned to the faces on her desk. Three women gazed up at her. The casting had been impossible. She had met them along with a hundred or so others – or was it more? – only a few hours earlier and had tried to view the faces and bodies of her visitors with professional interest. There was seldom real logic in client selection, Elle knew that. Models were chosen for all kinds of reasons. But at least she had brought to the table a basic agenda.

She peeked down one more time to take in a woman in her mid-twenties with corkscrew curls, caramel skin and an adorably round and curvaceous body. Then there was an older woman – almost aged by fashion-industry standards – with raven hair and soulful eyes. And, finally, a young blonde with elegant, even haughty features.

Elle carried the photos over to the large white pinboard behind her desk. It was where she stored anything of inspirational value, from beautifully shot images of women from fashion magazines, to fabric swatches, packaging and typography samples. Even dried flowers and Japanese sweet wrappers had their space. Ceremonially removing some of the clutter, Elle made a clearing and pinned up the pictures one by one. She stared hard, looking into the eyes of the women she had chosen, trying to bond with each cardboard Aphrodite until the light began to fade.

These three beauties would become the face of Esteem, groomed to spread the word with their effortless grace and pleasing smiles. They'd greet her as she entered the office in the morning and wave her off at night. It would be they who would glow, happy and fulfilled, inviting others to be part of their world. A fantasy world, constructed by image technicians and computerized machinery. What a strange existence, thought Elle, where the future survival of a company could be riding on the manufactured allure of three strangers.

'Goodnight all,' she said as she shut the door. And then, a little more self-consciously, she added, 'See you in the morning.'

8

'one is not born a woman, one becomes one.'
SIMONE DE BEAUVOIR

'YOU'RE joking,' said Tess. 'Nice one.'
'Thank God,' breathed Charlotte.
'Yes, Yes, Yes,' chanted Becks as she jumped around the room.

The morning after the casting, as each model celebrated the good news from her agent, Elle sat at her desk with a pencil-slim cigar between her fingers. Today was more significant than anything she could think of; it signalled the beginning of better things. Esteem was ready to take on the market place and enjoy a new-found direction. As her media family beamed down on her from the pinboard, Elle allowed herself the smallest self-congratulatory smile.

Trena had already nicknamed them 'Elle's Belles'. 'We need to do make-up tests,' she said, moving a few papers on Elle's desk before finding a place to settle and investigate the contents of the paper bag in her hand. 'I think,' she continued as she pulled out a lavishly garnished bun, 'that we should define something that works as a daytime look for the pictures, but can be accentuated for the show.'

Trena curled back her lips and carried a large smoked salmon and cream cheese bagel to her mouth. Before inserting breakfast, she managed to add: 'I mean, it makes sense to overstate for catwalk. We don't want tacky, though. Let's get someone who can give it a bit of an edge.' She worked large white teeth through her catch. 'Elle, I know what you're thinking, but Esteem has got to get in there. This is the big one and you've got to say something with everything you send down that runway. Mmm, this is good. Anybody want one? I've got more.'

'No, thanks,' said Alicia. 'How come you can shovel it in like that? I had nothing this morning and I'm starving. I wish I had your hips.' Alicia sipped black coffee. 'I still think that fairly bare skin with lots of shine is going to be around for ages. That would look good with the stone and slate colours, and with those lemons and greens –'

'She'd look great in some of the brighter stuff –' interrupted Trena, pointing to Becks with the remainder of her bagel.

'I want her in the tailoring,' said Elle decisively. 'I want to show those twenty-somethings that this look is the business. When are they having fittings?'

'I think we should organize the shoot for next week,' suggested Trena, wiping herself of crumbs as she rose from the desk. 'Let's check on Petra's diary, then we can load on some show fittings as well, and get an idea of who looks good in what. By the way, Alicia, can we talk props?' Trena was walking towards the door and homing in on the coffee machine across the studio like a woman on a mission. 'I've got a few ideas about breaking the show down – you know, into stories,' she said as she moved.

Alicia looked longingly at the remaining bagel in the bag.

'Let's go to the sample rail and you can take me through the range. Here,' said Trena, removing the bag from Elle's desk and handing it to the hungry assistant, 'take this bagel and call it lunch.'

Elle watched the two of them exit. It was good to have her design assistant deal with the nuts and bolts of it all. Over the years Elle had wished for someone like Alicia. Someone she could nurture and bring along. More than a business arrangement, she wanted ... well, the chance to pass on something of herself. It wasn't a case of grooming a successor; she wanted ... Elle sighed; she could have had the chance a long time ago. She thought about the mother she could have been. Plenty of her friends were now looking forward to their first grandchildren. Some unfortunates had already got a whole litter of sticky, messy tykes climbing over the furniture, making slimy hand prints on everything they touched. And they loved it. As she got older, Elle had begun to feel sad for no particular reason. She could have, should have ... Oh, not again. She felt her eyes sting and watched the room and everything on the desk blur. The decision she had made all those years ago had seemed so right at the time.

'Maddy,' barked Elle in an attempt to distract herself, 'let's get this show on the road. I want a list of the proposed guests for the show. Did you remember to call round and check our celebrity support? I'd like to get Nanette Newman and her daughters to sit in the front row ... And what about ...'

But Maddy wasn't listening. And no wonder, thought Elle to herself testily. There was much commotion as a biker arrived with yet another sweet-smelling parcel. Maddy's desk was stocked with more roses than a florist's on Valentine's Day.

'Maddy,' called Elle jealously, 'in my office – now.'

'Well, I think Tom was simply trying to make me smile,' said Maddy curtly as she stood by the door. Her body language signalled the desire for an exit.

Elle had never known a time when she and Maddy had been so far apart.

'You've known him for less than a month. This is too sudden. How can you . . .' protested Elle, trying somehow to find the right words '. . . be so sure?'

'Elle, I'm thirty-one,' said Maddy seriously. 'I want to do other things with my life. I want babies, and I want to be a mother. I want more.'

'And I want more, Mad,' Elle interrupted, unsure of her ground. 'I want more time for you to think about what you are doing here. You hardly know him. Is he pressuring you? What is it?'

'I just know, Elle,' was all Maddy could say. She wore a dreamy faraway look on her face like they did in all the bridal catalogues.

'Look,' said Elle as she paced the room, waving her hands about like a mad woman, 'he could be a nutcase. How do you know he's all the things he says he is? I mean, a guardsman of aristocratic descent – he could be anything. He could be a mass murderer, or he could be extremely wet. I seriously think you should ask yourself what kind of man sends a grown woman a fluffy teddy bear through the post.'

'Elle, I've met his parents,' explained Maddy patiently. 'They live in Salisbury. They have a farm. They love their youngest son. He has a degree in animal husbandry. In his spare time at university he worked with underprivileged children. He had a dog called Laddie when he was a boy, and when it died he didn't eat for two days. He once took a bird that had been savaged by a cat to the local vet – he was six when he did it. He's a kind person. I know everything there is to know about him, Elle. He's a good man and I'm a lucky woman.'

'Oh, yuck,' challenged Elle. 'Maddy, please take a little time –'

'Don't!' roared Maddy. 'Don't say anything more. I'm happy and you're not. You're feeling put out because I'm in love, and I've got more in my life than . . .' she searched the room, as if hoping for some kind of inspiration '. . . than this,' she finally blurted. Maddy composed herself and lowered her voice. A hush had fallen upon the studio work force as they busied themselves, not unconvincingly, while alert to the latest drama unfolding. 'Look, Elle,' she said, 'I don't know whether you understand this . . .' A Virginian accent surfaced with a twang and she sank it instantly amongst rounded vowel sounds. Maddy had a horror of her roots. 'I need to belong. I need to make a family around me. I know it's not the way you run your life, but, well . . . I don't want to spend my entire life worrying about hemlines. I don't want to race through life prioritizing meetings, production schedules, and shipment agreements. And I don't' – she pushed her hair from her eyes and straightened her jacket – 'ever want you to talk about Tom that way again. I'm going to my desk now and

93

when I step back into this office,' she said, looking Elle straight in the eye, 'I'll expect a bit more understanding from you. This is the happiest time in my life. I am beside myself with excitement. So don't . . .' Maddy thought about it some more and struggled to hold her poise. 'So don't handle me like you're my mother, because you aren't.'

With that she turned on her heel and stormed off in the direction of the ladies toilet, leaving Elle feeling like she'd been slapped across the face by a love-struck teenager. Maddy seemed to be changing in front of her. If only her droopy lieutenant could hold it all together until after the show, then Elle would be only too pleased to design the wedding dress herself and wave the happy couple off for a few weeks. Just a few weeks, though.

Minutes later, Maddy returned, calm, sweet-smelling and freshly glossed. In silence she delivered some post to Elle's desk and turned her back once more.

'Maddy,' soothed Elle, 'I'm sorry.'

Maddy nodded her head and reached for the door.

'And, Maddy,' Elle continued gently as she watched her once sophisticated assistant head back to her desk, 'take your skirt out of your pants.'

Elle returned to the day in front of her. It was going to be long and hot, but not without the odd comedy interlude. Heat seemed to reduce people to maximum ineffectiveness. Looking out of her window, she watched a man in his middle thirties argue with a traffic warden. He had bought a bunch of flowers and was holding them in his left hand. In his right hand he had a mobile phone, which he slammed on to the bonnet of his car. While he was digging deep into his pockets for his car keys, he shook the bouquet – mostly gypsophila, rose and peonies – at his opponent and shouted some more. *These are loaded with pollen*, he seemed to be snarling. *So get back unless you want them to go off in your face.* Hay fever was clearly not the threat he hoped it would be, for the parking official – a woman about the same age as Elle – stepped forward, undeterred, to hand him a ticket. He snatched it and threw the traumatized blooms into his illegally parked vehicle. His face distorted with anger, he revved the engine and delivered one final remark accompanied by a spectacular hand gesture before swerving off.

Shaking her head, the woman made a few notes in her book. She would have to make a report complete with expletives and floral-thrusting manoeuvres.

'I'm sorry I stayed out last night,' said Rick as he slapped his parking ticket on the kitchen bar. 'I was really wound up. I'm under a lot of pressure and, well . . .' He handed Charlotte a slightly crumpled bunch of flowers. 'I went to Groucho's for a drink. I thought I might see Jimmy there. Anyway, I met a few people and we stayed there talking . . . you know how it is. Jimmy came later and I went home with him. I thought I might give you time to cool off.'

Rick smiled at Charlotte and moved closer. He put his hands round her waist and sandwiched the flowers between their bodies.

'I'm sorry. I . . . I just don't want you to throw away your career. I've been thinking about you all night.'

'Well, you needn't have worried,' said Charlotte, pulling away. 'I got the job. I'm back on course.'

'Fantastic,' said Rick. 'Well done. Now you can lend me that money and you won't even notice it, not with the fortune you'll be earning. Thank you, God,' he said sky-wards. 'It's all taken care of. Oh, Charts, I'm so pleased. Let's celebrate.' Rick helped himself to a large carton of orange juice from the fridge, and drank straight out of the container. 'I've got to go back into town now for a really important meeting,' he said between slurps, 'in Soho. Then this afternoon I'm going to look over a new facilities house. Might be a good one.' He returned the juice to its shelf and wiped his mouth with his hand before checking his reflection in the mirror. 'When I get back,' he said, as if talking to himself, 'let's go out to dinner. Somewhere special.'

'Why didn't you stay in town for your meeting, Rick?' asked Charlotte, reading the parking ticket. He had already been to Islington and back.

'Charts,' said Rick in a voice that told her he didn't have time, 'I needed to come home to you first. Let's speak later.'

'But you didn't know I would be here,' said Charlotte strangely.

Rick continued his journey out into the hall before turn-ing briefly to look at his inquisitor. 'Charts, don't go getting all *X-Files* on me. I didn't know you'd be here, but I hoped you'd be here. Besides, Jimmy lives in Waterloo. I was that close, there seemed no point borrowing his stuff when I could come home and change completely. Where are the clean towels?'

Charlotte had been about to point out that if Jimmy lived south of the river there was no need to go north, then she decided to save it. 'So why didn't you come home last night?' she persisted.

'Oh, work it out for yourself, Detective Scully,' said Rick in exasperation. 'I didn't come home because you pissed me off with your tight-fistedness. You were being selfish and I was angry, but it's gone now. It's all over. Let's forget the whole thing. Everything is great. It's better than that. Well done, Charts. Look, I gotta go upstairs and have a shower. I'm gonna be late at this rate.'

Charlotte searched Rick's eyes. He was lying about something. He held her glance for a short while and then disappeared upstairs. His face had been closed for business. She transferred her enquiry to the woman in the mirror and locked eyes with herself. She always kept a mirror on the fridge. It was a good light in the kitchen. White surfaces reflected the daylight and making up was easier here than in any other room. The woman in the mirror remained calm and motionless. She, at least, did not seem ruffled.

'It's easy for you,' said Charlotte to the green-eyed woman. 'All you have to worry about is knowing the right things to do, you don't have to actually *do* them.' She longed to climb into the mirror and live in a world that looked so uncomplicated. Life this side was messy and traumatic. The woman in the mirror seemed to be telling her something. Charlotte knew instinctively what it was.

She fed herself four more laxatives. The last lot had finally worked, but Charlotte could feel the food that remained. Rotting food, clogging up her system. Four should do the trick. Four should course through her body and cleanse her sluggish soul of all the putrefying slime that festered within. She drank them back with a whole glass of water.

'There,' she said out loud to her glassy companion, 'I

don't know why I didn't think of this before.' Pleased with herself, Charlotte put the laxatives in her bag and resolved to buy a larger pack. Here at last was a way of purifying her body. A few after every meal would allow the food to pass through neatly and cleanly. What she put in would come out instantly. No more bloated, swollen belly, choked and overloaded with decomposing waste. The woman in the glass frame watched with eyes unblinking, each bright green iris tinged with a knowing and conspiratorial hue.

'Charts,' called Rick, 'have you seen my shoes? The ones with the flat toes.'

Charlotte released herself from the mirror and returned to her world. The one where untidiness was the norm. The shoes were in the front room. She had watched Rick kick them off two days ago and there they had stayed until now. She had been determined not to put them away.

'They're by the sofa, where you left them the last time you took them off.'

'Thanks, doll,' he said as he breezed down the stairs. 'OK, I'm out of here, I'll see you later. Book somewhere nice. How about that new one in Farringdon? Everyone is talking about it. It will be great, but tell them we gotta sit upstairs – they put all the celebs upstairs, only nobodies sit downstairs. Oh, and by the window, Charts, not near the toilet. If they can't do upstairs, let's do Caprice. I know it's pricey, but we're worth it – and you'll be on an earner soon, so who's counting?' He kissed her on the forehead. Charlotte felt like she'd been stamped and nothing more. 'Gotta go,' he said over his shoulder. 'See you later.'

The door slammed and Charlotte enjoyed the silence. She was alone, but not lonely. Sometimes she felt lonelier when Rick was in the room. The loneliest time of all was when he lay sleeping beside her.

She padded through the flat to the bathroom and stood on the scales. Evidence of weight loss always made her feel good. More recently she had needed to see a reassuring dip on the needle each time she stepped on board. Something in her life was constant at last. The career worries, the arguments with Rick, getting older – all these things could knock her off balance, even send her to a gloomy underworld where everything seemed grey, flat and worthless. At least where her weight was concerned there would be no more fluctuations; no more depressing confirmations of weight gained as the scales careered past her usual marker. And there would be no more abstinence in subsequent months only to find the needle firmly glued in position, not registering any reward for those weeks of saintly denial. Now she had control. Tonight in the restaurant she could eat, knowing she had a dead cert method of staying on top of those calorie-laden banquets.

Charlotte smiled as she anticipated her next trip to the scales. At five foot eleven inches, she'd never seen the scales register under nine and a half stone. After this next lot of laxatives had done their job though ... perhaps at long last she would.

'learn early the immense difference between a photograph that is merely a photograph and that which is also a picture.'

FRANCES JOHNSTON

*T*WO HURT IN DESIGNER BOMBING. The papers were covered with news of the latest attack on the fashion world. This time the bombers had targeted the launch of a four-storey designer clothing emporium. The building had been packed with fashion press and celebrities at the time of the blast, but miraculously there were only minor injuries – a well-known journalist and a shop assistant cut by flying shrapnel. The designer himself had escaped unhurt, having left shortly before detonation to fly back to America on Concorde. He now appeared via satellite link, flanked by two security men, to express his shock and indignation.

Tess and Belle stood transfixed in front of their TV as

the camera panned over smashed glass shelves and broken mirrors. Surprisingly few clothes remained on the rails – perhaps fashion types, never slow to home in on merchandise going begging, had liberated some stock by way of compensation.

'I was nearly in that,' said Belle, gesticulating at the screen. Her hand knocked against the cup of coffee Tess was raising to her lips, spilling some of the hot liquid down her T-shirt. 'I was supposed to go,' Belle continued excitedly, oblivious to Tess's protest. 'I was pissed off that I couldn't make it. I had to stay late on a shoot. The models were gonna try and crash it with me. Then we got too tired – the shoot had gone on so late. Tess, I could have been killed!' And then with mock theatrical distress she added: 'And I could have ruined my Dolce jacket!'

'His prices are ridiculous and I hate his clothes,' said Tess, reaching for a tea towel, 'but there's no need for that.' She blotted the spillage and tutted. 'Belle, this is ma fave T-shirt. You have to get rid of the stain otherwise Bob and me are gonna be very upset.'

'It's those Global Defence people,' continued Belle in Kate Adie mode. 'This is going to cause more problems than you know. God, we've got a month to go before the shows. This is going to kill British fashion. The Americans won't come. The Japanese won't come. Remember the Gulf War? Nobody wanted to set foot on a plane.'

They busied themselves with the necessities of getting ready for the day ahead as the newscaster interviewed a survivor.

'Sorry about Bob,' said Belle as she retouched her lipstick hurriedly. She licked her teeth, sweeping her tongue from side to side. 'I'll get some Biotex on my way home. S'pose I'd better get into work. I know what Henrietta is going to want today.' Belle mimicked her superior's clipped upper-class delivery as she made her way to the front door: 'Let's do something on how to get the best out of your dry cleaner and how they can work wonders with that just-been-bombed look.' She turned and waved regally. 'Have a good day anyway, Tess. Oh, I nearly forgot –' Belle put her hand to her head – 'today's your big shoot day, isn't it? Have you met the other models yet?' She twinkled mischievously. 'Hope they're not bitches from hell,' she called devilishly before disappearing out of the door. 'See ya later.'

At the studio with another coffee in her hand, Tess waited patiently. No sign of anyone yet. The papers were spread out in front of her. The bombing was front-page news on all the tabloids. 'FASHION TO DIE FOR' screamed one; 'FASHION WORLD HELD TO RANSOM' proclaimed another. One paper even suggested that last night's bombing was a publicity stunt gone wrong. After all, it warned, designers have been known to do anything for a few column inches.

'Good morning,' said a boyish studio technician. He carried large flasks of tea and coffee, which he set down on a pine table. 'I'm Colin. If there's anything you want for today, I'm your man.' He returned minutes later with croissants and Danish pastries. Already on the table were cans of Coke and Diet Coke, and a large aluminium urn with boiling water for speciality teas. Tess walked over and helped herself to a sticky apricot concoction.

'Hello, a model who eats! How fantastic.' The woman in the dark-rimmed glasses scanned the table for tempting delicacies while her two assistants, Gillian and Lara, carried large boxes of shoes to the changing room. 'I'm Trena,' she said as she turned her head to look at Tess. 'We met at the casting. I'm show producer and stylist. Call me the creative director today. I've worked with Elle for years. You're Tess, aren't you? Nice to meet you properly.' She began investigating beverages. 'Do you want a cup of tea? Builder's, hairdresser's or hippie?' she said as she rifled through the contents of a few packets. 'There seems to be plenty of choice.'

'I'm a coffee fiend,' smiled Tess, warming to Trena.

'Good call,' agreed Trena. She tipped the aluminium flask, allowing a deliciously pungent aroma to escape as she filled the polystyrene cups. 'Colin!' she yelled. 'Where are the sounds? It's too quiet in here. Can you put something on?'

Colin obliged and as the room fired into action musically, Gillian and Lara returned with large amounts of clothes wrapped in plastic bags.

'Put them on the rails there,' commanded Trena. 'Gillian, do you need help?' Without waiting for the answer, she summoned reinforcements. 'Colin, could you get some of the clothes from the van? There's a dear.' She handed Tess her drink. 'You're gonna love Petra Mayhew,' she said as she resumed her search for the perfect bagel. 'She gets on with it. None of this faffing about, or flirting with models, or pissing everyone off. She's a woman's woman – know what I mean?' Tess thought she did.

The doors crashed open and in came Kevin. He was one of the top hairdressers on the circuit; Tess had seen him at shows before. His hair was auburn and curly, and he wore leather trousers and pointy boots. Behind him followed a younger and immaculately dressed associate dragging several black nylon holdalls full of equipment and products into the studio. 'Hello, everyone,' cooed Kevin in soft tones that carried a hint of his northern upbringing. 'Get that fucking kettle on, I'm gagging.'

Great, thought Tess as she clocked the assistant – a handsome man with skin several shades darker than her own – someone who knows how to handle my hair for a change. Tess had lost count of the times she'd had her tightly wound curls blow-dried straight and forced into a French pleat or, worse, been handed a wig. Was it because Caucasian hairdressers didn't know what to do with it? Or did they want her to look as European as possible?

'Ray,' instructed the head man, 'get out the brushes, the blowers and all the silicone products, then get me some caffeine.' Without drawing breath, Kevin swung round. 'Trena, darling, I saw you at John's, but I was backstage and I couldn't come out. Did you like it? He's done ever so well.'

Tess watched Ray do as he was told. Assistants were always the hardest workers on any shoot. The big names had earned themselves the right to mince around complaining about the lack of creative designers, honest agents, and tasteful campaigns.

'Hi,' said Tess to Ray as he stood astride the largest bag of all. 'You look like you're going on holiday for six months with that lot. What have you got in there?'

'Oh, you know,' said Ray quietly under his breath, 'just stuff we're not gonna be using. Kevin likes to make sure he's got everything: driers, rollers, tongs, gels, mousses – and then he brings back-up of everything.' Ray straightened up and smiled as he rubbed his back. 'If my man had to carry it himself then maybe he'd pack less, but . . . well, he needs his "tings" round him, you know how it is.'

Ray secured his hair in a black band and bent over the

bag to unpack further. One tendril fell endearingly across his face. Tess lingered upon the perfect tubes of jet-black curls – fashion locks, as opposed to 'roots' locks. She had once gone out with a guy who was far too roots for her taste. His locks were sectioned off into big clumps; some were even pressed flat where he had lain on them over the years. He didn't wear aftershave or even antiperspirant. He claimed he was a natural man. He said people concentrated too much on the superficial and that consumerism was an attempt to buy inner peace. She'd stuck it out for about a week before deciding that enlightenment might be important, but so was exfoliation. Tess had made up her mind that future suitors would require a basic personal hygiene routine and an iron. Ray definitely knew his adjustable steam settings. He wore a large silver ring on his thumb, and in his black T-shirt and immaculately pressed trousers he looked relaxed, stylish, and hetero. 'Always a bonus for this model,' thought Tess to herself.

'So where do you hang out?' quizzed Ray over his shoulder as he transferred the equipment to the brightly lit table surrounded by lights. 'I don't think I've seen you about.'

'Ray,' said Kevin almost territorially, 'stop chatting up the skirt and come over here.' Ray excused himself with a sheepish smile and went to join the crowd.

'I'm trying to tell Trena who it was in our salon the other day with nits,' explained Kevin, his face registering the smallest flash of triumph. 'She's very famous, you know,' he continued, putting his hand to his mouth and lowering his voice. 'On the telly. Oh, Ray, I can't remember her name.'

Tess mentally adjusted her antenna. It was getting harder and harder to tell these days. She didn't want to give off any signs if Ray didn't date women.

'Anyway,' shrieked Kevin loudly, 'I couldn't believe it. They were crawling about!' He put his hands to his face and rolled his eyes. 'She said she had an itchy scalp.' Kevin looked around at his audience; he punctuated everything he said with 'I mean' which he drew out theatrically.

'I meeeann, the old dear thought it was sensitive or something. I made some excuse and got the junior to wash in a bit of Prioderm and comb it through with a nit comb.' He subconsciously started to scratch at the back of his head. 'She pretended she was washing in a scalp treatment. I meeeann, it makes you want to scratch thinking about it. Oh, Ray, who was it?'

'Oh, some woman who does daytime,' said Ray, not really interested. He looked over at Tess, who was helping herself to more coffee.

'When I was a Saturday boy,' continued Kevin as everyone in the circle began to scratch, 'they'd send people home and tell 'em to come back another time. But you can't do that, can you? Not if they're famous – it's not good for business. Anyway, for God's sake, she's a glamorous woman.'

'Oh, yeah, of course,' said Trena. 'Famous people, and glamorous women especially, don't have head lice or farting fits. They don't pick their noses and they don't have messy periods. In fact, they don't even go to the toilet, do they?'

'They do go to the toilet,' said Kevin knowingly, surveying his little crowd of listeners. 'They're in that toilet all the time. But they don't use the pan, darling.' He groomed his hair as he spoke. 'The ones I know spend most of their time jacking up.' He raised his eyebrows. 'You can't get them out of there. Mind you . . .' he paused for breath and folded his arms '. . . nobody seems to keep it secret any more. I'm not kidding you, I did a big one a couple of weeks back for – oh, Ray, what's his name? Huge photographer, does all the top mags. Anyway, he had a big dish of powder on the table next to the fruit bowl. The models were all helping themselves. The magazine paid for it. Nobody cared.'

'What did you do?' said Trena.

'I had some, of course,' said Kevin indignantly. 'God, it's horrible when you're the only one who's straight.' He roared at his own joke. 'Chance would be a fine thing! Nah, look, it was free. I'm there all day. Coke doesn't mess about with your head, you do your thing. When I've had a bit of coke, I think I'm bloody marvellous. I can go on for hours. In fact, I think we did. It was a really long job. Went on till about three or four in the morning. Everyone else was buzzing and I didn't want to look like some downbeat in the corner, out cold. Anyway, I'd rather feel like that than be worrying about, you know . . .' He raised his shoulders. '"Do they like it?" "Do they hate it?" Those kind of shoots can get you down, there's always too much pressure.'

'Well, Kev,' said Trena, laughing, 'you're on your own today. The only drugs in plentiful supply are caffeine and nicotine. Look, I gotta go and sort out the models.' Tess had now joined the crowd. She turned to the brown-eyed beauty. 'Tess, come with me, will you? That's Charlotte over there; we'll start some fittings now the stuff is on the rail.'

Ray watched the two of them move off. He would have to bide his time. Models didn't like eager men; a life basking in other people's adoration and approval had made them impervious to sincere or even subtle appreciation, and slightly haughty as a result. But it was only an act, disguising a penchant for compulsory adoration like it was a medical necessity. In his experience, models were high-maintenance creatures, and Ray wondered whether Tess needed to be drip-fed compliments.

'Last chance to gorge on chocolate croissants before you put on a powder blue suit that will show up every mark, Charlotte,' instructed Trena. 'This is Tess, by the way. Do you two know each other?'

Charlotte was pleased to be reacquainted with Ebony Woman and both exchanged smiles.

'Hello, again,' beamed Charlotte. She had liked the look of this model from the start, and standing next to her in a campaign would enhance her new trimness further.

'OK,' rallied Trena, 'let's get into some clothes, then. You can leave your stuff here. This whole space is ours for the day.'

Trena walked her two models to the fitting room. Sandwiched between Tess and Charlotte, the diminutive creative director – only five foot two in her bright yellow trainers – looked like a child on a day trip with her parents. Becks arrived and joined them, making Trena look all the more stunted.

'Trena,' said Kevin as the foursome passed, 'grow up, pet. Honestly,' he said to no one in particular, 'what's she like?'

Time flew by as each model stepped in and out of clothes; fittings for the catwalk show were an important part of the day. Finally Trena had a good idea of what suited each of them. Kevin had gelled Becks' hair right off her face and when she tried the brown and slate tailored trouser suits she looked fantastic, years older than she was. Tess wore oranges, lemons and limes, and looked splendid in the wider trousers – her clothes had been specially tailored to fit her since conventional sample designs were cut to standard model sizes. Trena put a sliver of silver metal round her neck. 'Perfect,' they had all chorused. Charlotte had donned the navy knee-length skirts and jackets, opening a few buttons on the jacket to reveal nothing underneath but porcelain flesh. She exuded an earthy sensuality that contrasted with Becks' flighty refinement. With Tess the most businesslike of the three – and possibly the look most likely to appeal to American tastes, if the campaign were to travel – Trena felt she'd got the balance right. She called Petra in to see.

'Looking good,' she said. 'Let me take a few Polaroids, then I can work on the lighting while you organize hair and make-up.'

Tess, Becks and Charlotte made their way to the marker Petra had set down in the white infinity cove. It was a daylight studio, but lighting to bleach out shadow and highlight skin tones was still needed. They arranged themselves together and smiled.

'OK,' said Petra, 'I'm going to do a couple of tests here and then after make-up we'll get down to business.' She fine-tuned the threesome. 'Tess, move into the middle. Charlotte, turn outwards slightly. Becks, you're fine as you are. Yup, fine.' Petra looked down and into the viewfinder for a sighting. The Hasselblad, mounted on a bayonet tripod, was her most trusted piece of equipment. Satisfied, she released the shutter, generating a fantastic blast of brightness from industrial lights stationed around the tableau. For a split second, Becks, Tess and Charlotte were bathed in supernatural luminosity, radiating a faultless beauty, brilliant and vivid, while an image was harvested.

Petra slid a metal plate across the rear of the camera, and commanded: 'OK, one more. Becks, to me a fraction, just with your eyes. Yep . . .' She fired the lights. 'Got it. Good. Relax.' All three models assumed their position in the real world while Petra handed her camera to Sam.

In the meantime, Karen the make-up woman had arrived and set out her things. She was a striking blonde with long eyelashes who often followed Petra from job to job. The two of them were old friends. Everyone loved Karen. She gave great massages in between shoots and would often have a stylist in her chair for a little cranial rub-down while the models were doing their thing for the camera. Karen had recently crossed over into films, having made her mark in the fashion industry some years before. She knew all the latest gossip about who'd had what lifted.

'First customer, please,' she called and beckoned to Becks with a big smile.

Kevin coaxed Charlotte over to his chair. 'Let's get some Carmens in there, Ray. Have they been switched on?'

The stylist stood behind Charlotte, examining her in the mirror, his hands constantly working the hair. He flipped it one side and then the other. The contact was firm and strangely intimate. Charlotte had always like having her hair touched.

'Do you always wear it centre parting?' enquired Kevin.

Charlotte replied by shaking her head at the mirror. He wasn't an attractive man, but there was something about the gentle stroking and more urgent pressing and kneading that made her feel warm and loose. Rick hadn't touched her like this in a long time. He had mislaid the ability to touch for purely touching's sake shortly after the first date, and now – like all the men she had dated – he seemed to believe that women needed only to glimpse a pair of comedy boxer shorts in order to be uncontrollably aroused. Was that why so many male hairdressers made it to the top? she wondered. Did women employ the touch of a creative professional – one that could massage, fiddle, talk, and send her home looking and feeling like a goddess – as a substitute for foreplay, even sex?

Kevin piled it all on to her crown and pulled down a curl to fall over her face. 'I'm only playing,' he teased. 'It's gonna be simple and shiny today. But first I'm gonna give the crown some lift.' He dug his hands into her hair and pulled it slightly. Charlotte felt the hairs on the back of her neck rise. It had been a very long time since she had thought about pleasure and sensuality.

'No one said anything about flat,' he said, looking her straight in the eye, '. . . did they?' Charlotte nodded obediently. No, they didn't, she thought to herself, yet her relationship had all but collapsed into a flat and lifeless mess. Was it her? Was Rick unhappy? She would speak to him tonight.

'Now then,' said Kevin, as if he were about to get down to some serious business, unaware that his beautiful patron had been mentally reworking her life. 'Who cuts your hair and where are you going on your holidays?' He laughed. 'It's a hairdresser's gag, pet.' Charlotte was elsewhere. 'Oh, never mind,' said the hair man. 'Ray, get the other side of me, will you?'

'And then,' said Karen, addressing the room as she applied base in light feathery strokes to Becks' forehead, 'she threw the wig on the floor and said, "I want what she's got!" "But you can't," said the director. "You're playing a historical role, they didn't have root perms in those days." Well,' said Karen between issuing instructions

– 'eyes down,' 'head back' – to Becks, 'she was off to her own Winnebago and we didn't see her for two days. I gave everyone on set a manicure. We had to be there in case she came out. The director, poor love, was doing his pieces. She came out eventually and he was sacked.'

Karen laughed and shook her head. 'Then she went and had some face-lift – or was it her eyes? – done. Anyway, she disappeared for a week. Her agent said it was exhaustion, but I knew there would be trouble. Right in the middle of making a film. I mean, continuity or what.'

Karen focused on Becks for a minute and added some gloss to her lips. 'Press,' she said, offering a tissue, and then resumed her story: 'And then I get a call at about one o'clock in the morning to go to her hotel with full kit. When I get there, she's covered in bruises.' Karen shook her head some more. 'They were all over her face. She says to me, "Karen, what can you do for me, darling? I'm on set tomorrow at 7 a.m." Well, I worked right the way through the night. She dozed while I was doing it, but her face was swollen and it was so painful for her that she couldn't really relax. She took pain relievers on the hour. I don't know how she got herself through the next day. Well, I do, actually.' Karen put her hand to her face and mouthed theatrically: 'Chemical support. Not for me. I crawled around until wrap time – which was so much later anyway, because she was too high on pain relief and everything else to remember her lines. Honestly!' She squared Becks' face to the mirror and, looking at her reflection, applied the blusher to her cheeks. 'There you go, my dear. Give me models any day. Tess, are you ready?'

Tess marvelled as Becks vacated the chair. The smallest amount of cosmetic definition, added to clothes and hairstyle, and the blonde had become a different woman. Becks met her eyes and laughed. 'I know. Sometimes I'm not convinced it's me, either.'

'Come over here and be an Esteem girl, luvvie!' Kevin went to work with gusto. In his hand he flourished a small, pale blue jar. Immaculately designed and formulated by British Hairdresser of the Year Charles Worthington, Results had won awards across the board. It was Kevin's favourite hair-care range, and he was forever extolling its virtues.

'You know, Ray,' he announced, 'I'm not going to do much more. It's good off her face. Hey,' he quipped, '*I'm* good when I'm off my face.' He winked at his model and dug his fingers into the gooey concoction and kneaded the scalp before him. Becks watched him in the mirror as he passed a comb through her hair, transforming the short cut into an artful arrangement.

'I've just come back from the States, you know.'

Becks was listening. This stylist had a way of mixing conversation with comical anecdote and it made her smile.

'He's huge over there,' Kevin gestured towards the ergonomically packaged hair potions. 'Charles Worthington – what a geezer. The Americans love anything English, and the range has taken off big time . . .' Kevin flicked his fingers in his assistant's direction. 'Ray, pass me some spray.' With the metallic aerosol in his hand, Kevin continued his monologue in between tweaks and blasts as he teased the hair into place. Becks sat obediently under the hairdresser's hands and waited for him to finish his craft. 'Well, anyway,' he resumed, 'they started importing the range and, God bless 'em, they thought he was a made-up name. I meeeann, "Charles Worthington" – it's *so* English. The man is blessed with a branding miracle by accident of birth. Anyway, he goes over there to promote the products, and when the marketing department realize they've got the "man on the can", so to speak, they just can't believe it. They treat him like Elvis or something. I meeeann . . .'

Kevin stepped back, mumbling to himself, and motioned for Becks to move off the chair. She didn't hear him tutting as he screwed the lid back on his beloved pot. 'Kevin Christopher Crapper is hardly likely to get anyone moist in the gusset, is it? And look at it!' he declared, pointing to himself indignantly. 'What was my mum thinking of when she married my dad? I don't think I'll be launching an award-winning range this week. Oh, away with you, wench!' cried Kevin theatrically as Becks swung round to witness her hairdresser's heartfelt lamentations. 'Leave me to my woes. I meeeann . . .'

Charlotte observed the scene around her. She had worked with Kevin before. He deserved his own chat show, never mind a range of shampoos. The studio was bustling now, and from her vantage point facing the mirror, she could monitor everything. Behind her, Petra adjusted large chrome lights as she had seen photographers do a thousand times. Petra's assistant, Sam, stood on a box in the centre of the whiteness while she held a light meter to his face and clicked. The lights flashed. She held it to the other side of his face and repeated. Petra returned to her table full of equipment and answered the phone. 'Yeah, hi, I'm gonna be sending some processing down later . . . About fifty rolls, maybe more. I want a test strip on every third . . . just a few frames . . . Yup, OK, thanks.'

Charlotte sighted Tess in the make-up chair. 'You've got beautiful colouring, Tess,' gushed Karen as she worked a sponge across Ebony Woman's cheeks. 'I've brought out the orange highlights in your skin. This powder is probably a bit darker than you normally use, but look how it evens out that area round your forehead – and it really makes your eyes shine.' Charlotte admired Karen's handiwork.

Tess loved it from the start. 'I normally sit in this chair and get lightened up,' she said, surprised to hear herself say it.

'This is an American range,' offered Karen. 'You can take these products home with you. I'll get more next time I'm out there.'

Colin arrived with heavily laden plates. Charlotte felt her stomach lurch and her mouth begin to water as the smell of herbs and seasonings wafted across the room. The warm comfort she had enjoyed at Kevin's hands disappeared instantly. The hunger would soon rise inside her once more, provoking yet another weary clash for domination. Colin moved the croissants and coffee flasks to the end of the table and placed an enormous vegetable quiche in the middle. Other studio hands added bowls of new potatoes, assorted salads, cold meats, roast peppers, courgettes and plantain. There was rice with saffron and pine nuts, and there was crusty French bread. This was standard fare for a campaign shoot. Most large studios employed caterers.

Charlotte instinctively reached for a large handful of tablets from her bag. She could pass them off as vitamins and pick at her food as she usually did. In fact, over the years she'd developed a variety of ways to avoid eating too much. Sometimes she'd fill a plate and then gradually leave items of food about the studio. Other times she'd rest sandwiches on her lap and then clear them away with the napkin or secrete them in her pockets. Once she had even emptied a meal into a carrier bag and taken it home for disposal. She had become an expert at spreading the food round the plate and making it look as if it had been nibbled at. No one would concern themselves with the contents of her plate, anyway. Meanwhile the remainder of the crew tucked in like breakfast had happened yesterday.

Kevin was the first to light up a cigarette. 'I've only been smoking for a few years,' he confessed to Charlotte as she toyed with a peach. 'I don't like the taste much, but it keeps the old weight down. It's weird, isn't it,' he pondered between puffs, 'how many models actually smoke. Do you think they all do it to stay thin?'

'Sure,' said Trena, joining in as she covered the sole of the shoe she was holding with thick white tape to stop it from scuffing when it was worn. 'But it's a good crack. I still get the urge for the odd one now and then. It counters the terminal hanging about for a start.' Trena looked up and squinted through her glasses. 'Could we make sure all the sample shoes are taped, Gillian?' She lifted a sculptural foot-piece from its box. 'I got these for a favour, and since he's not going to get credits . . .' Trena had to make sure each pair was returned to Jimmy Choo's PR in pristine condition. Her helpers began carefully stripping masking tape over the sole of each shoe and trimming off the excess with scissors.

Trena looked at Charlotte and pushed the glasses back along her nose. 'I think,' she said, motioning with her head to the food, 'they'll probably clear all this away once we get the clothes out – I don't want grease on the samples. So you might as well put something on a plate for yourself. Nothing more is coming until seven-ish. It's a long time to leave it.' She raised her voice to reach the others. 'I don't want any of you modelling lovelies to keel over under

117

the lights through lack of nourishment. You know what you're like.' With that she departed to organize yet more clothes.

Charlotte was angry. It was as if Trena was watching her. Who did she think she was? Nevertheless, she added a few crudités to her plate. Common sense told her not to draw attention to herself. It would be a bad move to faint. Standing still for long periods of time while the roasting lights sapped all energy made many models vulnerable, and most had passed out at some point in their careers. It usually happened around show times when the pressure to fit catwalk designs was at its greatest.

'OK, everyone – first outfits, please.' Trena clapped her hands. 'Let's get on with it. Tess, you go with Gillian there. Put on the lemon pant-suit first and give me a shout. I might pin it at the back if it looks too roomy. Charlotte, put on that sage jacket with the skirt – Lara will help. And Becks, slate slim-fit trousers and waisted jacket. I'll help you.'

For the next five hours models earned their money and assistants fussed and clucked. Grouped together in the centre of the studio, Charlotte's long limbs and jet hair gave her a panther-like sleekness; Tess with her golden-brown face and perfect cheekbones opened her mouth wide and lit up the room with her smile; while Becks posed with an angular grace that danced through her body adding years to her once girlish demeanour. Warming to each other, and silently working together to make the best poss-ible picture, they locked bodies and legs and leaned over the large silver reflector that Sam held close and low to scoop up and redirect light to their faces. On command, they laughed, they smiled, and flirted, each revealing a serene facial composure that ensured perfect shots time after time.

'Good – to me,' coached Petra. 'Tess, look at me full on. Charlotte, eyes left. Becks, more profile. Sam, hold the reflector closer. Everyone this way. To me. Great! Becks, I want to see more of you – you're disappearing behind Tess. OK, relax. Can someone get some tape on that collar? It's creating a shadow on the material below. And I think Charlotte's jacket needs to be pinned at the back – I'm seeing a wrinkle every time she turns.'

During periodic bouts of flashing intensity in which various lights would release their charges like firework displays with sound effects to match, Kevin would slip into shot – the hairdressing world's equivalent of an SAS man – and settle a rebellious hair arrangement. With speed he would tweak curls, flatten stray hairs or dig his hands into Tess's crown to lift her shiny ringlets away from her face. Then he'd back out, standing attentively to the side, serum in hand ready for the next assignment.

Each time Petra finished a roll of film, Sam would pass another cartridge, already loaded. Like a relay runner grasping for the baton, she would flip off the back of her camera and exchange equipment with her attentive assistant. Other times she would switch tackle completely, using a smaller camera.

Meanwhile, Karen, having spotted her chance, would deftly glide past the industrial battery packs, negotiating a multitude of wires, thin metal tripods, lamp stands and a cold-air fan to reach her beautiful team. With seconds to spare she would powder each face, paying careful attention to the area above the top lip and the forehead to remove any tiny droplets of perspiration. Then, with a quick squirt of iced Evian, she'd be off back to the real world.

In the wilting heat, and under the glare of the large and powerful lights, each model did her best to re-live every memory of windswept beach and cool water she'd ever had. Their facial expressions and bodily movements gave no indication of the discomfort that new shoes, sticky tights and tailored grandeur might generate in equatorial heat. And, as they projected the very essence of carefree abandon, each woman feigned her own private paradise, for this was what modelling required. Fantasy moments. Fantasy lives. Fantasy women.

Petra recorded the heavenly trio in every outfit, with every colour combination, angle, position and facial expression possible – each shot as perfect as the last.

The group shots gave way to single as each woman was whisked off to change. Then once again the threesome would unite to perform as one. And as the polished and melodic strains of Betty Carter, Marlena Shaw and kd lang drifted from the open windows of Studio 4, the gathering inside laboured into the evening, all quietly working at their craft and offering the very best of themselves until Petra's camera required no more.

'OK, I've shot the arse off it,' she announced, reaching for a can of Coke and checking the clock as she wiped her hand across her forehead. 'I've got thirty rolls of two and a quarter and I did twenty rolls on thirty-five mil. That's three sixty . . . four eighty. OK, we got eight hundred and sixty-four shots. Sam,' called Petra, 'speak to Joe's – tell 'em I'll be down in an hour.'

Charlotte and Becks were chatting happily together. 'Thanks for that tip,' said Becks. 'I would never have thought that something so simple would make so much difference.'

'Well, Steven Meisel is supposed to have told Linda Evangelista the same thing and it worked for her,' explained Charlotte. 'I use it all the time. Opening your mouth very slightly makes such a difference to the shape of your face. I've got loads of those little tricks.'

Tess joined in. 'I know some model who taught herself to sleep only on her back, so she doesn't wrinkle up her face in the night. You know – like munch it up on the pillow.'

'Obsessive,' agreed Trena, standing in the middle of the gathering like a games mistress on her day off. 'I've got cars coming at nine, but we need to do make-up and hair tests yet. Models, you can eat as we go – there's food coming round – but let's crack on, can we? Charlotte, I want Kevin to work on you. Tess and Becks, let's look at make-up.'

As instructed, Charlotte took her place in the stylist's chair while Trena issued directions. 'Kevin, these are going to be the catwalk looks I spoke to you about. We need something extra. The poster look was perfect for commercial tastes, but on the runway we gotta go for big statement. Alicia is working on extra outfits for effect, but we're gonna style up some of the more dressy looks. I was thinking about some hairpieces for Charlotte. You know, a bit of high-priestess height. What do you think?'

Charlotte listened as Kevin and Trena discussed what she could and couldn't take. Large and square with bulbs right round the edges, the mirror covered the wall. A few bulbs were missing but the rest shone brightly, lighting her face and sending those behind her into shadow. On the long bench area in front of her were Kevin's tools, all laid out on a black towel. He had various kinds of gleaming aluminium apparatus. Like some mad hair doctor, he could work miracles on the thinnest of coverings, and would have the woman in question looking like a full and fecund glossy-maned nymph in no time. It was well known that he did royalty.

'Look,' said Kevin as he moved Charlotte's head to give Trena a better view, 'I can nail it on to her head so it'll stay there during changes. She's gonna have to get clothes over it, isn't she?'

There was that reminder again, thought Charlotte. One moment they were a team: model, hairdresser, stylist, all working together to achieve the best result. But the next minute she, or whoever they were working on, was little more than an obedient dolly. No one said, 'Charlotte, do you mind if I just jerk your head round 180 degrees and talk about you as if you were not of this world?' Nobody liked working with models who were too opinionated. It was always best to keep quiet and give in. As a result, some pretty horrific outfits had found their way on to her body – though there were those who thought otherwise. When trapped inside a giant meringue or encased in rubber corsetry, Charlotte would always smile. Twelve years of smiling had paid the rent so far.

The pizza arrived. It smelled heavenly. Maybe she would reward herself with a slice. After all, she hadn't given in at lunch-time, had she?

'Yeah,' said Kevin to himself, 'this is good. It doesn't weigh too much, does it, Charlotte? I don't want you crashing through the runway when you get up there. I meeeann, I know what you models are like; always trying to lose a bit of weight before the show. I don't want you worrying about it.'

This man was extremely irritating. Was he deliberately trying to make her feel uncomfortable? Charlotte's eyes darted to the other end of the studio to take in her colleagues. Becks was drinking cola like it was water. Several spoonfuls of sugar in every can, and she'd had about half a dozen during the day. Tess was munching a piece of cheesecake. Charlotte felt her stomach cramp up. It was usual about now. The laxatives she had imbibed had started to work.

Kevin carried on oblivious: 'It's amazing the amount of girls who don't eat in this business. Or they do and then they stick their fingers down their throat. I did a job in Japan about two months ago. Ray, who was that model? Quite well known . . . She was American, wasn't she? Does all the shows. Anyway, we were working with her and I had the hotel room next to hers. Every night she would make herself sick. I could hear her – the walls were like paper. Horrible nasty sound. She would gag and cry and gag some more.'

Kevin looked at Ray. 'It was awful,' he grimaced. 'By the end of the shoot, I couldn't stand to be in my room. I made Ray sleep in there. She thought no one knew. I didn't know what to say. I meeeann, what do you say to someone who's doing that? What was the matter with her?' Kevin looked to Charlotte in the mirror for an answer. 'I meeeann . . .' He shrugged.

Tess helped herself to another piece of cheesecake and moved closer to join in the conversation. She offered the plate to Charlotte. 'A lot of women do that in this business,' she said with disgust. 'I couldn't find it in me to abuse myself for some precious designer type.' She made a face.

'Are there really models who do that?' Becks asked, horrified. 'Why? I mean, all the models I know . . . they're naturally thin, aren't they? That's why they're models, surely?'

Tess dipped her body into Charlotte, and Kevin leaned in closer. Becks stepped forward to listen. 'There was a pair of trousers going around last season,' she said indignantly. 'Sample pair, straight from the catwalk – so some anorexic had managed to squeeze herself into them, at least to model them down the runway.' She wiped cheesecake crumbs from her mouth. 'Anyway, I was on this job when they were produced, and I couldn't even get them past my ankles. Not one model on the shoot that day could fit herself into them and there were some real thin girls, too,' added Tess incredulously as she looked at Charlotte in the mirror.

'It rots your teeth, you know,' said Kevin, still working with Charlotte's hair, 'being sick all the time. It's the acid in your stomach. Not nice.' He grimaced.

'And then there are the art directors,' continued Tess, bristling. 'Failed designers of some sort or another. A friend of mine was told her legs were too fat for a jeans commercial. To her face!' Tess was incredulous. 'Some smug little git with a paunch as big as his bank balance wrote her off. The woman is five foot eleven and ten stone, for God's sake!'

'It's not a guy thing,' protested Kevin. 'Some of those fashion editors are stick thin. I've heard them talking, you know. One told a photographer that his model had thighs like a sumo wrestler and he wasn't to use her again.'

'Why does thinness equal perfection in advertising terms? And why,' quizzed Tess, 'is a larger woman considered to be less attractive? Can anyone answer that?'

'Not now,' said Trena. 'Look, I hate to break into this little union meeting, but we've got to be out in less than an hour. Becks, I want Karen to experiment with your make-up for the runway, so go and sit in her chair and let her play.'

'Ray,' said Kevin, 'sit down with Tess and work with it.' He pointed to her hair and involuntarily made the smallest of faces.

Ray stopped handing pins to Kevin and turned to welcome Tess to the seat beside him. He winked at her in the mirror. 'Could do something a bit nice – like braiding. You know, Kevin, I could section off this whole piece and bind it nice and tight into tiny pieces. Wow, man,' he said with humour, 'the sista would look funky.'

'Don't start getting all ethnic on me, Ray,' issued Kevin like he'd heard it all before. 'I don't want anything too Black. Take it back off her face and give it some lift. There will be some headdresses for the show – maybe we could tie it all back and stick it in one. I think it's best if we don't try anything too adventurous, don't you?'

Tess watched Ray in the mirror. She liked him; it was rare to find someone on her wavelength. What few Black hairdressers there were on the circuit had given up even trying to work in a little African originality and had become skilled in the art of persuading Black hair to behave like the European stuff. Fashion hairdressers seemed to agree on one thing: there was hair, and then there was Black hair. And the hottest looks on the runway, which would later influence all the salons, featured styles exclusively for European locks. The sleek, blow-dried, straight cuts which dominated the catwalks over the last few seasons had not been easy to emulate. Most Black models disguised their natural curl underneath synthetic straight extensions.

Tess's friends were always giving her an ear-bashing: 'Like to see you jus' locks up and mash up that catwalk, sis. Those White gals look nice, but why can't a sista be herself? Why has Naomi gotta wear blue contact lenses? An' why has Tyra gotta look like Pamela Anderson? All those blonde streaks in her hair, cha. The woman look like she wanna be a White gal. What's wrong with a sista looking like an African Queen?'

She had tried to explain an industry untouched by nineties notions of political correctness. Beauty, it seemed, was defined according to seasonal whims of variation on a theme. Black super models would never earn as much as their Caucasian sisters because they would always be perceived as other: separate from the norm, not part of it. It was entirely possible that she had been chosen for this job *because* of the colour of her skin. Tokenism had launched a few Black modelling careers, but never sustained them. Tess thought of her own portfolio, brimming with fantasy shots of her as a smouldering untamed tigress; or a she-devil, mysterious and malevolent. Black models would always be expected to portray an edgy outsider quality for stodgy-minded image-makers.

'Why is it that the pretty White gal is always the princess and the pretty Black gal is always the prostitute? Tell us that. And why do you work in an industry that treats you like meat?'

Tess never found a good enough answer. Her friends weren't left-wing militants but ordinary women who took an interest in fashion and appearance. And thank goodness for them – she needed the sassy energy of her West London compadres to stay sane. Trena's loud voice penetrated her thoughts, yanking her back to studio time.

'OK, people,' she yelled, looking at her watch. 'That's it. We've got to get going with a few pictures now.'

'I'm nearly finished here,' called Karen as she wiped her

hands on a tissue. 'Only got one more thing to do.' She turned to Becks and continued. 'Oh, and none of them had any eyelashes,' she declared as she applied large spidery legs to Becks' eyelids. 'They came off with the glue after a while. All the top ones looked like bush babies until we got hold of them. Why do you think they always wore dark glasses? Sit still just a little longer.' Karen was centimetres away from Becks as she pressed the lashes home. 'These won't be on long. Nothing to worry about – I'll take them off gently.'

'I'm going to take a few Polaroids of the finished looks,' announced Petra as she approached Becks with her camera and flashed. 'Wow, Karen, you've done a great job. I like the silver. Hold it, Becks. Nice eyes.'

'OK, everyone. A few more Polaroids and we're done,' said Trena. She had nearly finished parcelling up the clothes and they hung on the rails covered in a thin sheath of transparent plastic. Colin entered the room and signalled time up by clearing the discarded film packaging from the top of the bench.

'Colin, is the van here yet?' asked Trena.

Becks, who had nearly finished wiping off all the make-up that had been applied only minutes earlier, rushed to the table and folded over the lid of a large uneaten pizza that had lain waiting for interest for some time. 'If no one minds, I'll take this home to my mates,' she said excitedly. 'Oh, Petra, are there any Polaroids going spare – you know, to show my agent?'

Petra pointed to the bench she'd been working at. All the good ones were taped into her own book with aperture settings and f-stops recorded helpfully by Sam at the side. The others lay dog-eared in a pile.

With a slice of pizza in her hand, Becks bounced over.

Clad in her old trainers and jeans once more, she sorted through the pile. With the make-up removed, save some muddy smudges around her eyes, and her hair roughed and rinsed of hair gel, Becks looked like the awkward, boyish nineteen-year-old that she was. She turned to offer the others a few pictures and everyone was struck by her transition from sultry sophisticated woman to urchin.

'What?' she said, slightly unsure of the message in their looks. 'These are going spare.'

Kevin broke the silence. 'Who cut your hair, pet? Was it the council?'

Petra laughed. 'Becks, it's just ... well, you look so different now. You barely look like the worldly woman who inhabited our studio a short while ago.'

'I'm not,' said Becks oddly. 'You lot made me look like one. Until seven months ago, I hadn't set foot outside of Devon. I'd never tasted champagne. I'd never been shopping down Oxford Street. I'd never been to see a band play or sat in an all-night burger bar. Hey, I've never even been on a plane.'

'And was it a nunnery that you lived in?' asked Kevin as he packed away his driers.

'I didn't know too many people,' said Becks quietly.

'What does your mum think now, then?' asked Trena. 'I mean, it's a bit of a different life now, isn't it? Is she pleased for you?'

'I dunno,' said Becks, shifting uncomfortably from foot to foot. 'I don't see her any more. We kind of ... well, I don't think we'd get on now. We disagreed on a lot of things ... I kind of trashed the house a while ago and I thought it was best not to go back until I'd got some money to give her.' She brightened. 'That's why this job is so good – because I can earn some money and say I'm sorry.'

'Who do you live with in London, Becks?' said Charlotte, suddenly concerned. 'Do you have somewhere to stay?'

'Yeah, I've got a place in Hackney. I'm fine. I've got friends – Lal and Marcia. They're great. Real, you know? We have a good time. I'm taking this pizza back to their house. They'll be waiting to hear how it went today. I can't wait to tell them. You're all much nicer than I thought. I mean,' she blushed, 'it's just that ... well ...'

'Becks,' said Kevin, 'if anyone asks you, tell them we're all bitches. My God,' he put his hand to his head with exaggerated desperation, 'I didn't get where I am today by being nice. You tell them,' he boomed, bringing himself up to his full height of five foot five and wagging his finger above his head, 'that Kevin Crapper is the foulest, most frightening old queen of them all. That way,' he mouthed in his most camp voice, 'they won't take the piss when they see me. I meeeann, please –' he winced and gestured at his own body – 'there's nothing to be done with it. I'm a tortured creative genius trapped in the body of a flabby cab-driver. I can wrap myself in Versace from head to toe, but I still look like a pub landlord in drag on a good day.'

Colin was standing at the door with his arms folded. Kevin looked at him and made a face. 'Yes, all right, love – keep your knickers on. Time now, ladies and gentlemen, please,' he bellowed, flapping a small salon towel around and cleaning surfaces. 'Haven't you got no hotels to go to?'

As the hairdresser cleared away his chrome-and-black accoutrements and the make-up artist packed all her bottles and potions expertly into the tiered black hamper, Gillian and Lara scurried around like worker ants to remove boxes, screwed-up tissue paper, empty hangers and stray garments. Petra and Sam left carrying cameras and cases.

The lighting fortunately would stay where it was. 'I'm off to process these,' said Petra, 'so I'll see you all later. Thanks, everyone. Sam,' she called as she took the stairs two at a time, 'want a lift to Camden or not?'

The room rapidly emptied. As the rest of the troop decamped, spilling out and pausing by the lifts with an assortment of carrier bags, boxes and holdalls, Colin pushed a large metal bucket of whitewash past them all and into the now vacant studio. With a mop he began re-painting the photographic area, erasing the scuff marks and faint footprints that marked the place where Tess, Charlotte and Becks had stood earlier. Lining the lights to one side and shutting off the music, he closed the windows and straightened the magazines. Once again the silent room was clean, virginal and ready – standing by for the next ad man or woman's fantasy.

'We'll be at Holborn studios next time,' instructed Trena to her beautiful brood as they waited on the pavement in the balmy summer air. 'Be sure not to acquire a sudden tan or a radical change of haircut in the meantime.' She looked at Becks.

'Well, I mean, it can't get much shorter, can it?' said Becks defensively, unaware that she was rubbing at her scar and pulling strands of hair to cover it.

'Oh, don't be too sure,' quipped Kevin as he stopped amongst the crowd to secure a small bag over his shoulder while Ray struggled with the rest of the kit. 'I once worked with a girl . . . she was flippin' bonkers, pet. Overnight, after a bottle of Jack Daniel's, she decides to shave her hair off!' Kevin rolled his eyes for the hundredth time that day. 'The silly tart hadn't even forgotten that she was in the middle of a catalogue job. Didn't wanna do it any more, I s'pose. See what you're like!' he flashed in Becks' direction. 'Anyway,' he resumed, 'they had to fly in some-one else the next day and she went off into the sunset on the back of her boyfriend's motorbike. He was some nasty grungy rocker and she was a nutcase. She wanted to have a holiday with her bloke, I expect. She could have done well, but . . .' Kevin shook his head, 'she took too much nose candy.' On seeing Becks' confusion, he explained, 'You know, Charlie . . . Billy Wizz . . . Coke.'

'Oh,' said Becks, doing her best to conceal her embar-rassment at not knowing the lingo.

Straightening his shirt, the hairdresser spoke wistfully. 'She couldn't handle it,' he said sadly. 'Some of the girls play around – you know, dabble a bit – but this one was on self-destruct. It was such a waste . . .' He looked around as if trying to make some sense out of his story and decided to hurry it to a close. 'Anyway, things got worse. The next time I worked with her, she was out of it. Looked a bit of a mess. I dunno what she's doing now . . . This is going back a bit.' He shook his head some more.

'Honestly, you models!' He brightened, not wanting to stay with the moment any longer. 'Oh, lawks, is that the time? Must dash! Kiss-kiss, all – missing you already. Ray, bring my other bag, can you?' Kevin opened the door of a black saloon car and issued instructions to its driver before turning. 'OK, everyone,' he said, making a thespian-style curtsey, 'hairdresser signing off.' Kevin climbed into the car and waved regally. 'Bye now.'

Before getting into her own car, Charlotte looked for Becks. Ten years separated the two women. One was just starting her career, and the other was considering its close. In other circumstances, Charlotte might have felt less than generous towards someone like Becks, but the awkward beauty had inspired a sisterly yearning. Having never had a sister, and after listening to Becks talk about her mother, Charlotte felt a protective urge to adopt the girl. She also wanted to make new friends; her own had fallen by the wayside, what with the travelling and . . . well, if she was honest, she had let them all go, preferring to concentrate on Rick.

'Let's meet for coffee,' she said decisively. When she got home, she would tell Rick that things had to change. 'Do you ever come south of the river?'

'No, but I'm in town a lot,' replied Becks, flushed and pleased to have made a contact within an industry that had so far made her feel like she didn't really belong. 'Do you want my number?'

'Yes,' said Charlotte. 'I'd really like that.'

10

'do you titter, or snigger or guffaw? All unpleasant habits which need suppressing.'
THE YOUNG GIRL'S GUIDE TO INTELLIGENT DRESSING

CHARLOTTE fumbled with her keys at the front door. 'I'm home,' she called as she shut it behind her. There was silence. She looked at her watch. It was nine forty-five. She'd said she would be home for ten o'clock. True, shoots always ran over; perhaps Rick had thought she would be much later. But his car was in the drive. It would have been nice if he could be at home for once. She had something important to say. The woman in the kitchen mirror greeted her as she passed on her way to the fridge.

Soon a reassuring fizz came from the stove. Charlotte poured the soup into her bowl and sat at the kitchen table, hands cupped round the warm dish. She preferred eating at home and on her own. Here she could concentrate on her relationship with food, mentally rewarding herself for stalwart adherence to the path of discipline and order, and pledging further dedication like a disciple at the altar. The watery meal burned her mouth – a penance perhaps for her unbridled greed.

More and more, lamented Charlotte to herself as she held her hair out of the way with one hand and fed herself with the other, she was finding it hard to control her cravings. Today had been a particularly difficult day. And the way that everyone had gorged themselves had turned her stomach. But then there was Becks ... And she had the results of the shoot to look for. It would be so good to see herself in a large glossy campaign once more. Charlotte enjoyed a *frisson* of confidence as she thought about the conversation she would later have with Rick. She had to learn how to stand up for herself. And he would have to understand that she deserved better.

Charlotte returned to her bowl. She had drained it without realizing and the cracker box beside her was also empty. She must have gorged the entire pack of wheaty squares without even realizing it. Thoughts of bettering her relationship with Rick flew out of her head.

'God, this is getting out of hand,' said Charlotte, appalled not by the invasive presence of an eating disorder, setting up home like some cancerous growth in her mind or indeed in her life, but by her lack of restraint where food was concerned. For Charlotte the wrong was her own doing and she must govern her body with more authority.

As if to quell any hint of suppression, the devil in her belly roared for more. Frightened, Charlotte searched for the woman in the mirror. She who lived in the perfect world would know what to do. They locked eyes. Beside the frame the laxative tablets waited in a box. Charlotte helped herself to ten, fifteen maybe. The demon was rising, festering, growing. She must starve it. The food she had eaten would pass through her body and lend no nourishment to the beast.

'I've got to get rid of it,' she explained to her glassy companion. 'Then I can live my life the way I want to. I've got to be stronger.'

The door slammed and Rick came into the kitchen looking flushed. 'Who were you talking to?' he said, wiping his hair away from his face. He looked odd.

'Oh, no one,' said Charlotte hurriedly. 'Where have you been? Your car was outside, I thought you were home, I...'

'Got to get rid of who, Charts?' Rick persisted. He marched into the front room and, as if in the vain hope of uncovering another person, moved the settee and checked behind the door. Charlotte noticed him gently pull back the window blind to gaze down at the forecourt. A car pulled away.

'Didn't the car work today, Rick?' Charlotte looked at him. 'Did you get a lift home from Jimmy? I didn't hear you draw up.'

He looked at her seriously. 'Look, I don't know who you were on the phone to, or what you've heard, but I'm not going anywhere, Charts.' He was indignant. 'You can't chuck me out.'

'Rick,' said Charlotte, startled, 'I wasn't asking *you* to go.' Then, aware of how peculiar that would sound, she explained the voice. 'I was talking to myself, that's all. I was reminding myself how well I've done with my diet. Anyway, there's something I want to talk to you about. I've been thinking and –'

'Charts, I gotta go out now,' said Rick as he lifted a pile of her things to look underneath. He wasn't listening. 'Jimmy and I have gotta see a client,' he said as he searched. 'Seen my keys, Charts?'

'I thought there was something wrong with the car,' she said.

Rick swung round, his face registering confusion. 'No, I didn't say that – you did. The car's fine.' He appeared disoriented. 'Where are those fucking keys? Jeez, Charts, this place is a mess. I'm in a rush.' Stopping in his tracks for a minute, Rick turned and bolted upstairs. 'I found them,' he called as he descended the stairs and let himself out of the front door. 'Don't wait up.'

Charlotte listened to his footsteps as he clattered down the stone stairwell. She heard the communal front door slam and then more footsteps as he crunched across the gravel. There was the clunk of the car door and the guttural fanfare as the exhaust pipe coughed up its toxic emissions. All very distinctive noises, and none of them audible upon his arrival. Charlotte meditated on the particulars as Rick's Karmann Ghia faded into the distance. He never left his pride and joy at home. And then there was ... Rick couldn't have heard her talking to herself from outside the apartment. So he had been in the flat all the time. Had someone else been here too?

Upstairs in the pastel blue room, things looked disappointingly ordinary. Sitting on the bed, Charlotte watched the hands of time adjust to the passing moment. Her silver Habitat alarm clock lay on its back. This smallest of clockwork procedures made such a deafening noise in the still room. Perhaps it was trying to draw attention to its predicament. Could it have been knocked by flailing arms in a recent embrace, Charlotte asked herself. And as ten o'clock struck, she experienced a pressing need to pick up the fallen timepiece and hurl it through the window.

'This isn't how I planned it,' she announced to herself angrily. 'My life is spinning out of control.'

Now Rick was no longer a lazy (but generally constant) boyfriend in need of threatened separation to jolt him into appreciativeness. He was a lying, cheating . . .

In the kitchen Charlotte Davis threw open the cupboard doors and surveyed her kingdom. Packets of food stood in regimented rows. When problems were insoluble she could always console herself with the orderly arrangement of her universe, but tonight, for once, Charlotte could see further. Today's shoot had not been the answer to everything – she had returned home to feel the same nagging doubts about herself, despite having lost the weight she set out to. And on top of that, she now had a partner who didn't care any more. Her life was a pathetic shambles and tidy cupboards did not make everything all right. A bilious, foul slime rose in her throat and the taste of her own anger turned her stomach.

In a faraway compartment of her head, someone began to shout. They were still kicking and shouting as Charlotte made the decision to join in. Releasing a coiled fury that swept through her body like a raging current, she aimed several blows at the contents lining the clean white shelves and watched with satisfaction as the calm gave way to turbulence and disarray. Containers fell to the floor and broke, biscuits scattered, shattering into small crumbly bullets as they hit the ground, and paper and Cellophane packets spilled their cargo of tea leaves, sugar and pasta.

A loud thud caught her attention. A pot of jam lay fatally wounded. It was split in two, and as large shards of glass folded themselves into its entrails, a gummy pink liquid seeped slowly across the terracotta tiles. Charlotte bent down to survey the damage. Sitting on her haunches, she poked at the scene of the accident with an outstretched finger, exploring the mess from all angles. Like a small boy using a stick to prod a dead animal, she occupied herself for a good while. As Charlotte began removing pieces of glass from the site, the heady perfume rose to her nostrils. Sticky sweet strawberry glue attached itself to parts of her hand.

Instinctively, she put her fingers to her mouth. The sugary fruit paste tasted like a lover's embrace and instantly she wanted her whole body to experience the sweet, sweet ecstasy. Quickly, as if someone might catch her in the act of such sinful lust, she filled her mouth with the contents of the broken jar.

Charlotte was suddenly conscious of the battleground before her, strewn with opportunity. A box of almond pastries had landed over in the corner and some had tumbled free from the packaging and waited for her attention. Looking furtively around the kitchen, she gathered them in her hand, and, with an urgency that surprised her, shoved them into her mouth. Chewing so hard that her jaw began to ache, the green-eyed woman cleaned everything off the shiny floor tiles and into her body.

Halfway through a packet of dry pasta, Charlotte leaned back with exhaustion and listened to her shrunken stomach as it struggled to accept the latest menu. The large mirror outside the bedroom beckoned and she struggled to her feet; her stomach was distended and painful. Her heart was hurting too, but no man could come anywhere near to matching the loathing she could summon for herself. The woman in the mirror agreed. *Let's really teach her a lesson*, she seemed to say. *Let's show her what her punishment will be from now on.*

Charlotte found her tormentor in the bathroom mirror. Go on, she leered, or can't you even do that? More tears rolled down her face as she stood over the sink, poised. The woman in the mirror lowered her voice to a whisper. 'Now is your chance,' she cajoled, 'to punish that grasping, gluttonous monster you have given life to. Now is the time to tie it up like a wild dog. Now,' she urged, 'you must do it now.'

Charlotte reached across the mirror and removed her toothbrush from its holder by the windowsill, then she lowered herself slowly to lean over the toilet. For the second time that evening she held her hair back and away from her face. Watching her tears spill into the clear water, Charlotte slowly inserted the handle of the toothbrush into her mouth and paused. She took a deep breath and jabbed the plastic instrument gingerly into a fleshy lining at the back of her throat. Her diaphragm heaved but, as the muscular convulsion subsided, Charlotte realized dismally that nothing had happened.

'I can't do it,' she whimpered.

Fear hung in the air. It made no noise, but she could feel it cloaking her body, covering her in desolation. Charlotte thought about changing her mind, but knew that the woman in the mirror would never allow such spineless conduct. There was no way out. Catching her breath and with her heart thudding deafeningly, she tried again.

Stabbing harder, keeping the spatula firmly in place, Charlotte registered first the pain of blunt instrument bruising soft tissue, and then a violent spasm. A low scream coursed through her body, gathering momentum as it travelled from her belly to her throat, and she roared as the contents of her stomach hit the pan with a satisfying splatter. Coughing and choking, Charlotte sobbed as she emptied herself of everything she had eaten. Her eyes and nose stung as the air filled with the pungent smell of food in a semi-digested state. At last, silence. The beast could howl no more.

Wiping her mouth, Charlotte stood up. The tempest had passed. She checked in the mirror to make sure her companion was still there. A woman with red-rimmed eyes and a grey pallor greeted her. *We have broken her*, said the voice in her head. *She will do as we say now*.

It was nearly midnight as Charlotte swept the floor in the kitchen. Tomorrow she would slip out early and restock the now barren shelves. Everything would be like it was. Only the woman in the mirror would know differently.

11

'while beauty is a "timeless" quality, the beautiful woman is tightly fettered to time. Female beauty is a state to be attained and lost.'

WENDY CHAPKIS

'WHAT do you make of America so far, Becks?' enquired Petra as they sat in the back of a yellow cab. Wire mesh separated them from the driver, who had not been particularly apologetic about the lack of air conditioning in his vehicle.

'I love it,' gushed Becks with her eye on a giant picture of a British super model towering over the freeway from a billboard. They passed her in the cab. 'Everything is so much . . . well, it's . . .' Becks caught herself in time and took a deep breath. Stay cool, she cautioned herself, exhaling slowly. 'Will we have time for some shopping? I'd love to visit one of those really big stores, like Macy's or Bloomingdale's.'

'I expect so,' said Petra. 'You know, I'm very glad you could do this shoot. I think it will be an important one for you. When we get to the hotel, I need to make some calls, and then I have appointments. I think you should order room service and get your head down. Don't forget, on British time you're five hours ahead. Soon you'll begin to feel pretty tired, and you need to look good first thing.'

Becks nodded obediently. She was still reeling from the phone call two days ago. Her agent had excitedly explained that after the Esteem shoot, Petra Mayhew wanted to include her in a set of pictures for the American magazine *Harper's Bazaar*. So Becks was going to New York. Rebecca Cotton the country bumpkin was making her mark.

Lal had been particularly excited. 'Can you get me something Nike from Delancey Street?' he asked, handing her a twenty-pound note. 'Don't pay full price,' he tutored. 'Only tourists do that, and you're not a tourist, you're a top model. Soon you'll be in and out of New York all the time. Hey, you'll probably get a flat there and forget us because you'll prefer to hang out with posh people all the time.'

'Don't forget to have a pastrami on rye,' advised Marcia. 'You can't go to New York and not have one.'

'What's pastrami?' quizzed Becks.

'How do I know?' said Marcia. 'It's what they always have in the films. Oh, and "cwaoghfee". You know, "Gimmee cwaoghfee,"' she barked. 'Don't go around saying "please", whatever you do, you'll get followed and mugged.'

Becks remembered the helpful instructions from both friends as she folded her things away into the closet. Now, in her tiny hotel room, she felt restless and lonely without them. It was tempting to flick through the cable TV channels. There were hundreds, it seemed, and Becks stood transfixed as each channel revealed its bounty.

'I'm gonna show you how to get fullness,' said a hair-dresser working the head of a model. 'OK,' the presenter interrupted. 'Already selling well. If you've just joined QVC . . .' Becks switched again.

'. . . Germany used to be synonymous with copious amounts of beer drinking,' issued a brisk brunette on NBC News, 'but figures now show that Germans have been steadily reducing their intake.' Becks enjoyed the game and flicked again.

'. . . They often get very noisy in training,' explained the shaggy-haired dog trainer to a toothsome child. 'I'm going to command your dog, and let's see how obedient he is . . .'

America was going to be fun, there was so much of everything and Becks was in a rush to try it out. With her thumb she continued her journey and clicked once more.

'Secondly, Master Pip,' declared a Dickensian gentleman from a black-and-white screen, 'you are to understand that the name of your benefactor is to remain unknown to you. I bid you a goodnight.'

'Oh, Biddy,' said Pip breathlessly as Becks searched for the off-button on the remote, 'I must travel to London.' The screen turned black and fizzled slightly and all was quiet once more. She was determined to appear fresh and bright-eyed in the morning and dutifully prepared to sleep.

On the shelf next to the bed was a ruby red book. Thick, with gold-edged pages, it was a bible, very like the one her grandfather had kept. Perhaps America was not so far away, after all, if God could reach her this easily.

As a child, Rebecca Cotton had thought that everyone prayed. God had played a big part in her life, for she and her mother lived with Him and her grandfather in a musty house with dark wooden panels.

The atmosphere in the house of her childhood was as lifeless as the yellowing lithographs of Moses and the scrolls that hung in the living room. Or the dead room, as Rebecca used to call it. Dead, because the walls were covered with images of dead people: saints, prophets and other biblical types. Dead, because her grandfather, during snatched daytime slumber, would give the most convincing impression of a corpse listening to Radio 4. Dead, because the grey room with its antique books, listless ferns and shabby carpet smelled like a morgue.

The kitchen was where she spent most of her time, glued to the small but perfectly functional colour television at the end of the counter. The beige Formica surfaces were kept spotless by her mother, who would often insist that Rebecca lift her plate or cup mid-mouthful to facilitate the passing of yet another cloth on germ patrol. This little room with strip lighting that flickered for an unbearable length of time before bursting into life was her mother's kingdom and every evening the outside world was allowed to visit. Neighbourly types from Australian soaps; good-looking American policemen with a penchant for writing off people and cars; girls in Lycra dancing to hit records; murderers, villains and 'ne'er do wells'; women with superior cooking skills and sumptuous worktops; or pop stars with inferior social skills and sulky smiles, and a host of faded film stars from the olden days: these were just some of the people Rebecca spent her time with as she shared tea in silence with her mother after school. Her grandfather would take his meal alone in the room up the hallway.

After tea, Patricia Cotton would leap into action. The water would be hot as the plates disappeared into the washing-up bowl and the windows above the boiler would quickly steam over. Rebecca preferred to dry the dishes and would hover by the draining board, cloth in hand, waiting for them to cool before handling them. Her mother's hands were always red because she never adjusted the temperature in the bowl with cold water. In the early days Rebecca had tried to be helpful by washing up herself, until her mother had sampled the warm but not nearly hot enough liquid in the basin and done the whole lot over again. The room always smelt of ammonia, as her mother wiped all the surfaces she could find. They weren't dirty, but as if trying to cleanse some persistent blemish that would not go away the worker and her cloth methodically and purposefully sought out invisible stains.

Once finished, her mother would invariably withdraw from the kitchen to her room, leaving Rebecca with the whole evening to pass on her own. As the day drew to an end, Rebecca would have to make her way upstairs. Having put this moment off until it could be delayed no longer, lingering over a final cup of tea or late-night television programme, she would finally launch herself into the shadowy corridor. Body braced against the cruel chill that lurked in the hallway, Rebecca would race through the house – shoes clacking on floorboards and old York stone.

The banisters, grimy with use, were also in dark wood, which might once have been highly polished. There were still small amounts of varnish at the bottom of the carved limbs where they joined each stair. In the daylight, the foot of the stairs used to be her favourite place. As a child she would separate the ornately carved wooden bust from its post at the beginning of the handrail and lift it clean away to reveal a hollowed-out space the perfect size for secret documents or stolen treasure. Staring for hours into the little wooden cavity, she made up all kinds of stories involving brave adventurers who, even on pain of death, refused to reveal the location of their valuables. This to her was the most secret place in the whole world. Not even God knew of its existence.

God knew about everywhere else though; her mother had said so. He knew when you were doing something wrong, even thinking it. He was with you all the time. For a long while, Rebecca had thought He was some kind of invisible man with telepathic powers who sat watching every move. This was disturbing, and as each birthday passed, bringing with it a heightened desire for privacy, she began to resent the presence of her mother's holy sentinel.

'What have you got to hide, Rebecca?' her mother had probed one evening as they tidied away the remains of the meal. 'God is there to guide you. When we stray from the path, He feels pain. We must always try to observe His way.'

'But how do we know when we are doing it the right way, and how do we know if we are wrong, Mum?' she had asked with girlish innocence.

'God will show us,' was all her mother could say. Only recently turned thirty-one herself, Patricia Cotton had led a sheltered life. It had been spent in service to her aged father, and at his knee she had received most of her education. 'God will show us how angry He is when we have done wrong,' she repeated like a mantra.

Rebecca noticed her mother's shoulders were trembling as she spoke. 'I know what I'm talking about, Rebecca. He's never really forgiven me,' said Patricia Cotton, gesturing in the direction of the living room. But was she talking about God or Grandfather?

Later that night, Rebecca had listened to her mother in the next bedroom. It was always the same. The movements were jerky and noisy, followed by periods of calm. Occasionally there were murmured words, but nothing intelligible, only the familiar conspiratorial whispers and the clinking sound of glass bottles.

In fact, Patricia Cotton was rifling through a pile of empty wine bottles in her wardrobe. She did not bother to stand up the ones that had fallen, but climbed further in to investigate the darkest corners of her cupboard for anything that could be used to quell her craving. Clothes and shoes obscured her vision, making it hard to seek out the bounty. For a moment, she seemed to forget the purpose of her mission, and extracted herself from the murky depths for air. The room was dimly lit; faded rose-patterned curtains shut out the world and bathed the room in a pink glow. The pink candlewick bedspread matched a dusky pink rug that had seen better days. The floral-patterned walls were dismally bare except for a small wooden figurine on a cross above her bed. From His lofty post, the crucified man watched everything.

'This is the last time,' she had pledged, returning to the wardrobe with renewed intent. Empty bottles lay like discarded friends around her feet. Promises meant nothing really. Patricia Cotton had grown up on broken promises. Her own mother had promised to take her to a million wonderful places but never roused herself from the old armchair in the front room. 'I promise we'll go next week,

Trish,' she would say as she drifted into drugged oblivion. The child had hidden all the bottles in the garden one summer's day, reasoning that now her mother would take her out. But that night, reaching for a secret supply on a top shelf, her mother had lost her balance and slipped from the chair on to the tiled floor. The old man wept at his wife's funeral, a sight his daughter had never seen before, and would never witness again.

For a while Rebecca would hear nothing from her mother. This was always the way for a few hours, and then she would be woken by thuds and clattering noises as the disoriented woman in the next room crashed about. There would usually follow laments or cries, and finally praying. Low and slurred, the relentless whimpers of her mother's pleas for forgiveness echoed around the house.

The stuffy, cramped hotel room in New York was a million miles away from the cold and musty bedroom Becks used to sleep in as a child. But a lingering odour that reminded her of distant times hung in the air and followed her everywhere. She tossed and turned, waiting for sleep, until at last a comforting grey fog arrived. She slept fitfully, however, and in troubled dreams real life merged with ghosts and monsters.

Becks had only meant to make a small but dramatic exit by dropping the match into a metal bin. A bit of a smoke stain on the ceiling, and a few charred papers, that was all. Surely it couldn't have got out of hand? The dreamer watched transfixed as the hellish flames licked at windows and shattered glass panes. Fire engines and angels were trying in vain to rescue a woman who had climbed to the top of the house.

Patricia Cotton stood on the roof clutching her crucifix to her breast. She looked ready to flee the towering inferno. Becks screamed: 'Someone help me! Don't jump, Mum! Oh, please don't jump, Mum . . .' The sound of thunder filled her ears. A priest stood nearby to administer the last rites. He seemed to lose his temper and in a voice that sounded far away he barked, 'Tell her to jump and we can all get some sleep.' The banging continued; it seemed to be moving closer. A black cloud covered everything and prevented Becks from seeing. 'Mum!' she called urgently into the darkness. 'Are you all right?'

'Did you hear me?' said an agitated voice from behind a wall. A wall right by her head. A wall that separated her from the next hotel room. 'Quit yellin', there's folk tryin' to get some sleep around here.'

The air conditioner rumbled and jogged her memory, reminding her of the vast transatlantic distance now separating her from Marcia and Lal – the nearest thing she had to family. As dawn broke across Manhattan, Rebecca Cotton waited for the homesickness to pass . . .

'Wake up, Becks,' said Petra as she changed lenses later in the day. 'You look washed out. Paul, can you give her some more colour?'

The shoot was in full swing and Paul the make-up man ushered Becks into the chair. He was softly spoken for an

American and pretty. He wore black biking leather, as if to counter the public schoolboy looks. He'd even dyed his hair black. The fine blond hairs round his hairline were there to give the game away for those who looked close enough. 'It's that time difference, isn't it, girl?' he said knowingly. 'You look like you didn't sleep much last night, honey. Lily might have something to wake you up, if you need it. You know, a little candy. She's always prepared. Hey, Lily, get your fanny over here, girl! You got anything for poor little Becky here?'

'Sure,' said Lily. A six-foot ash blonde, Lily was draped in layers of coloured silk all held in place with a satin bodice. With her hair swept into a sophisticated chignon and plain bands of silver round her fingers and toes, she looked the epitome of elegance. This vision was shattered, however, as she advanced, chewing furiously with large red lips and teeth.

She spoke in blasts, throwing the gum from one side of her mouth to the other with her tongue. 'Here, girl, this'll . . . slurp, slurp . . . make ya feel a lot better. Don't share it with anyone else, though . . . slurp, slurp . . . I ain't that generous.' She produced a small container. 'It's already cut. It's good stuff.'

As if to prove a point, she opened the screw-top and licked her finger before dipping it into the white powder. Paul did the same and they both slid index fingers backwards and forwards across their gums.

'I hate it when they won't supply anything, don't you?' Lily said testily. 'I got Jack to get me some this morning because I knew there would be nothing on this shoot.' She jerked her head in the direction of Petra, who was bent over her camera. 'Some photographers are so dull.'

The lenswoman on the other side of the room continued

unaware. 'Good,' she boomed to her model, yet another svelte flaxen-headed beauty. 'Relax while I reload.' Petra shifted her gaze to take in the scene at the make-up mirror. 'Paul,' she asked accusingly, 'you're not teaching Becks any bad habits, are you? Just throw a bit more of that tawny powder on to her cheekbones and give her back to me now, there's a dear.'

With glowing cheeks, Becks extricated herself from the chair and returned to the white studio area for more shots. She had gold sprinkled in her hair and dusted over her shoulders. The sequinned suit shot dancing beams of light around the room as she walked.

'That's much better,' said Petra and then, more quietly: 'Great make-up artist but lousy friend. Don't cosy in with Paul, his friends are all junkies. OK, Laticia, you're done in that look, go get changed.' She directed Becks to a point in the white space and returned to her light meter. 'I'm gonna do a Polaroid.'

Becks turned her face to the light and directed a steely gaze to the camera. Petra snapped efficiently and trans- ferred the Polaroid from its moorings to her armpit. Becks was getting used to this sight now, although at first it had made her laugh. For three minutes Petra held the developing image under her arm and let the warmth of her body incubate the newborn goddess. 'Excellent,' Petra boomed as she peeled away the flimsy top sheet and then separated the positive from the negative. She studied the print, intently searching out shadows that needed bleaching out or hot spots that required attention. Becks looked at the reverse image on the remaining square of film in Petra's hand.

'I'm gonna move that light to fill in here,' instructed Petra as she approached Becks to show her the results.

'Here, see. Watch out for that slouch of yours. Straighten your shoulders and don't be afraid to lean back on your hips a little.'

Once Petra was closer, she whispered to Becks: 'Don't go out with him tonight. It won't be what you think. He's not in with a good crowd. See a film, maybe. Eat out. Get a manicure – anything! You've got castings tomorrow and you can't afford to be looking rough.' Petra stepped back and, hoisting her black box to her face, she worked to capture the goddess on film. 'You only get one chance in this town, Becks!' she warned quietly.

Becks listened and shifted her body. Her gentle movements, punctuated by Petra's rhythmic flash, were in time to the music. With the lecture now forgotten, both women exercised well-choreographed actions. Lone dancers on a deserted stage, the audience otherwise engaged.

It was wrap time and Paul wanted to talk about England. 'You doing the shows?' he asked casually.

'Yeah, any good ones?' enquired Lily between cigarettes and gum.

'I'd love to get some work over there,' enthused Paul. 'I could take my book around.' He sucked hard on his Marlboro. 'It would be nice to meet some people with a bit of class for a change. Hey!' he burst out, flicking a spiky quiff northward, 'maybe you could introduce me – I'm coming over soon. I could sort you out while you're here. There's a great party tonight, a lot of good people will be there – you should come and meet them. They'd like your look. They just lurve anything English, honey, and you are such a doll. I know them all. I'll introduce you. Say you'll come . . .' Paul was very persuasive in a relentless, pleading kind of way. 'I won't take no for an answer, girl. You gotta get out while you're here. Oh, Lily, tell her she's just gotta come.'

Becks looked for Petra; she was on the phone.

Lily was helping herself to one of Paul's cigarettes. 'You gotta go, honey,' she said distractedly.

'I'll come by in a cab at about ten o'clock. I'll take you there,' persisted Paul. 'You should wear what you've got on now: you'll kill them all.'

It was hard. Becks didn't have many friends. Surely you couldn't have enough? Paul wanted to know her – for now at least. He was funny and almost cosy, like a big brother. He'd look after her. He could be her friend in New York. She could write to him like a penfriend, maybe, or send him a Christmas card. When he came over she'd introduce him to Marcia and Lal. They'd be impressed.

Paul was smiling expectantly. 'Say you'll come, girl. Don't be dull.'

Becks cast a furtive glance towards Petra, who was still on the phone. 'Yes, OK. But I can't wear this. I've got something at the hotel. I can't be late, though.'

'How sweet,' cooed Paul. 'Isn't she a darling! You'll be having such a good time, you won't worry about going home. I don't know any model in New York who worries about home time, honey.' Paul looked in Lily's direction. 'Life is just one long shoot, isn't it, Lily?'

Lily smiled at Paul. 'Hey, I get all the beauty sleep I need. I found some great little pills. Double the dose and I'm out for thirty-six hours straight.' She shot a defensive grimace at Becks. 'He talks a lot of shit,' she said quietly but unconvincingly. She raised her voice again. 'Like you don't have mood swings, smackhead boy. You can't afford to jerk around any more people in this industry.' With that she picked up her coat and bag and left.

Paul turned to Becks. 'Ten o'clock, honey.' He turned and gathered his bags. 'I gotta catch Lily, we live in the same block.'

'OK, Becks,' called Petra, 'let's get you into a taxi.' As they made their way down out into the street, she handed Becks a scrap of paper with an address scribbled on it. 'I've got you an appointment with *Cosmopolitan*. The new editor likes Brits – you'll do well. Gotta be there first thing though, so get your head down tonight. I'll see you on Friday. I may have another job for you then.'

A cab pulled over and Becks was bundled inside. 'Read a book,' Petra yelled as the cab pulled off. 'Expand your mind the traditional way.'

Becks smiled warmly and waved out of the back window. An hour or two at the party wouldn't hurt. Maybe it would even tire her out so she wouldn't have to lie awake struggling with homesickness. A few hours and then she'd go back to the hotel room.

After a soak in the bath and a drink from the mini-bar, Becks slipped on a pair of jeans and her favourite top, made by a Belgian designer whose name she couldn't even pronounce, and waited in the foyer of the hotel for Paul. After half-hour or so, she had decided to return to her room, maybe take Petra's advice and get an early night. But she changed her mind when a yellow cab pulled to a halt in the middle of the street and Paul's head emerged from the rear window.

When they arrived at the club, Paul greeted the man at

the door and bounced in without paying. 'She's with me,' he said as they bypassed the queue. As Becks made her way into the crowded room, the music hit her like a wall and the heat covered her like a warm duvet. Paul was at her side, holding her elbow protectively and guiding her through the throng. 'Hiya, honey,' he yelled to a passer-by as they travelled into the dim and secret belly of the club. Becks moved behind him to squeeze through a wall of bodies.

They reached a small clearing. Lily was leaning against a dirty pink wall drinking from a bottle. 'Nice ta see ya, Becks,' she drawled as she spotted them. 'Come over here, girl.'

In contrast to the bright lighting of the studio earlier in the day, Lily was lit from the side by a dim bulb which hung from a broken plaster fitting on the wall. She looked drawn and tired. 'Hey, Juliee, meet Becks,' she called, still chewing. 'You know, I was telling you about her – she's from London. She's gonna show Paul around when he gets there.'

Becks watched Paul tip the waiter for his beers and took one as he approached, arm outstretched. 'Yeah, she's a doll, ain't she.' Paul wasn't asking, he was telling. 'When I get to London, Becks will put me up for a few days – won't ya, girl?'

Becks was about to protest, but Paul had moved on. Staring greedily at a large smoking joint coming his way, he intercepted it as it went from one hand to another.

'Paul!' wailed a blonde waif, irked that her turn had been cancelled.

'Staceee,' mirrored Paul right back at her as he transported the goods to his mouth and sucked hard, 'don't be so greeedeee,' he mocked between two generous lungfuls.

He held his breath for a while, holding the cigarette out of her reach, then let out a jet of smoke as he spoke. 'Now that's what I call quality blow. Here, Becks, go on girl, Little Miss Puff Head can wait a while.' The sulky blonde retreated to the corner. 'I've put enough stuff her way,' he said, loud enough for her to hear.

Becks enjoyed the pungent odour of marijuana. The smoke reached down into her lungs, delivering instantaneous serenity. The slow-motion sensation always made her smile and, as she leaned against the wall and toked again, the lonely model revelled in the agreeable sensation of new-found camaraderie.

After leaving home, Becks had decided that smoking weed was no big deal. At a late-night party in Peckham she had come to the conclusion – aided by a considerable quantity of vodka – that if she was as bad as her grandfather always insisted she was, then a few drugs weren't going to make anything worse. Since then, Becks had thrown herself into clubland life with its late nights, excessive partying, and the almost compulsory imbibing of any hallucinogenic substances, with a vengeance. After all, she had to make up for lost time. And – even better – there was no one to administer punishment when she returned home late. In New York, she saw no reason to behave differently. Becks felt comfortable with Paul, he seemed to have a way about him.

He was holding court, talking between puffs of smoke while Lily and the others listened. 'So, anyway,' he said, 'then she said, "You can stuff your contract up your arse! Your sales have gone through the roof since you signed me, honey, and these breasts just went out and got themselves a business manager."'

Becks laughed. It was a good feeling. She liked to laugh;

she didn't find life all that funny. Paul made everything seem humorous. It could also have been the weed: sometimes when there was good grass, she got the giggles.

'And whadda ya know,' he squealed, enjoying the audience he had gathered. 'She ripped open her shirt and stood there with her assets hanging out, and then she said, "I own these babies, and unless you want to talk business, that's the last time you'll see them or me, capiche!"'

The crowd fell about. 'Anyway,' Paul said seriously, 'I heard she's gotta make as much as she can pretty quickly. With all that silicone she's had injected into her face, she hasn't got long before it all goes nasty.' Paul's concern was momentary. 'Hey,' he said, raising his voice and laughing, 'she's had so much surgery on those eyes that she already has to tape her lids shut at night so's she can sleep.'

Becks laughed. So what if some mad American had overdosed on cosmetic surgery?

'We call it beauty surgery,' said Paul, as if reading her thoughts. 'Hey, girl, I can get you anything you want. I'm a model's best friend. You know, prescription-strength Glycolic acid – you don't want to mess about with those silly pots of stuff that you get over the counter. Come to me instead.'

Becks liked the fact that she had found her own Mr Fixit. Petra was old and boring. Paul seemed like someone who knew his way around the industry and he made her feel warm and accepted.

The dance floor beckoned and she followed the musical trail, which got louder as she turned the corner. In the middle of the throbbing mass, Becks melted into the crowd. The bodies of everyone around her belonged to the beat and she lost herself in its embrace. Surrounded by people she was content and, for a while, life was right and good.

But eventually evenings had to come to a close. It didn't matter how many clubs she visited, there was no escape from the never-ending darkness that arrived at the finish of every party.

Back in her bed, silence and stillness would envelop her as she waited for sleep to come. It was her worst time. Cold and empty, she would often sit hugging her knees, listening to echoes of her mother whispering to an almighty presence in the next room. She hadn't seen her mother in nearly a year. Perhaps, when she got back to England, she should contact her after all.

Becks returned her attention to her new friends. Lily was scattering conversation amongst her modelling confidantes. She had a glass in each hand and a cigarette in her mouth, which jigged up and down as she talked, sprinkling ash to the floor. Becks caught Lily's eye. Lily winked and turned towards her, raising both arms over her head and spilling some of her cargo. It didn't seem to bother her as she closed her eyes and moved gently and completely out of time to the muffled music. The muted light from the dim bulb danced around Lily's body as she stepped in and out of shadow, highlighting the sheen on her second-hand cocktail dress. In Dolce & Gabbana mules, with hair and make-up slightly dishevelled, she looked like a character in a faded fifties film. Without the studio lights and a top make-up artist at hand, Lily seemed kind of ordinary. Tall and thin but ordinary.

Suddenly she lurched to one side and fell over, barely managing to prevent her liquid freight from spilling. Determined to drink both glasses dry, she staggered to her feet, downing one and then the other in swift succession, hardly noticing the grimy mark on her dress and her laddered tights.

'I think it's time I got Lily home,' said Paul, intercepting the hapless damsel. He removed the glasses from the hands of his charge and held her firmly by the shoulders. She wavered quite spectacularly, threatening collapse once more.

'Becks,' he said, concerned, 'come with me, girl. We need your help.' He propelled Lily out of the darkened cavern and towards the stairway, talking quietly to her. Becks obeyed, collecting one of Lily's shoes from the floor. 'Bye,' she called to her new-found friends, who seemed strangely unconcerned with recent events, as she made her way after the exiting couple.

The taxi ride had passed quickly. Lily dozed quietly on Paul's shoulder while he rolled another spliff. The climb up the stairs to Paul's fourth-floor apartment had been something else. Lily seemed unable to wake and so they had both struggled to manoeuvre her up step by step.

Once inside, Paul dropped Lily on the couch. 'She's had a little too much Harry,' he proclaimed. 'Wake up, Lily!' he yelled. There was no response, so Paul began to tap her face. 'Wake up,' he insisted. Lily's head rolled. 'OK,' he said crossly, 'I'm not going through this again,' and with that he shook her roughly and slapped her cheeks.

'Paul, let her sleep it off,' pleaded Becks.

'Honey, I've got to get her up and moving about. Lily,' he shouted, looking into her eyes and examining her pupils, 'get up, bitch!'

With this, Lily seemed to surface. She was disorientated and grumpy. 'Leave me alone. I'm all right.'

'The hell you are. Now get off your fanny and make

some coffee. We've got a guest – you can't crash out now.' Paul stood Lily up and pointed her in the direction of the kitchen.

Lily seemed to seize the moment and stumbled out of the room. Paul appeared visibly relieved. 'It'll do her good,' he said, flopping on to the couch. 'She's gotta move around. Last week I was that much away from calling 911. I swear, one day she's gonna . . .' He lost interest in the end of his sentence, distracted by an old wooden box on the glass coffee table.

'Now,' he announced, pleased with himself as he opened up the container, 'you can't say we New Yorkers don't know how to give a gal a good time!' Then he lifted out the contents and immediately began levelling a piece of tin foil. When it was as smooth as glass, he laid it down gently on the wooden surface.

'Chasing the dragon is much less of a health risk than shooting up, but you gotta be patient. Lily in there is craven. Me, I say it's worth taking your time to do it right.'

He broke off for a short while, concentrating as he liberated some powder from a small Cellophane bag and piled it in the middle of the foil. 'Then,' he resumed, 'you don't get those nasty abscesses.' Paul leaned towards Becks and spoke with the grandeur of a newly qualified physician. 'When you shoot up, everything goes into your bloodstream.' He pointed at his chest. 'You know, like whatever it's been cut with goes straight into your veins. A lot goes through the needle – bacteria and shit. That's how you get blood poisoning, or the shakes and AIDS.' He stopped to let the words sink in and then shuddered. 'Anyway, needles,' he hissed, 'I can't stand them.'

Lily limped back into the room with some cups of hot

liquid. She set a mug down in front of Becks, and tottered over to a leather armchair the other side of the table. Becks looked briefly around the flat. Once a luxurious apartment with plush furniture, it was now somewhat unkempt and shoddy. Things looked like they needed a good clean; even the white mug in front of her was chipped and caffeine-stained.

Paul continued his tutoring. 'This way no toxic substances get into your bloodstream because clever ole Mother Nature provides you with an extra filter: your lungs. And,' he cautioned like a seasoned salesman, 'you can check the stuff out. I've got good connections, but s'posing you don't have a good dealer and some bum slips you shit or sells you a bad deal? If you mainline, you could be feeding your body talcum powder or flour, but you won't know until it's already in your bloodstream. Now, with smoking,' his voice took on an even grander resonance, '*I* can tell after one puff.'

Paul held a flame under the foil and peered intently at the substance in his hand. 'Good-quality dope melts when you heat it. Like this, see? Look how it moves around the foil. When it leaves a trail of little black specks, then you're OK. Not all kinds of Harry are good for this trip, though. You'd think Chinese would be just the ticket, wouldn't ya? But you'd be wrong. Best I know is Turkish.'

'Turkish what?' quizzed Becks, shaking her head.

'Turkish heroin, girl,' chimed Paul, turning to face her. 'You're not really following me, are you? But don't worry. Uncle Paul is going to show you everything you need to know and, believe me, you are gonna love this one.'

'I've never done heroin before,' stammered Becks. 'I mean, heroin, that's . . . Well, people can die. I don't take those kinds of risks.'

161

Paul laughed. 'You've been listening to too many stories, my dear. Nobody overdoses any more, unless they want to, or . . .' he paused looking at his flatmate, 'they get careless. There's a lot of models do it over here, girl. It's good for the skin – you know that pale, almost translucent look some of the top girls have? – and it certainly keeps the weight down, doesn't it, Lily?' He didn't wait for an answer. 'Trouble with Lily,' he said, like she wasn't even in the room, 'she's not clever enough. Lily likes to inject. She's got to: it's cheaper that way. She's been on it for so long that she has to keep up her maintenance and shoot extra for any sensation at all. Lily gets a better buzz with the needle, but it ain't pretty.'

He lowered his voice. 'I'd say she even goes to bed with those shoes on.' Paul pointed, and added in a conspiratorial whisper: 'She injects between her toes, but she's gonna have to look elsewhere soon, because after a while the veins dry up. And if you get scabs on your feet, it's too painful to walk.' He raised his voice. 'But you've tried everywhere else now, haven't you, Lily?'

Seeing Becks' glance shift to Lily's arms, he said: 'Well, she can't do it in such an obvious place – she's a model. That's why it's better to smoke. There are loads of your favourite models that do.' Paul winked and laughed. 'Hey, we made it fashionable. I know people in this business who've been using it for years.'

'Like who?' quizzed Becks.

'Ah, now that would be telling, girl,' teased Paul. 'If you keep your dose level, you're safe. And it reduces your appetite.' This was his trump card, like he thought that might clinch it for Becks. 'Most of the girls on Harry like a burger or two, but that's about it.'

He turned to Lily. 'Did you hear about Gemma Baxter?'

Lily shook her head. Paul continued, turning back to Becks. 'She's big over here,' he said by way of explanation. 'From New Zealand, I think ... Anyway, she was doing some shoot with clients all over the place. I can't believe you never heard about it, Lily. It was that cosmetic campaign she's got ... So,' he resumed the story with enthusiasm, 'they were in the desert somewhere and she had her own enormous top-of-the-range Winnebago. Come to think of it, everyone did. And they had a catering company on set. The full works. I'm talking fantastic food with everything you could think of: salmon, lobster, and champagne ... OK, so midway through they break for lunch. Now, Gemma's supposed to come out and decorate the set a bit for all these suits. You know, like sit with them and laugh at their jokes while they try to kiss her arse. Anyway, all the clients sit down, the photographer and his six assistants ... And she won't come out of the Winnebago. The little minx says she's gotta have McDonald's and nothing else will do. So ...' he paused to adjust the flame, 'she held up the shoot for hours while Ronald McDonald cooked the fucking thing himself and biked it over. This is in the desert, remember. And then, when it gets there,' he said gathering momentum for the punchline, 'she picks at a few fries in her caravan! Won't let anyone in to retouch her make-up for hours. They had to hire huge generators when it got dark because they hadn't finished the shoot.

'You've seen the ad.' Paul was incredulous. 'Honestly, butter wouldn't melt in its mouth! You must have heard that one, Lil. I mean, what is that woman on?' Paul laughed at his own joke. 'Well, I know what she's on, Lily!' he called, using a silly voice. 'Do you know what she's on?' he asked theatrically.

'OK, Becks,' he announced, pleased with himself, 'try

this for size. You just suck up the vapours like this –' He held a thin tube to the fumes and drew the smoke into his lungs. He acted as if he was going first to show his protégé the way. Becks had yet to learn that heroin addicts never offered anyone else a turn until they had satisfied themselves. 'It's the best fucking feeling this side of earth,' he said, offering the tube to Becks. Lily watched, salivating as Becks tentatively accepted his offer. 'Go, girl,' he said dreamily. 'Don't waste it.'

Becks took the tube and leaned over the melted resin mixture. This was what they all did here, and if other models could enjoy it, so could she. Paul sat dreamy-eyed on the sofa, saying nothing. In less than ten seconds Becks was floating in a sea of love as euphoria spread to every blood vessel in her body. All of life's problems seemed suddenly irrelevant. Her mother and grandfather became a jumble of sensations that lifted clean away from her body. She was floating, happy, ecstatic even. Becks had never known that life could be this good. Oh, life was fantastic. This was what she'd always dreamed of.

'How do you like that, honey?' cooed Paul. 'Didn't I tell ya?' It seemed like he was a very long way away and Becks made no attempt to answer.

A lifetime passed, or was it simply a moment or two? Becks had found a new way to be. Swimming high above the planet, she could look down at everyone and know them all. Life was simple when you knew how to live it. So very simple . . . If only this could last forever.

Becks began to feel restless. She shifted her body in search of the effortless existence she had enjoyed seconds earlier. Her mind called out for the calm that had given way to something else now. She struggled to sit up.

'Paul, I . . .'

'Get into the bathroom, honey,' he soothed. 'It's all right.'

Becks did as she was told, resisting the nausea that had taken hold of her body. Fluffy white towels tinged with grime hung limply over the bath as she rushed for the toilet.

After being sick, Becks returned to the living room with Lily and Paul, and drifted in and out of companionable silence. She stayed that way until Paul offered her a square of chocolate. Or was it when he used the silver wrapper to cook up some more heaven? 'The sky is the limit, Becks,' he said as he passed the smoking dragon her way. 'In this town you can have whatever you want.'

12

'when girls get older, they start to think for themselves too much.'

NEW YORK MODEL AGENT

'WHAT a result,' said Trena when she saw the enormous framed print of three happy and immaculate faces hoisted into place behind the reception desk. Tess, Charlotte and Becks glowed, goddess-like, from their shiny world. In large white letters, a single word was reversed out of the dark shadowy greys: Esteem.

'Great, now I'm gonna look like a dog every day of my working life with those three behind me,' wailed Kirsty.

'Maybe,' observed Trena. 'But don't forget, your body is only a sensible place to store your brain. Perhaps you could out-charm them, competitively speaking. You know – your mouth moves and theirs doesn't.'

'But you can't compete with a fantasy,' said the perfectly

167

packaged brunette sorting the day's post. 'You know what men are like. I thought I was in with a chance with that biker – the one with the long brown hair and leather trousers. I'm not gonna get a pout in edgeways now.'

'Oh, get a grip,' said Trena as she peeled back the wrapper of a chocolate bar – her first of the day. 'Anyway, haven't all bikers got long brown hair and leather trousers? Aren't you getting lost in a little fantasy of your own here? I mean, is it the man or the image? S'posing he walked in here with a haircut and suit and asked you out now?'

'Yuck, gross!' exclaimed Kirsty, wrinkling her nose in distaste. 'I don't think so. Not a *suit*. Anyway,' she said smiling coyly, 'I like the way he grunts when he hands me a package. And all that grease is divine. He only looks good in leather. You know, rough and ready.' Kirsty pronounced the word rough like a playful dog bark.

'God, you were right, Kirst. You've come over all canine. I hope it's not catching. Maybe it's a hetero thing.' Trena leaned on the desk with one hand. 'It's all right, I'll still lust after you. All the women I know look like they could give anything at Crufts a run for their money, but they've got fantastically sexy, curvaceous minds. I find it's better that way.' She returned to her chocolate for a brief moment. 'Anyway,' she said, chewing, 'how come Mr Leather doesn't do it for you in ordinary attire?'

'Oh, Trena,' said Kirsty, exasperated, 'it's a *loin* thing. Anyway, what's it to you? You don't have to worry about looking like Miss World just to get a man to pay you some attention.'

'What, you think dykes don't care about appearance? And after I made such an effort for you this morning, Kirst.' Trena sniffed melodramatically. 'You're a cruel woman,' she pronounced and marched off in the direction of Elle's office, laughing.

'All I know is that, with these three behind me, I'm gonna have to wear a lot more lip-gloss!' Kirsty called after her.

Elle was seated at her desk, beaming, when Trena walked in. 'They look great, don't they?' she said, pivoting to look at the large poster behind her like a proud mother of triplets. 'Look, Trena, I've got to go to a meeting at the British Fashion Council headquarters and I want you to come too. They're stepping up security because of the bombing, and it seems other designers have been threatened. Those of us doing runway have got to pay extra for bag checks, and there's even going to be a police sniffer dog at each show.' Elle rolled her eyes. 'I mean, this is getting ridiculous, what are these people on?'

'Well, I was reading a piece in the paper this morning, Elle. Some journo sounding off, but I think they've got a point,' said Trena sitting on the corner of Elle's desk in her favourite spot. 'I'm not saying it's OK to hurt anyone, but you know how it is in this business. No one will take any notice otherwise. Look at the anti-fur campaign. You've got models all over the place coming on a touch anti-fur. There's a pretty picture of a whole group of them, buck-naked – nice little effect there – and for a short while they say they'd rather go naked than wear fur. That was then, of course. Now it's no longer trendy to be concerned about minks – since they've started running wild in the countryside, killing indigenous mammals and birds – and they're all having a pelt party. Those fur people pay big money to persuade designers to use it and models to wear it. Money can do things, but if you haven't got it, you need to come up with a way to make people change their minds.'

'Yeah, but violence is not the way forward.'

'I'm not saying it is,' continued Trena, folding her arms. 'But when was the last time any of us worried about how much chemical waste fabric manufacturers release into our rivers and streams?'

'Hey, I do what I can,' said Elle testily. 'I couldn't be in this business if I had such a big conscience. And neither could you.'

'Look, Elle,' soothed Trena, 'what I'm saying is that we're *all* involved. It's not simply the biggest names. It's all of us. Sure, you gotta sell next season's clothes, otherwise a whole group of people who depend on you for wages are struggling. Hey, I'm happy here, I don't want to look for another job, but maybe a few changes would be good.'

'Well, there's a team of loonies out there called Global Defence who'd happily employ you, Trena,' snapped Elle. 'Look, I know what you're saying, but I'm running a business and every week I –' Elle gestured with melodramatic gusto – '*I* look at the figures and worry about how to survive the next skirmish with the Inland Revenue. It's a lonely business. And, speaking of survival –' Elle checked her watch – 'I've got to get some caffeine into my system before I can cope with any more from those right-on frock sisters. It's only ten o'clock and I've got to do two interviews, one for *Draper's Record* and the other with the *Telegraph*, then meet with Harold to agree the budget for pre-show press. I've got to oversee next season's production schedule and write a programme intro for the show. Oh, and I've got to get my photo taken for the press office. All before lunch. Now,' said Elle, drawing breath, 'how about making us both a cup of coffee? Medium roast and fair trade, I believe, produced by a farm co-operative in Nicaragua.' Elle winked. 'Maddy insists on it.'

The Crow watched her staff like a fretful mother hen

keeping vigil over her chicks. High-profile survival was every bit as hard as plain old struggling. No one in the office had any understanding of the panic she felt each time Harold called her on the phone. Would this be the day he would tell her that he couldn't hold the business together any longer? For the millionth time, Elle wished she had someone to share her problems with, someone to listen attentively, to partake of a glass of wine and enjoy a sunset at the day's end. Maybe it was because she had no one that she needed the business all the more keenly.

Even as a girl, Elle had never really shared anything with her brothers and sisters. As the eldest, she had been expected to get on with it. Her only solace back then was a method she had devised for sending her troubles elsewhere. She would go down to the seafront near where they lived in Kent and scour the grey shingle beach for exactly the right pebble. Sometimes she would look for heart-shaped rocks, other times she might wait until she came upon a craggy piece of flint that felt right in her hand. And then, as the waves crashed into the jagged shore, sending spray high into the air, she would clasp the stone to her mouth and tell it everything. There would be days when she would cry while recalling some injustice or family fight; reliving it blow by blow, she would be angry and indignant. When she had finished expelling all the wretchedness from her body, leaving out nothing, not even the embarrassing bits, she would hurl her stony confessor as far as she could into the horizon and watch it sink below the spumey brown depths. Then she would wait for the sea to do its magic. Because the sea knew everything. It knew all her secrets and it knew her better than anyone else alive.

When the family left Whitstable and moved to Tottenham, Elle had missed the familiar cacophony of seagull cries, the bracing wind and salty air, but she got on as best she could with her new job in a clothing shop. Only once did she return to that stretch of seafront, on a crisp October morning when she was twenty years old and burdened with a sadness that nothing could heal.

But that was nearly forty years ago. A lifetime of autumn days had since passed with watery sunlight glinting through trees of russet and gold, and wind playfully dancing amongst the fallen leaves. There were always blustery days that made eyes water and tears fall as she recalled her brush with motherhood. That had been back in 1962, yet Elle remembered as if it were yesterday.

'Now, dear, you've got to push,' urged the midwife. 'You can't expect anything to happen unless you put your back into it. You got yourself into this mess,' she chided, 'and you're the only one who can get out of it.'

Elsa tried her hardest to eject the infant from her body, but either tiredness had taken its toll, or the child itself resisted, clinging tightly to the mother she would know for only the briefest of moments.

Not for the first time did Elsa believe she was alone on that cold October night. At twenty, she felt world weary; the anxiety of the last few months had taken its toll. The no-nonsense lampshade offered little protection from the bleak, laboratory-like brightness in the small room. Elsa had already laboured for sixteen long hours and, staring hard at the ceiling, she'd had plenty of time to reflect on the events that had conspired to land her where she was now.

'Elsa,' snapped the midwife, 'you're not trying hard

enough. I'm going to leave you alone while I find the doctor. If you don't change your ways, he'll cut you. Your baby is beginning to show signs of distress. Now, Elsa,' she cajoled, softening her tone, 'you don't want to be cut, do you? Come on, there's a good girl. Let's try one more time.'

Nineteen sixty-two had been a good year, or so Elsa had thought. She was living in a time of new beginnings, of upturned rules and new sexual codes. Unlike her mother, she was free to continue her education if she wanted to, or build a business for herself based on her natural talent as a dressmaker. The exciting possibilities of financial independence and equality loomed large, and the icing on the cake for Elsa had been meeting John, a shy and softly spoken art student from the local college. It seemed the two of them were perfect for each other and she looked forward to the years ahead, proud of their harmonious and loving match. But then she had discovered she was pregnant.

John had recoiled at the news. It couldn't possibly be his, he reasoned hastily. She, like he, must have slept with so many people – surely neither of them could be certain.

Elsa, who had slept with no one else, cried into the night, long after John's departure.

She had cried in the delivery room too. Not tears of sadness, but frustration, anger and hopelessness. Excruciating pain mixed with fury and gave way to madness. She heard her own wails as she alternated between begging the midwife to help her – 'Please take this pain away. I can't do it any more. Please stop it now. The baby . . . Oh, please help me!' – And then calling upon God or anyone else who might influence the situation. 'Is there a God? Will the doctor help? Oh, why won't he come? I'm so tired . . .

the pain . . . Just cut it out. Get the doctor, please,' she blubbered.

But the midwife stood her ground and held on to Elsa's flailing arms. 'You can do it, my dear. One more push, that's all. A nice healthy girl like you – you can push this baby out of your body and into the world now, if you try hard enough.'

Elsa, however, did not want to cast her child out into the cold night. This was not such a joyous earth, after all, for she had mistakenly assumed that a brave heart bolstered by fierce independence would be enough to see her through. When Elsa learned of her impending motherhood, she had also discovered that with the absence of a golden wedding ring proudly displayed at all times came recrimination. She was not simply pregnant, as she had first thought, but a mother unwed and unwanted. Pretence offered a solution. It was easy to disguise her spinsterhood with a cheap gold-coloured band and a title, but her sad eyes glistened from behind the hastily made mask.

'Mrs Crabtree,' said the doctor over the top of his reading glasses in a voice heavy with displeasure and intolerance, 'you really must think about what you are doing, my dear. Do you honestly believe that this is the best start for a new life?' He seemed to be focusing on her expanding girth. Caught out, Elsa began to cry. More softly he continued, 'You are a young woman with your life ahead of you. You have a job and one day you'll get married. But think about this child: it needs a mother *and* a father now. Don't you think it would be better for everyone if you gave your baby the very best start?'

Elsa had wept at the thought of deliberately sabotaging the life of an innocent. And like so many forlorn young women of her time, she had surrendered, agreeing to give the most precious love she had ever known into the care of strangers. 'They are a decent married couple,' she was told repeatedly. 'He is a religious man, and his wife is a respected member of the parish.'

Elsa had pictured them waiting in their quiet, calm house, the nursery decorated and full of toys. After crying some more at the thought of never seeing the person she had carried around inside her for the last nine months, she had summoned all the energy left in her body for one more evacuation attempt. At last the wails were no longer hers alone. She had stopped for breath and hoisted herself up on to her elbows to focus on a small human being wrapped in a towel. The child stopped crying and fixed her gaze on the woman who had brought her into the world. Then she was gone, carried off to another life by a matronly attendant in an identical uniform to the midwife who had spent the night by her side.

'It's better that way,' said a voice from high above her head. 'Try not to think any more about this. One day you will have children of your own and be able to give them the life they deserve. That little girl will grow up wanting for nothing. They are well off, I hear.'

But Elle never did have any children of her own. More and more she thought of the daughter she could have known, and the mother she should have been. Perhaps her daughter had a child of her own now. Maybe Elle was a grand-mother. She was still reflecting on this possibility and wondering whether it would be possible, after all these years, to re-trace the footsteps of her past, when Kirsty bolted into the room, white-faced and wide-eyed.

'Elle,' she said strangely, 'I think we've had a bomb threat, but I can't be sure.'

'For God's sake!' snapped Elle. 'Either we did or we didn't. What the hell did they say?'

'They said . . .' stammered Kirsty. 'Well, there was this voice – it was a he, although I could hear someone else in the background. He whispered something about getting out. He said something would be on fire soon. I could hear something else that sounded like fans – you know, electric fans.'

'Yes?' urged Elle expectantly. 'And . . . ?'

'Well, that was it,' explained Kirsty, running her hands through her hair. She looked about the room as if to detect the whereabouts of a large black orb with BOMB written across it.

'Oh, for pity's sake,' said Elle in exasperation. 'How do you know he was referring to a bomb? There are several different businesses in this one block. We'd have to get them all out.' Out of the corner of her eye she could see Jason, Harold's assistant, larking about with one of the new work-experience recruits.

Elle made her way to the front desk and picked up the handset. She dialled 1471 – that helpful BT service which allowed for number playback – and jotted down a few digits. The Crow dialled the number and nodded with satisfaction as a telephone trilled at the other end of the studio.

'Could you haul your arse into my office for a tongue lashing now, please, Jason,' she barked into the phone. 'Oh, and if anyone's pants are on fire, it will be yours. OK?'

Elle replaced the receiver and looked at Kirsty. 'Don't phone the police. Do get on with your work. Don't put any calls through to me for the next five minutes.'

Kirsty settled back into her red swivel chair and self-consciously plumped up her hair at the sight of a young man in leather carrying a parcel. 'Well, hello,' she breathed, pulling at her shirt, bosoms remembered and bomb threat forgotten.

Elle left them to it. Business as usual at front desk. Kirsty was the quintessential babe – all big lips and bouffant. Men were like panting dogs around her. And Jason, poor Jason, had been trying to ingratiate himself with Esteem's receptionist for weeks. Everyone had noticed except Kirsty, who only responded to grungy couriers in battered Lewis leathers, or crumpled pop stars in dodgy clubs.

'Jason,' said Elle as he slithered into the chair in front of her, 'tell me something . . . Why Kirsty? Why not Alicia or Maddy? I'm not trying to marry you off here – I merely want to understand what sells and what doesn't, so to speak.'

'I can't say,' said Jason defensively. 'Look, I'm sorry about the phone call. I know it wasn't very PC of me. I thought Kirsty . . . Well, you know. She likes that kind of thing.'

'Jason, apart from the fact that you've plummeted in my estimation, and apart from the fact that I nearly hyperventilated back there, Kirsty thought it was a bomb threat. There's a lot to do and I expected more from you. I don't just mean I think you should be working your arse off right now – although you should and you'd better start the minute you leave this room – but I mean, well . . .' Elle struggled to find the question. 'Don't intelligent women interest you?'

Jason shifted, even more uncomfortable with the fact that the Crow was asking him about feelings when a bollocking would have done the job. Next minute she'd be tearing out his entrails like a giant bird of prey and feasting upon them. The only way to escape was to roll over and play dead – that might lull her into a false sense of security and then he could flee, back to his own territory. 'I don't feel so comfortable around Alicia ... She's like ... you know, uptight. She's witchy. I mean, she's good looking and all that ...' Jason stopped. He looked at Elle. Was this what the old bird wanted? 'She's clever,' he continued self-consciously, 'and I sort of feel like I'm wrong, like whatever I say will be wrong.' Now Jason was on a roll. 'Kirsty looks good. She knows how to talk to men and she doesn't give a bloke a hard time for being a bloke. She's the business.' Jason finished his assessment of the receptionist's charms. 'I almost got carried away there,' he said, looking sheepishly at Elle, suddenly remembering that this was his boss he was talking to. 'I dunno if that makes sense,' he said shyly, looking longingly at the door.

'Jason,' said Elle with a faraway look and a sigh, 'women give men a hard time for being insensitive, ignorant wankers.' Turning to face him squarely and adjusting the volume so that others hovering nearby might listen, she added: 'The bloke bit they just put up with. Now, sod off and get something done. Oh, and ask Harold to send down those figures I asked for, will you?'

Jason smirked uneasily and Elle watched him adopting a humble backing out of the room sort of exit that boys probably kept in reserve for escapes from malevolent dowager types. She smiled. This made him whimper slightly en route. She liked that also. He reached for the door, exhaling loudly with relief, and fled.

Turning back to look at the poster behind her chair, Elle tried to bond with her beautiful monochrome daughters. These were the women she felt closest to at this moment.

They would never disappoint her, shout back, throw tantrums or, worse, join the Green Party and wear those embarrassing hippy shoes that looked like buckets. They would all make sensible choices men-wise, mix co-parenting responsibilities with fulfilling careers and live happy ever after. Life looked marvellous in their world. If only it were really like that.

13

'models have such an obsession with minor flaws. The average receptionist has a better self-image than the average model.'

LYNN SNOWDEN

CHARLOTTE was not aware of tears, only dizziness. The hunger in her belly was like a pain reminding her that she was inside a body. She couldn't control life, but she could control her own flesh and blood. She was in charge, withholding privileges or bestowing them. She had come to rely on pain to keep her focused. Watching everything and everyone, particularly herself, with intense scrutiny, this was the way Charlotte had learned to live. It made her feel as though life could be kept in check. Her body, too, needed to be planned and organized. Not given a moment's freedom in case something went horribly wrong.

The woman in the mirror watched quietly as Charlotte

devoured the contents of a supermarket carrier. Subsisting for days on starvation rations left a hunger that howled like a banshee, invading every waking – and sleeping – moment. When the torment became intolerable, Charlotte would silence the screaming beast's demands by stuffing her body with groceries by the bag-load. Behind the bathroom door, as Rick snored contentedly in the next room, she gorged, filling up a giant hole inside her that cried, wailed and pleaded for more. Once the uproar had subsided, Charlotte positioned herself over the toilet. Everything that had entered her body through her mouth would shortly leave by the same route. The ruby-red cherries she had eaten first of all would serve as a marker; she would keep going until she saw the maroon pulp in the pan, then she would know it was all out.

'It's better like this,' said Charlotte to the onlooker in the glassy frame as she hauled herself on to her knees. 'Laxatives don't work like they used to.'

The spectator seemed to agree. *Sure*, she mouthed silently, *your body has grown accustomed to increasing amounts and it takes a whole packet to get any kind of result, doesn't it?*

The presence of the tablets in Charlotte's bag served to ease her conscience. The discovery that supplies were low would propel her panic-stricken into the car for an impromptu drug-store spree. Charlotte didn't use the local chemist any more because over a period of weeks she'd bought excessive supplies. Last week she had found a late-night chemist who didn't hold a large enough stock; having paid for the six remaining packs on display, she had spent the rest of the evening driving round South London in hot pursuit of Ex-Lax reserves. At the time it had seemed a completely normal thing to do, but something Guy said had lodged in her head and refused to leave. Guy was a photographer Charlotte had met on one of the many shoots she'd been booked for since the Esteem campaign had hit the streets, catapulting her career into new heights.

'No one can love you until you love yourself, Charlotte,' he had suggested quietly.

'Oh, believe me, no one spends more time on themselves than me,' she had reassured. 'You know us model types! I'm afraid as I get older, it takes extra time to bully these bones into shape.'

'That's kind of what I'm talking about,' Guy had replied. Then, very gently, he ventured: 'There's really no need to be so hard on yourself, Charlotte. You're so sweet-natured with others, sometimes when they don't even deserve it, yet you give yourself the hardest time.'

Charlotte had been unnerved by Guy. Off balance even. After the shoot he had given her his card and invited her for coffee ... if she was ever in his part of town. He wouldn't have bothered if he had known what type of person she was.

She leaned further over the porcelain bowl. Being sick was very easy now. Like a Pavlovian dog, she could feel her stomach begin to cramp as soon as she started to eat. Her body shuddered and Charlotte closed her eyes in readiness. She felt a familiar ocean of fury well up inside her, then like a foamy wave hitting a woody breakwater it rushed at her rib cage. The taste of this bilious sea was more reassuring than anything she had ever known.

'Something's happening to you and me, Charts, and it's not the way it used to be,' lamented Rick as he sat across the table one morning. Charlotte rarely bothered with Rick these days. Her preoccupation extended little beyond the perimeter of her plate.

'I think we need to think hard about us,' he said, fixing his eyes on hers. 'A baby will make sense of what we have, Charts,' he pronounced confidently, 'and I know a woman who wants a family when I see one.'

'Forget it, Rick,' she said quickly. The thought of seeing her body widen and bloat up horrified her. The woman in the mirror would never agree to such a thing. 'I'm not ready. I'm not even sure if . . .'

'Think about it,' said Rick as if he had found the answer to everything.

And Charlotte did. Fashion editors loved her new lean look and bookings were coming in from advertising agencies. At her age, absurd though it was, the chance to work on so many top projects would never come again. But that wasn't all . . .

Rick's mobile phone burst into life. Still holding her gaze, he flipped open the gadget with a flamboyant 'Kirk to Enterprise' gesture. The ridiculousness of the situation struck Charlotte right in the funny bone and with relief she laughed out loud.

'Yeah, I know, I know,' he said looking at his watch. 'Look, something's cropped up here . . . No . . . Hey, do I sound like I'm having a laugh? . . . No . . . All I'm saying is that I can't get there straight away, but I'll be on my way shortly . . . Yep, will do.' Rick slammed the phone back in place and fixed his eyes on Charlotte. 'What you've got out there, that's not real. You've told me that more times than I can remember.'

'What I have out there is a career,' began Charlotte. 'I really feel . . .'

'Oh, spare me,' winced Rick, gathering up his car keys. 'What's with this "I" business? What happened to "us", Charts? And what happened to you? Mr Photographer going to take you away from it all?' he mocked. 'Yes, I know something's going on with this Guy fella. He left a message on the answer machine. Oh –' Rick put his hand to his head – 'silly me, I forgot to tell you. They're all the same, those types, you've said so yourself. He wants to get into your knickers, Charlotte. Wake up and smell the cappuccino!' With his coat over his arm and his Filofax in the other hand, Rick stood in the doorway. 'I'm not having some camp little git move in on my girl. Look, I've got to finish a bit of business that I should have sorted sooner. Then I'm coming straight back home. Let's make plans to go away and sort this out.' Like a teacher issuing a demerit mark to a wayward pupil, Rick smiled indulgently. 'You gotta learn, these guys are only in it for one thing, Charts,' he called as he shut the door behind him.

As his car rolled out of the communal drive and sped off, there was a familiar and extremely irritating electronic rendition of 'My Way'. There on the kitchen counter was Rick's mobile phone. Charlotte flipped it open and put it to her ear.

'Where the hell are you?' said an irritated female voice. 'I'm not some piece of fluff you can keep waiting whenever you feel like it.'

'Who is this?' asked Charlotte.

There was silence and then a click. The caller had hung up.

Charlotte was suddenly aware of the afternoon heat. She paced the room. It was all falling into place. 'They need a bit of slack and will love you all the more for the odd fling. That's how I get a new wardrobe,' Charlotte's mother had once declared when Charlotte was about sixteen. 'He comes home feeling so guilty that I can almost get him to write me a blank cheque.' Charlotte had thought that women like her mother were realists; saints who got the best of a bad deal. But her father wasn't such a bad man and she'd seen the way he would try and hug his wife, who'd freeze at his touch.

Checking her reflection for no reason, Charlotte came face to face with her mother's daughter. The woman in the mirror was every inch her mother's desire. 'But I am not you!' insisted Charlotte to the face in the glass cell on top of the refrigerator. The heat was making her feel dizzy and her heart was thudding so loudly she thought it might leap out of her chest. 'I am your daughter,' she exploded, 'I am not you.' The words ricocheted around the kitchen and in the silence that followed, ghostly echoes mimicked the sentence like a chant: '–ter . . . your . . . daughter . . . your . . . dau–'

She ran from room to room, shouting at each mirror in turn: 'I am not you!' Lack of food and exhaustion made her feel light-headed, and a rushing noise in Charlotte's ears told her to cling on to something to remain upright. Unsuccessfully she grasped for the wall as her legs folded beneath her. Then Charlotte hit the floor with a thud.

The wind rushed in her ears and tiny spots swam before her eyes. Charlotte felt the warm varnished pine underneath her body and tried to focus. How long had she lain here? Someone else was talking. Perhaps she had been taken to a doctor's surgery . . . but the ceiling matched her own, right down to the faint brown stain in the corner.

'I don't think you know who you are,' said a voice coming from somewhere above her head.

Could there be somebody else in the flat?

'You've always been content with being what others wanted you to be,' said the woman.

Charlotte climbed shakily to her feet. Now she was hearing things. God, what was happening to her? The woman in the mirror stared as Charlotte walked towards the glassy doorway to examine the face that was now a short distance from her own. 'Is it you?' she asked. 'Was that you?'

Rick's mobile called for attention in another room.

'He just left me,' complained an anonymous caller. 'In fact, he dumped me, and he thinks it's going to end all neat and tidy. But it's not. Perhaps you'd like to know what we've been up to for the last couple of months.' There was a silence before the female voice added, 'Perhaps it will help you to make a decision about your future.'

Working as a model had taught Charlotte to fear the future. For the future would shortly mean invisibility. In the advertising realm, clients – mostly bloated old men – created a perfect world and then photographed it to sell clothes, cosmetics and accessories. To the women who read the magazines or bought the products, she was the future; she and her modelling colleagues were always next season. But for Charlotte, the past held more pleasure. The past, her past at least, was a portfolio full of pictures of a younger woman, a younger Charlotte.

The woman in the mirror read her thoughts. 'Allowing Rick to treat you badly is merely another punishment to add to the collection you heap upon yourself for not being perfect,' whispered the clear-skinned beauty in the glassy frame. 'This is a face and body that pleases other people, so why not you?'

Charlotte felt the confusion like a sickness. Her mother had fed her a virus long ago. She almost retched with the taste of anger.

'Life isn't like a magazine spread,' continued her glassy companion, 'and every day doesn't come with make-up artist and hairdresser. But there's more, isn't there? You need Rick to do this, don't you?'

'I don't know what you're talking about,' said Charlotte, 'I...'

'And knowing that he'll soon be at your feet with flowers and champagne, begging forgiveness and threatening to die on the carpet in front of you if he can't have you again,' sneered her reflection, 'has been your reward for being a good girl – hasn't it, Charlotte?'

It was true. Seeing his pathetic grovelling had always made her feel like a goddess. These were the golden minutes when Charlotte felt loved, desired and desperately needed. The power was always intoxicating and had proved to be enough over the years to sustain a substandard romance.

'But there is still more, isn't there, Charlotte?' said the woman in the mirror.

'The hunger,' murmured Charlotte. 'The hunger is gone.'

'Yes, the hunger you've always known is sated for a tiny moment. You can gorge on your own righteousness, licking your lips and stuffing your empty belly. His demented apologies will always signal delicious confirmation of your own human perfection. And as you feed like a ravenous vampire, sweet saintly superiority flows through your veins. Forgiveness is yours to bestow whenever you want.'

The woman in the mirror looked knowingly into Charlotte's green eyes.

'You feast on your faultlessness, like a beggar at a banquet, but you will always be starving, Charlotte.'

The door slammed shut in the hallway. Rick was home. Charlotte turned away from her reflection and walked downstairs into the kitchen. Rick was pleased to see her.

'Right,' he said happily, 'let's talk about our future.'

'You are seeing someone else,' accused Charlotte. 'I know it and this time I've had enough.'

'Don't be daft, sweetheart,' he said, still smiling.

'Rick, I've just spoken to her,' said Charlotte as she headed for the kitchen.

'You're paranoid,' he stammered. 'But if I was, no one could blame me. You've been so self-obsessed recently, only thinking about your own life. Never bothered about anyone else's.' Rick was on the attack. 'Too selfish to think about others, too selfish to have a baby. You don't care about me because you're too busy plucking your bikini line.'

He followed her into the kitchen and removed the cork from a bottle of red wine. Pouring himself a glass, he continued. 'You've got to change your ways, little lady. And don't start whining on about me drinking too much.' Rick glanced down to momentarily inspect the contents of his glass. 'I think I bloody well deserve this.'

Charlotte caught sight of the woman in the mirror. Her glassy companion looked back at her. 'Go on,' she said. Charlotte hesitated and the woman in the mirror spoke again. 'Now is your chance, Charlotte.'

'What?' snapped Rick.

'Rick,' said Charlotte carefully, 'it's over for me.'

Rick thumped the wine glass on the counter. 'Right, we're going down that old road again.' He looked at Charlotte squarely. 'Well, I'll be at Jimmy's for a few days. When you've had time to cool off, let me know.' He started picking up a few things, not bothering to look her in the eye.

'No, Rick,' Charlotte insisted. 'I mean it this time. It's over. I hate this relationship more than I hate you.'

Rick stopped dead in his tracks and looked at her, unable to say anything. He was dumbfounded. Then he found his voice. 'Look, I met her a few months ago. We'd had a row and I was angry with you. One thing led to another and then . . . Anyway, she had me, Charts. She kept threatening to tell you. I swear . . .' Rick looked uncomfortable. 'She was nothing to me, nothing,' he said, gathering momentum as if he'd found his stride.

'I've known what you were like, Rick,' said Charlotte as she stood by the aluminium drainer at the sink. 'But I thought . . . well, I thought I could change you. I thought if I put up with the rubbish for long enough, you'd see how much I really cared and you'd settle down. I can't believe I ever thought that, but I did . . .' Charlotte removed the half-drunk glass of wine from the counter and disposed of its contents down the sink. 'I've finally realized after all this time that I can't change you.' She stopped momentarily to hear herself deliver the next sentence. 'I can change *something*, though. I can change this relationship, just like that, by not having it.'

As the words left her mouth, Rick began to protest. He was up in an instant, moving towards her, reaching out his arms. Charlotte pushed him away.

'Do you know how much I hate myself?' she asked quietly. She caught sight of herself in the mirror on the fridge and spoke to her own reflection. 'I thought it was me all along, not being good enough. I thought . . . I thought I had to be someone special and then you'd love me. I thought it was a matter of trying harder each time.'

Her gaze shifted to her feet. 'It wasn't only you, Rick. I've been working this routine for a long time. Because I never could be the perfect woman, I hated myself for it.' Charlotte turned to Rick. 'But, Rick, I don't hate me. I don't hate me any more.'

'Look, Charts,' said Rick carefully, 'hate is –'

'Yes, hate is a big word, Rick,' agreed Charlotte as she moved away from him very deliberately, 'and I want you to listen to me. I want you to know how much I hate what we have. I want you to know how much I hate your lies and your deals that never come off. I hate your promises and your empty words.' Charlotte raised her voice to hear the power in her own words. Here she was at last, saying exactly what she wanted and – more to the point – what she didn't want. 'I hate watching you in the morning, drooling over your own reflection as you shave, and I hate the way everything you do is about you. I hate the way you never pay for groceries or the cleaner. I hate the way you have never once . . . never once cleaned the toilet or the bath in the entire time we've been living together. And I hate the way you expect me to know where you last left your keys or your wallet or your shoes.'

Charlotte became more animated as she spoke. The woman in the mirror watched with glee. 'I hate the way you can watch the telly when we've had a row, and I hate the way you're convinced people think you're great. And I really hate –' she looked at Rick with new-found distaste

– 'I really hate the way you go to sleep with your hand covering your balls, like someone's going to try and steal your most precious possession in the middle of the night.'

Charlotte caught herself and continued with her voice even. 'It's over, Rick,' she declared. 'It's over. It should have been finished long ago, but it's taken me a long time to learn that I deserve better.'

'It's that poncy little photographer boyfriend of yours, isn't it, Charlotte?' leered Rick. 'I know people who will swing a baseball bat in his direction for a few quid, and if I hear that he's been sniffing round here, he's in big trouble.'

'No, it's not another man,' said Charlotte decisively. 'It's another woman. It's this woman.' She picked up the mirror and looked at herself. 'And I'm going to spend some time getting to know her better.'

14

'beauty is truth.' **JOHN KEATS**

THE Laurels was so called because of the laurel bushes outside the front door in the overgrown garden. Vivid green and sunshine yellow, those large leafy shrubs nurtured bright red berries and were as old as the house itself. This was where Becks had grown up.

When she had received the letter with her mother's handwriting on it forwarded by the agency, Becks had been glad to learn of her grandfather's death. His passing was definitely cause for celebration, but the funeral also offered the chance for her to see her mother once more.

As a child Rebecca would look out for the blazing bushes, watching them grow larger with each step towards the Cotton family home. The presence of such colour was always a final comfort as she passed under a heavily shaded porch and into the shadow beyond. Her grandfather's world was inhospitable. God was by his side, yet the devil lurked in every corner of the house. There were all kinds of demons and beasts to be fought on the way to the kitchen, and out there was a planet straining with the sins of wrong-doers and other low-lifers. Surrounded by biblical memorabilia, the old man used his religion to ward off the muck and muddle of real life and waited stoically in the lounge for the inevitable day of reckoning to arrive.

From her first day at kindergarten, school had served as an escape. Rebecca would spend her days wrapped in the realm of make-believe. In the little red Wendy house she could create the household she wanted. Babies would be tucked up in warm cradles, while tea – some plastic carrots, a papier-mâché apple and an egg-like ping-pong ball – simmered in the red pan on the stove. Until it was time to go home, Rebecca would be in her own sweet heaven, fussing over cherubic infants with saintly dedication and offering sustenance from her nourishing pot to weary passers-by.

As she grew older, Rebecca walked back to the house on her own. She knew many of the people in the village, and they all seemed to know her. She was Joseph Cotton's granddaughter and she lived up at the old vicarage. She could always see the bushes highlighted against the gloomy doorway as she rounded the corner. They were as much a part of her life as the house itself, and among her earliest memories were recollections of hunger for those jewel-like berries nestled against green leaves. Rebecca had heeded her mother's warnings until one day she could bear temptation no longer and crammed a whole fistful into her mouth. They had tasted bitter, but the need to swallow the scarlet fire was strong. They stayed in her stomach for a short while and then, from the depths of her small body, she issued a blast of gelatinous red fury that took both members of her family by surprise. Her grandfather, seizing on her Technicolor sickness as proof of Satanic infiltration, needed no encouragement to vacate the contaminated area and ever after treated the messenger of such foul verse with deep suspicion.

At the time, Rebecca had found it hard to believe that the gleaming crimson delicacies were capable of such deceitful trickery. She had stood bewildered and lonely in the kitchen as her mother rushed to clean off the cupboards and linoleum floor before attending to Rebecca herself. At the tender age of six, Rebecca considered a future where bad was wicked and now good was bad also.

Thirteen summers had passed, but Becks could remember that moment like it was yesterday.

Charlotte, who had been only too pleased to come along to support her friend, now touched her arm as they both stood staring at the house from a safe distance across the road.

'I was never bad,' said Becks, staring at the house. 'But I always felt like I was. Granddad didn't care for me, but I don't know why.'

'He was a sad old man, by the sound of it,' said Charlotte. 'He was too wrapped up in his own miserable world. It's a shame your mother chose to stay with him. She should have left him to it.' Charlotte rolled her sleeves back; it was going to be very hot and to protect herself from the sun she had covered most of her body. But in the dark funereal ensemble she had chosen for the day ahead, she was soaking up the heat.

'I can't go in there,' declared Becks, shaking her head. 'I shouldn't have come, I don't know why I did.' She sniffed and shivered. The heat could not reach the chill in her bones.

Without saying anything more, both women turned their backs on The Laurels and retraced their steps towards the village green. For a while they walked in companionable silence. Neither wore make-up or displayed about themselves anything that might hint at a career on the catwalk. Height could have been an indication, possibly explained as a family trait by those viewing from behind. But to onlookers close enough to compare characteristics, the two towering goddesses could not be sisters. Charlotte's dark hair and milky white skin contrasted with the golden glow of her blonde friend's freckles and sun-kissed nose. Becks rammed her hands into the pockets of her dark jeans and dragged her heels, shuffling along in her black leather trainers. Her angular frame appeared tuned and ready for action. Charlotte, meanwhile, glided like a gothic maiden alongside.

Soon they found a small newsagent which seemed to double up as a grocery store and post office. After purchasing ice-cold Cokes they continued their journey, finally arriving at the top of a small hill overlooking the cemetery. Insects droned in the sleepy heat and cats stretched out on tiled roofs.

'I don't know what to say to her, Charlotte,' confessed Becks as she unscrewed the cap of a small bottle of whiskey and poured the remains into her cola. 'I haven't seen my mother in a year and I don't know where to begin.' After a few slugs from the can, she lit a large roll-up and the unmistakable smell of marijuana wafted across the field.

'I dreamed of this moment, like she'd be waiting for me with open arms,' she said. 'I thought when she and I would finally meet, I'd have done something to make her proud of me and she'd want me as a daughter again.' Becks plucked a single stalk of grass and smoothed it along her cheek. 'I don't know how to love my mother, and I don't think she knows how to love me.'

'Becks,' soothed Charlotte, 'most people don't even love themselves. It takes a lot of learning.'

Becks gazed into Charlotte's green eyes. 'How does anyone begin to learn that kind of thing?' she asked quietly.

'I don't know,' said Charlotte with a faraway look on her face. 'It should be the first thing we all learn, and then it should be the first thing we teach our children. I've spent my life trying to find someone else to love me because I couldn't do it myself. I thought if I loved someone – a man – hard enough and gave him everything he needed, then he would do the same for me.'

Charlotte looked at Becks, and with a wry smile on her face announced, 'I've only recently realized that I should have cut out the "middle man" ages ago.'

They both lay back in the shade and listened to the village below go about its day. Soon there were the sounds of a small group gathering at the church doors. Gentle strains of 'The Lord's My Shepherd' wafted into the wind along with fragments of conversation. Charlotte and Becks both sat up.

'There she is,' said Becks with excitement in her voice. 'The one at the back of the crowd – that's my mother. Gosh,' whispered the daughter with dazed astonishment, 'she looks smaller and older all of a sudden.'

They both watched as the procession disappeared into the small dark building. Patricia Cotton was one of the last to enter, hesitating for a while before she reluctantly joined the others.

Then, only moments later, the church doors were thrown back open and a blast of angelic organ music signalled the earthly end of a mortal man. Becks smiled as each person stepped unsteadily into the bright sunlight, shading their eyes from the blinding rays.

Patricia Cotton was again bringing up the rear. After thanking the man in long flowing robes she looked around.

'Perhaps she's looking for you,' observed Charlotte. 'I'd say she's hoping that you will come even now.' Patricia Cotton made her way to examine the display of flowers and wreaths. With the others – mostly men and women in their winter years – she read the cards. The smell of lilies and roses made its way up the hillside.

'I want to go home – back to London,' said Becks suddenly.

'Oh, Becks,' coaxed Charlotte, 'if you really need to, then that's what you must do. But I don't believe it's what you *want* to do. You didn't come all this way not to do anything about the situation between your mum and you. I know you didn't.'

'But I don't see what I can do about it.'

'You can talk to her, Becks.'

'But what if words make it worse than it already is? What if I make it worse? What if –'

'Becks, she may not want to face the reality about herself, but she owes you the truth about yourself. You don't even know who your father was, do you? I mean . . .' Charlotte faltered. 'We're none of us perfect, but that doesn't excuse your mother shutting you out of your own life. Anyway,' she continued anxiously, 'I've got eyes and I can see that you're already shutting down ... Drink and weed aren't going to help things, Becks.'

Becks looked defensively at her friend. Here was someone who managed her life so effortlessly – she would never understand. Becks had been drawn to Charlotte from the start, impressed by her sophisticated ways, her knowledge of the business. Since Marcia and Lal had taken off to bum around France, Becks had come to enjoy the company of this sister figure. All that would come to an end if Charlotte discovered the truth about her.

'OK,' said Becks, 'you're right, I've got to do this. I know I have and I will. Do me a favour, will you?' Becks got up and brushed herself down. 'Walk with me to the house and then go back to the station. If it's not going to happen between me and her, then I'll know soon enough and I'll catch you up. If the train comes and I'm not there, see it as a good sign.'

Charlotte unfolded her long body and stood by her friend's side. The two made their way slowly down the hill and back into the village. They parted company with hugs and words of encouragement from Charlotte, then she was gone, leaving Becks to ponder the pledge she had issued earlier. 'I will sort this out,' she muttered under her breath, 'but first I need a little help.' The sun was mellowing as Becks found an off-licence at the other end of the village. She bought two cans of Coke and a large bottle of whiskey. This was not her mother's tipple, and Becks felt comforted in the knowledge that she had not embraced the family penchant for wine. Sitting by a duck pond, Becks poured away some of the Coke and added a large amount of whiskey to the can. With the bottle safely stashed in her bag, she sat facing the glowing red sun, slowly watering her soul.

As the large crimson disc sank behind the trees, Becks

began to shudder. 'Now or never,' she said quietly. A few minutes later, she stood with nothing between her and her mother but a wooden door. The knocker, dull and heavy, sounded the same as always. Becks heard the old wood creak as the lock was released.

'Mum?' said Becks apprehensively to the shadowy figure. 'Mum, it's me – Rebecca . . .'

'Rebecca,' said her mother emerging from the dark hallway and stepping into the early evening, the last few golden rays bathing her hair in light. 'Rebecca, I thought . . . well, I thought . . . when you didn't come . . .' The older woman seemed unsure of her surroundings. She used one hand to steady herself against the wooden frame. She seemed so small and sparrow-like in comparison to her daughter, who towered above her.

'Things have changed now, Rebecca,' said her mother, taking some time to choose her words. 'I don't drink any more.'

'Mum,' said Becks, 'there are a lot of things I want to talk to you about.'

'I don't want to discuss the past, Rebecca.' Patricia Cotton retreated and for a moment looked like she might even close the door. 'It's done and gone,' she muttered as she began to turn away.

'Mum,' urged Becks as she reached for her mother's arm, 'who I am now is because of what happened in the past . . . I'm so glad you don't drink any more. Maybe now I can get to know the real you. But, Mum,' Becks struggled to find the right words and subconsciously rubbed her forehead, 'you have to help me get to know myself. Please don't close the door to me now.'

Later that summer's evening, whilst sitting in the living room which Patricia Cotton had attempted to brighten with a cheery coat of yellow paint, mother and daughter talked for the first time. Becks discovered that she had known her father all along. She was not sad to have missed his funeral.

In the old armchair, now adorned with a pleasing throw, Becks crossed her legs and nursed a mug of tea as her childhood unfolded.

'When your grandfather . . .' Her mother stopped as if to correct herself and then thought better of it. 'Well, when he fell ill, he employed a nurse. It was shortly after you left.' Patricia Cotton looked into her cup.

'Towards the end, he became delirious,' she said tightly. 'He called out for forgiveness. I didn't hear much, but his nurse did. He cried a lot and he said he was sorry for what he'd done. One day while he was sleeping . . . she – the nurse – told me she knew what had happened.' Patricia Cotton seemed to find it impossible to continue and sat quietly for a while.

'I was fourteen when he started,' she blurted. 'I thought I had to . . . I thought because I'd . . . well, somehow I believed I was responsible for . . .'

Becks looked at the older woman, locked inside a world that held her prisoner. And watched as the memory of it all transformed her mother into a lonely teenager.

'She died, and I thought . . . well, I thought it was my fault because I'd hidden her drink.'

The person in front of Becks had become smaller still, lost within the framework of an old leather chair.

'I thought I had to . . . I thought God wanted me to . . . Well, comfort my father.' The woman stopped abruptly, as if shocked by her own words.

It was dusk now and Becks could not see her mother's face.

'I was the age you are now – nineteen – when I realized I was expecting you. After that . . .' The thin voice gave way to silence for a while, as if the story might be about to end, and then it continued: '. . . he stopped. He never said anything more about it. I refused to see a doctor until it was too late to do anything except have you.'

The speaker shifted in her chair and reached out to switch on a lamp. From the shadows emerged the older woman once more, and she fixed Becks with her eyes.

'We pretended that I had been careless with someone from the village,' said her mother, relaying the final details as though it was still a well-rehearsed story. 'I think,' she added, shaking her head, 'that he even began to believe it himself.'

All the times that Becks had listened to the sanctimonious old hypocrite lecture her about God crowded her head. 'I feel sick,' she said. 'We . . . you and me . . . we didn't have a proper family life, did we?' Becks rubbed her forehead and stared into the world she used to know. 'He robbed us both,' she said angrily.

The older woman thought for a while. 'I think it all went wrong when I was about three or four and we moved here from London. Mum was lonely, so she started to drink. I grew up not really knowing what a mother did, because it was like I didn't have one. And as for a father . . .' Patricia Cotton turned to face her daughter. 'I wasn't a good mother for you, Becks. I know I wasn't. But maybe we could try and do things differently from now on.'

Now it was Becks' turn to shift uneasily in her chair. She wanted to parade all her disappointment before her mother this very minute. She wanted to recall every incident

202

where her mother had almost physically recoiled from touching her, hugging her, even combing her hair or helping her dress. She rubbed the scar on her forehead, as she always did when perplexed or self-absorbed. It was one of the few presents she had received from the woman who brought her up – the result of a blow from a plaster Madonna, an impromptu and spiteful punishment for blaspheming. Now this woman in front of her wanted to be a part of her life, like a proper mother – whatever that was! Becks considered feeling happy, but it was not really an option – years of compulsory detachment had trained her well. If she could only feel . . . if not elated or blissfully contented then . . . gladdened or optimistic about this, then there was a chance for them both. But some other bittersweet love had taken her mother's place and now held her close – much closer than any maternal embrace.

Seeing the confusion in her daughter's face, Patricia Cotton tried to help. 'There's something else . . . I found out something about my mother . . .' she ventured.

'Not now, Mum,' snapped Becks, tired and hungry for the warmth she had come to rely upon to fire up her hostile heart. 'It's a lot to take in just now and I'm tired.' Her joints ached and cried out for much more than a hot bath. 'I really am tired,' said Becks like a mantra as she reached for her bag. 'Is it OK if we leave the rest until tomorrow, Mum? I need some sleep.'

Once inside her own bedroom, Becks acted quickly. It had been twenty-four hours since she had taken care of business and she could feel the flu-like symptoms beginning to take a hold. Heroin wasn't enjoyable. Heroin was much more than that, it was essential. For a month now Becks had taken heroin like a medicine. People didn't enjoy medicine, did they? But they still looked forward to it, of course.

This, Becks reasoned, was because medicine made the body better. Becks felt better after her medicine, always.

In New York Paul had been contemptuous of her initial reluctance. 'There's nothing to worry about, girl,' he had instructed. 'If you're clever, you can stay way ahead of the game. No one's saying anything about overdosing – that's for jerks. Hey, I don't hang about with sleepwalkers. If you know what you're taking, and you take it regularly, then everything's cool. Look at the options: you don't get like Mr Skyscraper, cokehead hotshot – "Let's all have some 'quality me time'!" – and you don't start talking to the fairies in the wallpaper like some space wombat on acid. Listen, girl, with chasin',' he had said winking, 'there ain't no better way.'

The words echoed in Becks' ears as she set up her medicine. Soon a river of liquid serenity would flow through her brain and veins like a velvet charger. Becks had come to depend not on the drug but its ability to fluff up her heart into a great big fleshy globe of happiness. On H, Becks was in love with the entire world and it with her. She could do anything she wanted.

When Becks had returned from New York, she had meant to leave it well alone, but the days and nights were too bleak without a little something. It had been so easy to find heroin in London, and it was cheaper than lots of alternatives. Surprisingly, there were a couple of models able to point her in the right direction and now, with a new crowd of ready-made friends to go with the drug, Becks never passed a day without a little 'partying'.

Today had been the lowest and the highest points of her short life. She had bonded with her mother and they had talked. But the price for the togetherness was the knowledge that she was born out of the craving of some nasty religious crank for his own daughter. She shuddered and sucked hard on the plastic tube that would carry heaven to her head. Within seconds, she felt warm and safe.

15

'**OF** course, while it is true that advertising never sets the pace, it cannot escape its share of the responsibility for confirming the view that "to join the club" you've got to look like this, smell like this, speak like this and dress like this.'
DELEGATE AT A SAATCHI AND SAATCHI CONFERENCE

$\mathcal{T}$ESS rounded the street corner to see yet another Esteem poster. They were everywhere.

'You don't think the fashion industry is such a shitty place now, do you, Tess?' Belle challenged as they passed. 'It's not such a bad business when things are going your way, is it?'

'Yeah, OK, Belle,' replied Tess warily, 'but that doesn't mean I'll be sitting pretty in a fur campaign next week.'

'Why not?' queried Belle. 'These companies have got

millions to spend on their advertising, you know. You could be rich in seconds.' She checked her reflection in a car wing-mirror.

'Because I've got scruples,' retorted Tess, feeling the stickiness under her arms. It was going to be a very hot day.

'Oh, don't make me laugh!' snapped Belle. 'You're saying that you would refuse a couple of hundred thousand – and you know that's small fry, 'cos they'd pay a couple of million for the right model. But let's just say two hundred thousand. You could buy a very spacious home for that amount, and you'd turn it down?'

Belle was almost incredulous and her voice was high and thin. 'You wouldn't be able to,' she teased. 'You only say you would now because you don't believe you'll ever have the chance to earn that kind of money. It's easy to be noble when you aren't going to be put to the test.' Belle sniffed and began rummaging in her bag for her purse. She put a pound in the hand of a young woman sitting by the side of the road displaying a cardboard sign, then dashed into a newsagents and returned with gum.

'Anyway,' she resumed, 'you could do the job and give all the money to some anti-fur campaign, if you really feel so strongly about it. Or you could give it all to your mum or a homeless person – or twenty homeless people.' Belle was on a roll. 'I know plenty of big-name models who refused to promote fur quite publicly when it suited them. But *then*,' Belle emphasized the word like a lawyer confident of conviction, 'then they slip quietly into a bit of mink or silver fox when their favourite designer asks nicely, and pays them a wad on top.'

'It would never happen,' Tess declared confidently to her flatmate.

'Well, you're in the wrong business, Tess,' said Belle gaily as the tube station came into sight. 'I'll be late tonight; I've got a shop launch. You can meet me and come too, if you like, but the clothes are mostly leather – perhaps you've got a policy on that too. And let's not forget the vol-au-vents and canapés that will be served by underpaid waiters . . .'

Belle was not one to be brought down by anyone. She loved her job every bit as much as she loved the schmoozing, the free gifts, the trips, and the company of vacuous fashion types.

'Belle,' called Tess laughing as they parted company, 'you're a career slag of the very worst order!'

'Call me Fashion Trash!' yelled Belle as she disappeared into the bowels of the earth.

Conscientious objecting, it sure took it out of you, thought Tess with resignation. She'd drunk more than a few beers herself last night while agreeing that the liberation of minks awaiting injections of weedkiller before reaching the skinning tables was imperative. It was a big bash with wall-to-wall paparazzi. There were lots of models there; the anti-fur protesters were stepping up their effort to re-educate the fashion industry and many of the new recruits to the cause were teenage models. Funny how Bambi-eyed beauties went in for the preservation of endangered species with such passion. Kindred spirits, perhaps? Tess pondered the presence of a modelling gene responsible for cute, fluffy and mute behaviour, and decided that there was definitely cause for scientific research. Or could it be that some campaigns were simply sexier than others? Would a top beauty affiliate herself with a much-needed sewage project in a developing country? Possibly not, if it involved *not* having her picture taken by a top photographer in a central London location. She resolved to research a more unpretentious way of 'giving', especially if it involved earlier nights and less alcohol. Now she had a stonker of a headache. But Simon . . . well, he was worth it.

The guy was a looker all right, stylishly attired in camouflage trousers and neon T-shirt, and an excellent conversationalist. They had talked all night, and in him Tess was relieved to find someone who did not pant open-mouthed at her modelling credentials. So many men were overcome with an attack of 'slimy git syndrome' once they heard her job description. Yes, Simon was definitely worth a second helping. He had been fiery and spirited and – even better – he didn't have a current girlfriend, wasn't living with his mother, didn't want a boyfriend, wasn't fleeing a string of ex's suing him for child support.

'Let's see', thought Tess as she passed yet another Esteem poster, 'how he performs in the cold light of day.'

At that moment, her mobile rang. 'Good morning, lovely woman,' said a voice she recognized instantly as Simon's. Her belly did a flip.

'Hi,' she managed. 'You're quick on the draw.'

'I don't play games, Tess,' he said warmly. 'I would really like to see you as soon as possible because . . .' he faltered momentarily. 'Well, because I don't want to let this chance go by. I hope you are pleased to hear from me, but if you aren't and you regret giving me your number . . .' he seemed to be choosing his words carefully, 'that's cool, I won't bother you again. It's . . . well, I think you must know how I feel.' He laughed self-consciously and Tess warmed to him all the more.

'And I hoped you'd call,' she said encouragingly. 'I'd like to meet. Yes, I'd like that very much.' Inspired by her own enjoyment of his voice and words, Tess was already planning the night ahead. 'How about tonight?'

'London Fashion Week,' said Simon, as they sat in the newly opened brasserie later that evening. 'I want to know all about it.'

Tess helped herself to a pistachio nut from the bar and thought about how best to explain this strange twice-yearly affair to an outsider. She had always been contemptuous of the egos and the hype herself and didn't want to be in the position of having to justify her involvement in such a business yet again. It was a living, after all.

'Well, I suppose I've got used to it,' she said with resignation, 'but it's the weirdest thing really. Everyone in the clothing world pitches up for some kind of mad week-long fashion fest. I mean, hundreds of grown men and women pack themselves into a minute space to gawp at clothes for days on end.' Tess smiled self-consciously at her companion, who appeared to be fascinated. His large brown eyes were fixed on her. 'It could be a tent, a gallery or even a night-club. Wherever it is, though, you can be certain that it will be too small and half the audience will be left outside threatening bodily harm to the person on the door. Once the chairs are full, they'll sit in stairwells, on the floor – anywhere to get a view. And then they wait, sometimes for an hour or more, before anything happens. Designers are not renowned for their time-keeping.'

Tess took a sip of her Bacardi and Coke. Simon really did have the dreamiest eyes. 'Anyway,' she said, anxious not to let her guard down, 'finally the show begins, but it's not really a show, not like a thing you see at the theatre.

We models don't *do* anything.' She laughed. 'We just walk up and down a raised area called a catwalk one by one. When we get to the end of the runway we smile – well, that's where all the photographers are positioned, there are hundreds of 'em. So they take a shot – the skimpier the outfit, the more they do – and then we get changed into another outlandish get-up and do the same thing all over again.'

Simon was incredulous. 'Is that all?' he quizzed, screwing up his face. 'And models can earn thousands for that?'

'Some of the supers do,' confirmed Tess, nodding, 'but the rest of us are working gals. Designers and their clothes are big business, you know. Their models are an important part of the sell. A picture of Kate Moss will be beamed all over the planet on cable TV, national news, even the Internet, in moments. Then there are magazines and newspapers . . . That's millions of dollars of free advertising.'

'So why do people need to see it live?' asked Simon. 'You know, why do they cram themselves into an uncomfortable tent when they can see it on CNN?'

'You're talking about the chosen few,' rounded Tess. 'Hell, these people live for fashion, they've got to be there watching it live and direct . . . Oh, and being seen to be seen. There's easily as much camera action off the catwalk as there is on it.' She laughed. 'These are the opinion-formers, the stylistically evolved . . .' She threw him an ironic glance. '*Allegedly*. You should see them, though – some of the front row look a right sight in the full battle-dress. Then there are the writers, the columnists, the publishers, the editors and fashion directors. These are the people who'll announce the next big thing to their readers. If they like a designer, they can make him or her into a star. They can champion their work by wearing it, photographing it and talking about it. Some of these fashion types take their jobs very seriously.' She thought for a minute. 'They'll even throw punches to get through the doors, you know.'

'What, you mean people without tickets will fight to get in?'

'Oh, they've got tickets, but they've all got to get inside the doors like yesterday – and they *are* prepared for a fight.'

'No!' exclaimed Simon as he acknowledged a signal from a waiter beckoning them to their table.

'Oh, yes,' continued Tess. 'Fashion editors in their little Elspeth Gibson dresses and Manolo Blahnik shoes, who take cabs wherever they can, who won't step out of the house in the wrong shade of kid leather . . .' Tess rolled her eyes. 'These people will take body blows from a Neanderthal doorman in a bow tie in order to get inside a dodgy old club and see half an hour's worth of frocks.'

'But why?' Simon moved off his barstool and politely gestured for Tess to follow him.

'Hey,' said Tess, knocking back the last of her drink as she picked up her bag, 'even I don't know the answer to that one.'

Once at their table, Simon had been engagingly intimate, touching her hand briefly, but not lingering too long.

'I'd love to see something like that,' he said as he reached for the menu. 'It sounds so . . .' he searched for the words he needed to explain himself '. . . other-worldly.'

They busied themselves with the menu for a while, perusing the list of beautifully styled food items.

'But what happens if you haven't got a ticket?' asked Simon casually as a waiter jotted down his order.

'Everyone who goes to a catwalk show has been individually invited,' explained Tess. She looked at the waiter standing beside her and pointed to a special on the board. 'I'll have that one, please.'

'Don't people slip through the net?' tested her companion. 'You know, merge with the crowd and get past the ticket inspectors?'

'Look,' explained Tess, 'each designer has his or her own press officer, and each press officer has a team of people who know practically all their guests by sight. Someone who isn't supposed to be there would be stopped half a dozen times by different security checks. Believe me, I've tried to get into a few myself.'

They whiled away the time, Simon probing for more details about security, tickets and press officers, Tess answering him as best she could. It was great to speak to someone who was attentive and curious about the industry. He was genuinely enthralled by her world.

'No chance for me, then,' lamented Simon finally.

'Not unless you know an insider who'd be willing to lend you a backstage pass.'

'But I don't.'

'You do now,' chirped Tess.

Simon visibly brightened. 'Fantastic, I can't believe my luck.'

Neither can I, thought Tess as she prepared to receive a plate of creatively arranged crustaceans. There was something about Simon that made her feel rather excited. She wasn't looking for Mr Right, but Mr Right Now was sitting across the table from her and that was good enough. 'I don't know enough about you,' remarked Tess, and then regretted her tone instantly. What a giveaway, she thought as she quickly continued: 'I mean, you haven't told me anything about you, and that's a little one-sided, don't ya think?' Tess was back on course.

This time it was Simon's turn to look slightly off-guard. He gathered himself. 'Ah, well,' he said putting down his fork. 'You could say I'm a teacher of sorts . . . I teach adults how to behave. You know,' he looked around the room and returned to Tess, 'people who exhibit anti-social behaviour need help . . . they can put us all in a lot of danger.' He stared at her intensely for a fleeting moment. 'I'm brought in to help them see things differently.'

'What, like a therapist?'

'Yes,' confirmed Simon, nodding and smiling. 'Yes, you could say that, although . . .' he thought again, 'I work with people in groups, not really one to one. I get better results that way.'

They talked and talked, and Tess learned that Simon came from a little village in Oxford, where he'd had a dream childhood. His father was a professor, always away lecturing somewhere, and his mother was a charming woman who kept herself busy with charity functions and fund-raising causes. His older brother had followed in his father's footsteps and he . . . well, he was more his mother's son.

Tess talked about her mum and her hopes one day to go to Trinidad and meet up with the father she'd lost contact with.

'It's not that I'm looking for him or anything,' said Tess awkwardly, 'but . . .'

Simon looked into her eyes. 'Everyone is looking for someone, Tess.' He hesitated. 'I'm very glad I found you. I know this is . . . er . . .' He laughed self-consciously. 'The thing is, I'm always being told that I'm too intense and that I shouldn't make my feelings so clear . . . like, it's just not cool. But I don't know how to be any other way.'

A waiter arrived with the bill. 'Anyway, don't say anything . . .' Simon rubbed the back of his neck nervously. 'You've got my number, haven't you? Ring me when you want to see me, and I'll be straight round.' He placed some crisp notes on the table. 'I'd like to pay – if that's OK?'

As if anxious to confirm a no-strings-attached clause to the money on the table, Simon leaned over and kissed Tess carefully on the side of her face. She thought she detected a whiff of her favourite Ralph Lauren cologne. It was guaranteed to dispatch her out of orbit and into oestrogen meltdown.

'I've got to go now,' he apologized. 'I've got a really early start in the morning. A conference up the other end of the country. Remember, even if you don't ring, you promised me a ticket for a catwalk show.' He flashed a row of perfect teeth and was gone.

As she left the restaurant, Tess wondered whether she had jinxed things by putting on her favourite underwear. Not that she was definite about asking him back, but it would have been nice to have had the chance.

She hailed a cab and climbed in. 'I know you,' said the driver turning round to look at her. 'You're that bird in the poster, aren't you?' He pulled out in front of a small car, ignoring the angry shouts of another driver as he sounded the horn. 'That's two famous people in one day,' he said, pleased with himself. 'This morning, I had Charlton Heston sitting right where you are now.'

They rounded the corner to see yet another Esteem poster. Her friends had been impressed, and at first the novelty had been fun. Her mother had been so excited and, if she was really honest about it, so had she. But seeing herself defaced in a variety of ways had not been part of the plan. There was the predictable moustache, and the eyes-gouged-out look that seemed to occur on the underground. Sure, she could take that. But the contributions from those waiting at bus shelters, where a more unsavoury form of artistic augmentation appeared to take place, were less to her liking. Line drawings of male members close to her face were disconcerting. A sure sign of men with time on their hands. Nothing would change until London Transport could provide more frequent buses. Or men grew up.

Viewing her face on billboards, however, looking huge and magnificent like some powerful giantess – now that was something else. And, yes, there had been plenty of work lately, probably as a result of those very elegant hoardings.

Once inside her flat, Tess checked her messages. Simon's voice made her heart skip.

'I guess you're not home yet,' he soothed. 'I'm sorry the evening ended so abruptly, but I've got a bit of a big day tomorrow.' He paused. 'I had a special night tonight, Tess. And I hope very much that you would like to see me again. Please ring me soon.'

Tess experienced a giddiness. She had never allowed herself to feel anything too intense about the opposite sex. Sure, she'd had lots of relationships, but she'd never wanted to get seriously involved.

'If you don't love someone too much, it doesn't hurt when they leave,' she said to a picture of Bob Marley on her wall. Emotional protection was a necessity for members of the female gender.

Tess found herself thinking about the last time she had seen her father.

She was about eleven years old. She had been sitting in her room drawing, and her father had flung the bedroom door open and blown her a kiss.

'Gotta shift, Peaches. Be good for your mama,' he had said.

'Say goodbye to your father, Tess,' her mother had said as she picked up his coat.

But Tess never said goodbye normally. David Douglas was a wanderer, a romantic traveller not suited to nine-to-five hours. Sometimes, after his departure, Tess would find small origami shapes made from Rizzla papers. Other times he would simply be gone. But this time, Tess knew it was different.

She had grown up understanding the meaning of piggy in the middle. It wasn't a childhood game she had played when the fancy took her, it was a state of being. She was that piggy in the middle, caught between parents who stood either side of what seemed to be an abyss. She was always the bridge they used to reach each other. In her they found common ground; in them she saw the division that can exist between two people firmly stuck in opposing camps.

'Don't go troubling her now, David,' her mother would say stern-faced.

'She needs to know, Debs,' her father would shout as

218

he left the house. 'Stop trying to protect her from the truth. My daughter needs to know what it's really like out there.'

Tess was used to the arguments and the fights. She felt loved by both parents but wished they could love each other with more understanding. Her parents weren't married, and neither seemed concerned about the open-house agreement. The two females – one in her early thirties, the other just into double figures – would quite happily carry on for days before the return of the restless man. Then, once again, the family would become three and they'd start over, all smiles and kisses until the next time – which was always too soon.

'And they've gotta learn that this isn't days of the empire now,' her father once bellowed. 'How are they gonna know things are different if you go along with it to keep the peace?'

'Don't talk about my parents like that, David,' Deborah Collins snapped back.

Once when Tess had crept into the hallway to get a better look at them both, she saw her father sitting on the sofa, talking softly to her mother who was standing by the window.

'There isn't anything here for me, Debs. I'm trying, but I can't do it. I've got two good hands, two strong legs and a brain. I'm honest, yet I can't get a job.'

'Because you don't stay in one long enough,' her mother had complained as she stood hunched and guarded. 'You had a driving job two weeks ago – why didn't you stick with it? You had an interview with the Post Office; you didn't even wait to see if they would take you on.'

'Debs,' her father had tried to explain, 'me and the boss didn't hit it off. And the driving job . . . I don't want to work somewhere I gotta wait in line behind White drivers for the worst jobs. I drove to one estate for a pick-up, and I saw National Front graffiti on every wall I looked at. I didn't see one brother on that estate, and I thought some geezer was gonna jump me an' trash the car as soon as I stepped out. I thought to myself, I'm not picking up from here again. And I told them back at base, "Don't give me bogus pick-ups. I could have got myself killed, for what – for a lousy fiver. How come I don't get airport fares, and this man here, he gets two or three a week?"'

'What did the controller say?'

'He said, "You don't like it, boy, then you ain't workin' here. My drivers do as they are told."'

Tess had watched her father stand; raising his voice, he said, 'I told him, "Forget that, and forget this job." Then I left that nasty little office; I wanted to cuff him there and then – calling me "boy" like I'm some piece of dirt. I'm no one's boy, Debs.'

Her father reached out to touch her mother. 'That man, he thought it was old-style runnin's, where he clicks a finger, and I run around like some nigga.'

At the tender age of eleven, Tess had felt so much confusion watching her father ram his hands into his pockets and stare resolutely out of the window. With his back to her mother, he had said, 'I'm not just off a boat. I was born here. I went to school here . . .' There was silence for a while then he continued in a voice barely audible: 'This is supposed to be home.'

David Douglas had turned round at that point to see his small daughter outside the door. Immediately he had walked towards her with his arms outstretched, talking gently to her: 'Your mum wants me to shut up and take it. She wants an easy life, but she's a White woman, and things are different when you look like her. You remember that, Tess: you've got to find a different way.'

After that day her father had stayed away for a long time and Tess had missed him, but she liked the calm that would befall the flat in his absence. Her mother would seem brighter and less troubled for a while, and then she would begin to agonize about where he was, and why he wasn't with her. Tess remembered how her mother would stare out of the window with a faraway look in her eyes and a Benson and Hedges between her fingers.

The weeks seemed to drag by into months and then one day Tess received a postcard from Trinidad. It was from her father and he was working a hotel's season. He said he would be back soon. When the snow began to fall, Tess had waited for his return. They both did. Waiting for the restless man was now a silent game to be played on quiet days when the wind blew and drizzle hit the windows.

One grey Sunday afternoon, as mother and daughter stared out from the window of their high-rise balcony observing the south of London coated in white dust, Deborah Collins broke the silence. 'I don't think he's coming, Tess,' she whispered before retreating into the kitchen.

Tess had stayed by the window. She waited an hour or more, keeping her eyes trained on the world below until the light began to fade. Finally, she too stepped away, turning her back on the dimming skies, and went to find her mother. The two of them hugged and cried softly until it was dark.

Fourteen years later, Tess remembered her father's last words like they were spoken only yesterday. 'Gotta shift,

Peaches. Gotta ... shift ...' Every now and then, she would pull out the dusty shoe box from under her bed and enter all she had of his world. A faded Caribbean postcard revealed his neat handwriting. An unfinished book waited for his interest once more. When she lifted one of the yellowing origami shapes to her nose, Tess could still smell her father, even touch him. For a while he was with her.

Her thoughts returned to Simon. He was someone she was willing to take a chance on. Simon wasn't some fast-talking, empty-headed charmer; he was committed, honest and ... well, gorgeous, actually. At last here was someone who sparked a fire in her heart.

'What do you think, Bob?' she quizzed casually as she placed a CD in position.

'One love,' began Bob.

Tess joined in. Kicking off her shoes and swaying gently to the rhythm, she crooned, 'Yeah, let's get together and feel all right.'

16

'adornment is never anything except a reflection of the heart.' **COCO CHANEL**

THE Family Records Centre was a disappointment. Becks had hoped for a magical citadel bursting with secrets about the lives of its subjects. Instead, an ordinary civic building, grey and lifeless, yawned before them.

Beyond the heavy wooden doors were rows of giant directories slumbering peacefully on never-ending shelves. Becks and Charlotte surveyed the inexhaustible collection of dull green volumes, each divided alphabetically, yearly and quarterly, and simultaneously gasped.

'This is going to be harder than I thought,' groaned Becks, eyeing the crumpled document in her hand. 'All I've got is this adoption certificate. It's nothing to go on, is it?' She looked around the room and flopped on to a wooden bench with a sigh.

'Was there anything else your mum could tell you?' quizzed Charlotte gently as she sat beside her friend. 'Did she ever try to trace her mother?'

Becks dabbed at her nose with a tissue. The sniffles she seemed never to be able to shake off were making her nose tender. 'She didn't even know she was adopted until my grandfather died,' she said. 'But she did find out her name. You know, the one her mother would have given her. It was Helen . . . Helen Crabtree.'

'Imagine that,' whispered Charlotte. 'She's only just found out who she really is.' In silence, the beautiful woman considered her words. 'I think I have a lot in common with your mother.'

Becks looked sideways at Charlotte.

Charlotte scanned the faces in the long corridor, all quietly consumed with the business of searching for someone. 'I've been looking for myself too . . . I thought that if I looked in the mirror for long enough, I might see me . . . There was always someone staring back at me, but I never liked her. I didn't take the time to get to know her for myself . . . Still,' she brightened, 'all that is changing. Let's see,' she twinkled, 'who we can find for you.'

The two women examined the shelves for 1962. Even the year itself was split into quarters. And so was the alphabet. Beginning with the first quarter of the year and with the largest of the four books open flat, they hurriedly turned the pages. Tracing the names from Crab to Crabbet to Crabtree. There was no Helen. They tried another and another until they came to the last portion of 1962. Becks held her breath.

'There!' she shrieked. 'There she is – Helen E. Crabtree. That's my mum!' Becks swung her head excitedly, announcing her news to the rest of the large room. One or two of its occupants looked up and smiled before returning to their own detective work.

'What now?' queried Charlotte.

'Look, there . . . that name . . . she must be my grandmother. My mother's mother.' She used her index finger to prod excitedly at the words on the page. 'That is the woman who gave birth to my mum.' Becks was beaming. 'I could have a granny out there, a little old grey-haired lady who knits. How exciting, I've never had a grandmother before. All we have to do now is trace this woman.' Becks was jumping about with excitement.

'That's not as easy as it sounds,' cautioned Charlotte. 'I mean, supposing she's . . . well . . . dead.'

'She won't be that old,' breezed Becks. 'If she had my mum in 1962, she must have been fairly young herself – you know, a teenager or something. She'll be in her mid-fifties, maybe.' Becks thought for a minute. Looking upwards and out of the corner of her eye she spoke softly but insistently. 'She's alive, I can feel it.'

'Well, you know, she may not . . . want to . . .' Charlotte was trying to choose her words carefully. 'I think you should . . .'

'I can handle it,' said Becks. 'Hey, maybe I don't want to meet her. I mean, she left my mum with a religious child-molester and a drunk. That says it all really, doesn't it?'

Not for the first time her thoughts turned to heroin. The need to suck up a little serenity was growing.

Seeking distraction, she turned to watch an old lady brush away a tear as she closed a large book. This was a library like no other. For some, like Becks, a name and date could be the beginning of discovery and adventure. For others, like the grey-haired grandmother opposite, this anonymous room full of fellow seekers was to be the final resting place of dreams.

They stepped out into the sunlight, each wrestling with the future.

'I don't feel so good,' said Becks as she made her way to a bench conveniently located in front of the registry. 'I think I'm coming down with flu or something. I need to go to bed. I'm going to head home to sweat it out.'

Charlotte hugged her friend. Her own body could be temperamental too. 'Will you be all right?' she asked, hailing a black cab.

'Yes,' said Becks. 'I'll be fine once I've had a rest.'

Charlotte leaned into the front portion of the taxi and furnished the driver with instructions while Becks opened the door and climbed in unsteadily. She managed a cheery wave as the vehicle pulled away, but turned immediately to concentrate on her bag. If she could have a little H and make this awful feeling go away, she'd be better, stronger and back in the land of the living. In a frenzy to get to her mobile phone, she tossed out a wallet and a pair of sunglasses, then scattered the contents of her Filofax on the seat beside her.

Becks had been trying to give up. In fact, she hadn't had any heroin all day. But now, with these dreadful cramps and the hot and cold flushes . . . It was going to be harder than she thought.

'Jerry, you've got to get to my place as soon as you can. It's business and it's urgent.' Becks had learned to use code. Everyone she knew who took heroin did. It made it possible to talk about it in the back of the cab without having some nosy driver know your affairs.

Just a little one to get me over this patch, promised Becks to herself. *Then I'll stick it out. I'll stay in my room and brave it out.*

Jerry was waiting outside Becks' door as the cab pulled up. He was a fixer of sorts: some models had used him to scare off persistent and unwanted admirers; others worked for him occasionally by escorting an assortment of unappetizing film types to premieres. He had long hair tied in a ponytail; it was thinning at his temples. Pretty women all over the city owed him favours and that was good for business.

'Had to grease a few palms to swing it for you, Becks,' he said, making sure she understood the extent of his loyalty. He would certainly require a return at some point. 'You know, express, like. But you sounded so eager.' As Jerry nudged at his nose with a crooked index finger, his overblown biceps bulged from his T-shirt.

Becks unlocked the communal front door and stood at her own doorway fumbling with yet more keys.

'There's some bad stuff out there at the moment, Becks,' cautioned Jerry, extracting the keys from his patient's shaking hands. 'Some people I know have gone down,' he said as he motioned her into the hallway. 'Seems like it's been cut with travel-sickness tabs ground to a powder. There are people out there hearing voices and blanking out. Now what I've got is pure, all right. No black flashes – I've tried it myself. But there ain't much of it.'

Becks dropped her things on the table and sank into the chair. At last relief was not far away. 'I don't care, Jerry,' she said. 'Give me what you've got now.'

Jerry opened his bag. 'I'm gonna cook it up for you,

sweetheart. You need help.' He laid out his apparatus on the table. Becks recognized it instantly as the tools of someone who injected.

'I'm not doing needles,' she snapped.

'You don't look like you got much choice,' said Jerry. He nudged his nose several times.

Becks thought about Lily. In the week she had spent at Paul's apartment, Becks had seen her inject in between her toes. She remembered how she had been overcome with revulsion.

'Backs of your knees, my dear,' said Jerry casually as he dissolved the powder into water.

'Jerry, this isn't how it's supposed to be. I'm not some disgusting junky,' protested Becks.

'Course you're not, sweetheart. I know some of those. Man, I've seen them grab at the stuff in the street with their arms already tied. They dissolve it in a dirty puddle, cheap wine – even their own pee, if they have to. That's what addiction does, Becks,' he stated matter-of-factly. 'You're not like that.' He filled a syringe slowly and squirted out a tiny amount – an air bubble could be fatal if introduced into the bloodstream – and advanced towards her. 'Now, turn over,' he instructed.

Becks obliged, lying on the settee face downwards. Jerry slapped hard at a point behind her knee and Becks felt a sharp sting. He did it again. 'I'm trying to get a vein to raise a little,' he explained. 'Relax, there's a good girl.'

But Becks could not. She held tightly to the cushion as he pierced her skin and sank the needle into her body.

'There,' he said, 'in fifteen seconds you are gonna be floating. I've given a lot of pretty women their wings.'

Becks knew this was heroin slang for teaching someone to inject themselves. As she waited quietly for the pain of withdrawal to leave her body, a phone rang in the distance. She heard a voice she recognized ... Was it from a long time ago or only yesterday?

'Did you get home all right? ... Give me a call later.' Click.

At last, peaceful warmth covered Becks like a soft and comforting blanket. Tomorrow she would answer the phone. Tomorrow she would give up taking this drug for good. Tomorrow she would get herself straight.

Charlotte hoped her friend was all right. She replaced the handset and began to sort through her own messages. There was one from Rick, as there had been every day for the last week.

'It's Rick ... Charlotte, I know you aren't going to pick up the phone so I'm leaving this message in the hope that you'll ring me later.' His voice was strained. 'Please try and ring me, Charlotte. I'm at Jimmy's and I'm desperate to speak to you ... Charlotte, I can't believe you want this ...' Click.

She listened to the next one more carefully. It was from her agent.

'Hi, Charlotte, it's Sally. I've got details of the Esteem film shoot next week. Give me a ring when you can. Oh, and there are a couple of bookings you might want to go through with me. You've had all the details about tomorrow's job, haven't you? Car to pick you up at eight. Be at the studio for nine. Oh, and Charlotte, one of the bookers saw you out the other day and said you were looking thin. Have you been ill? I'm a bit worried ... I know you've been having a hard time with Rick lately ...

I hope it's not getting you down. Please try and get some rest over the weekend ... and *eat*. Speak to you later.' Click.

There were other messages: one from her mother – Did she want to meet in town next week? – and one from a girlfriend – Did she want to meet in town next week? Charlotte listened half-heartedly. She was thinking about what to eat and how much exercise she would do later. Long and punishing training schedules conducted in the dappled streets at dusk were a much more refined way of civilizing crude flesh. Exertion had become a preferred alternative to expulsion and a palatable way of staying in control.

In the bedroom, the woman in the mirror greeted her as she kicked off her shoes.

'So what now, Charlotte?' said her glassy girlfriend. 'You may be eating, but you choose not to allow your body the chance of expansion. Why do you work so hard to get nowhere?'

'This is my way ...' replied Charlotte as she fished amongst her clothes for her running gear '... of taking care of my body.'

She changed into her cycling shorts, adding an assortment of extra layers including a fleece sweatshirt before finishing off with thick socks and trainers.

'It's 80 degrees out there!' objected the woman in the mirror.

'I'll sweat more.'

'Yes, then you'll come back and step on the scales and congratulate yourself on losing a pound or two, but it's only water, Charlotte. Your body needs water. In this heat you could shrivel up.'

She made her way into the kitchen. The woman had

taken her place in the small frame on the fridge. 'Why don't you get off my case?' Charlotte snapped. All these questions were irritating. She was eating, but carefully. Mostly vegetables, salads, soup, pulses and fruit. Lately, however, Charlotte had found herself fantasizing about the gastronomical delicacies she would lavish upon friends for some make-believe dinner party. She would deliberate with obsessive fervour over the smallest details concerning accompanying sauces and garnishes, or scour recipe books, reworking the recipes by substituting low-fat alternatives. In Boots she had recently stood by the display cabinets for over an hour speculating on the true calorific value of all their low-fat products. Adverts for foodstuffs on the television could root her to the spot with mouth-watering anticipation; gravy powder and Oxo cubes were her favourites. And sometimes at night, Charlotte was convinced she had emptied the fridge. Her dreams were so vivid she would wake in a cold sweat and run downstairs to reassure herself.

She busied herself preparing a meal, carefully weighing out amounts and cutting off portions. Sometimes she would adjust the final allowance on her plate, removing an extra sliver here and there before allowing the meal to commence. Watching her food carefully she would help herself to tiny amounts, letting each morsel dissolve into a paste on her tongue before preparing for the next admission. This was a practice that confirmed the gourmand as a sophisticated diner, not some ravenous glutton unable to exercise control. It could take ages to consume one meal. Charlotte never went out to dinner any more.

All was silent in the kitchen but for a peculiar whir emitted by the large white container, refrigerating its contents.

'Have you ever asked yourself,' said the voice, 'why Charlotte Davis needs an eating disorder?'

With bright sun streaming through the windows, the kitchen became a cell-like enclosure full of reflective surfaces. Charlotte watched a grossly distorted woman scuttle across the kettle for cover. Suddenly the room was alive with tortured mutants as each spoon, gleaming aluminium surface and glass exterior revealed a hideously deformed prisoner morphing past its shiny expanse. As each malformation scurried into the shadows, Charlotte addressed them all.

'I haven't got one,' she exploded. 'How dare you talk to me like I'm some kind of mad woman. I'm holding down a job and living my life. If I had an eating disorder,' she roared, jabbing a carving knife into the air to enhance her point, 'I'd be in hospital. Some sadistic doctor would be force-feeding me and I'd weigh half the amount I do now.'

The woman in the mirror replied, 'But you are weak, Charlotte. Look at yourself.'

'Ah,' said Charlotte triumphantly, 'then why am I being told how fantastic I look by photographers and fashion editors? Why am I getting more work now than I ever did when I was heavier?'

The woman in the mirror pondered this. 'They need you to look that way, Charlotte. They want you to prioritize the ability to fit into a size eight dress above sanity and serenity. As a reward for your immaculate existence, they will iconize you, worship you, bathe you in glory. If others will follow, dedicating their lives to the pursuit of perceived beauty and shrunken perfection, then, like some self-elected and corrupt council, they can elevate their fanciful little trade to a position of greatness.'

Charlotte reached for a glass jar and spun round to aim it at the speaker. 'This is my life and I am in control!' she screamed. 'Leave me alone, you with your jumped-up little theories.' There was a crack as the jar tipped the mirror to the floor and smashed against the wall, scattering coral-coloured lentils everywhere. The mirror had snapped in two and Charlotte stood over it. A muffled voice struggled to be heard as she crushed the shards into smaller pieces with her foot.

'How badly do you want to be a part of their world, Charlotte?' it asked, before dissolving into a hundred fragments under a clean white trainer.

'Can you show me where it all takes place?' asked Simon.

'Here –' revealed Tess twenty minutes later, pointing to a large patch of grass outside a museum – 'is the site for London Fashion Week goings-on.'

'But there's nothing to see . . .'

'Ah-ha,' said Tess, 'there will be soon. They'll set up giant tents with catwalks and exhibition areas. In a few weeks this place will be full of models, security, and women in black strappy shoes with mobile phones. Oh, and lilies, there will be loads of those.'

Simon was quiet.

'There you have it,' said Tess, laughing. 'It's a strange mirage that takes place twice a year in Paris, Milan, New York and London while everyone in the real world goes about their business. Hey,' exclaimed Tess, 'what's the matter?'

'Oh, nothing,' lied Simon. 'I hoped there would be something to look at, that's all.'

'There will be,' said Tess, blissfully unaware of her partner's frustration. 'There will be.'

D-day was only three weeks away and Elle was beginning to feel the strain like an impending cystitis attack. Why did designers have to go through such a ludicrous process in order to sell their wares? To stage a twenty-minute show during the London calendar she could spend equivalent to the going rate for a three-storey house – twice a year! And, as one of fifty or more exhibitors packed into the fashion week schedule – the week actually consisted of four or five days – Elle could not linger over subtle details. Like oversized conveyor belts, the giant white catwalks operated a fast turnover and she must slot in behind one frock fitter and ahead of another.

Abroad, where the competition was far greater, international names seemed to dispose of marketing budgets the size of Third World debts. In Paris, for instance, the underground Carrousel de Louvre played host to French Prêt-à-Porter week, but many designers exchanged the marble floors and air-conditioned catacombs for the preferred ambience of palatial banqueting halls and indoor courtyards. Some design houses repeated this formula several times a year for a multitude of lines including couture, menswear, children's wear and a diffusion range. But it was the franchising lines which sustained most multi-million administrations. Pierre Cardin had reportedly secured six hundred separate licensing contracts, from wine and food to bicycles and bed linen.

Even Harold had recognized the need to upgrade the business to stay competitive. 'You've got to address the market, Elle,' he had announced during a company brainstorming session in the wake of Esteem's poor performance the previous quarter. 'We can't afford another set of figures like these –' he said, waving a sheet of paper.

'Yeah, we need a fragrance, a Herb Ritts advertising campaign, and a franchised accessory range,' agreed Trena. 'We want new customers to notice us and existing customers to buy more.'

'We've got to create a lifestyle,' said Alicia. 'When they look at a jacket on a hanger, they want more than an acetate and rayon mix complete with a set of cleaning instructions and a spare gilt button sewn into the lining. They want to see a world that they can be part of and know that the only requirement for membership is a credit card.'

'It's the only way we're going to survive, Elle,' Trena had persisted. 'You know we all love Esteem. We all love what you stand for. But the buying public aren't as aware of you as they should be. We've got to tell them about Esteem. So what if it's all been constructed in a photographer's studio?'

Alicia held out a pink double-breasted jacket. 'Are we offering a lifestyle as part of the Esteem empire? Or just a few clothes in this season's colourways?'

Elle had taken the advice of her colleagues. It had been her dream to carve out a very British approach to tailored clothes, and when her aunt had died leaving a few thousand pounds to her favourite niece, she had invested it in a working space and an industrial over locker and set about making the business work.

For a while, she had enjoyed enough popularity to make the graft seem worth the effort. Esteem grew, and a few years later she had her first catwalk show. Elle Cartwrite could not compete with the big names in British fashion, but a small review in the glossies twice a year had kept things ticking over. Technically, the seventy-five thousand pounds or so that it cost to stage a modest show was her advertising budget. But times had changed and she must keep up. 'Branding' was the millennial buzzword; even magazines and model agencies were marketing their own range of clothing and accessories nowadays.

And so Elle Cartwrite was now on a mission to ensure that her clothes would be featured in top fashion magazines and worn by up-to-the-minute fashion editors. And she would produce tights, cosmetics, and designer eyewear – if that's what it took to stay in business.

She looked around her studio. There was a relentlessness to this cycle. As seasons not yet lived expired and made way for more neatly packaged moments in time, looking into the future took on a different meaning. For Elle, it was always divided into large brown card pattern blocks which hung from chrome rails like bloodless cadavers on a meat trader's hook.

The year ahead held no surprises at all ... Or so it seemed.

17

'I'm unhappy because I am too fat and feel that because of this I am ugly.'

HERTFORDSHIRE SCHOOLGIRL, AGE FOURTEEN

'OOH, mothers' meeting,' said Kevin as he entered the studio and headed for the saccharine-smelling croissants. 'Talking about tights and boyfriends again, I expect. You girlies, honestly – what are you like?'

'So,' continued Tess after feigning a smile in Kevin's direction, 'you've found your grandmother's name next to your mother's name, but how does anyone track a person down after thirty-seven years?'

'Well, there are ways,' said Charlotte. 'You have to get a copy of Helen's birth certificate.'

'Helen is the name my grandmother gave my mother before giving her away,' snorted Becks. She was feeling a little tetchy today. Jerry had rung late last night with a request she had been unable to refuse. After the shoot she would be needed to accompany one of Jerry's dodgy business contacts to a night club.

'It will show Becks' grandmother's address,' continued Charlotte. 'That's a starting point. Or if she got married and had more children – Becks' aunts and uncles – their births would have been registered in a town or a city. We could try local records like phone books. Maybe there are even grandchildren . . .' Charlotte smiled. 'Who knows!'

'There aren't any grandchildren and there aren't any brothers and sisters,' said Becks flatly. 'I've already looked.'

'Oh, that makes it harder then,' said Charlotte, discouraged.

'Well, no. I had a bit of a lead,' said Becks. 'I followed up the first address I found. A neighbour two doors up knew the family. It seems my grandmother is quite well known in some circles.'

'What's her name then?' quizzed Tess.

'Her name is Elsa Crabtree,' replied Becks, watching them closely for a reaction.

'Never heard of her,' said Tess.

'OK, people,' yelled Trena, clapping her hands, 'we're out of here in eight hours. Let's get this show on the road.'

Charlotte's mobile phone trilled. 'Darling,' said a voice she knew all too well, 'let's stop this ridiculous charade. You've made your little point and I'm sorry, so very sorry, but this is taking it too far. Jimmy says he's had a vanload of my stuff arrive at his house. And I've been back to the flat and you've changed the locks.' Rick could not contain his irritation. 'I mean, what the hell's got into you, Charts? And, anyway, there's furniture in there that we bought together. I want what's mine.'

'Don't call me again, Rick,' said Charlotte. 'Drop me a line when you've found somewhere to live and I'll send over your half of the kitchen table.'

'You're making a big mistake here, Charts. You've got to think about the rest of your life. You know: you and me, marriage, kids – the whole thing. Let's get married tomorrow. Let's do it now,' he said, gathering momentum. 'I know you don't mean this. Look, I'll come round and get the keys.'

Charlotte dropped the communication piece in her bag and walked towards the bright lights and large mirror in the far corner of the room.

'Here she comes,' said Kevin comically. 'Quick, stop talking about her.'

Charlotte smiled. Kevin was harmless. He was perfect for shoots, keeping everyone entertained, and Charlotte needed a bit of light relief today.

'Come on,' urged Kevin, 'get your knickers on, pet, and get yourself over here.' He welcomed her to his chair. 'Are you all right, love? You're looking a bit peaky.' He didn't wait for the answer. 'Now, we can't have that. Let's get some heat in there and lift it off your head.' He busied himself with her hair.

'You looked gorgeous in that poster, pet. Everyone said so. And I said,' Kevin stopped what he was doing and looked at her in the mirror, ' "You'd never guess she was twenty-nine, would you?" ' He announced this smugly, like twenty-nine was so old it was unthinkable to be modelling at such an age. 'Well,' he picked up the slack, 'you've all got a lot of competition, girls. Even Becks is an old lady

239

now. They start them young, you know. Ray, how old was that girl we did the other day?'

'Thirteen,' said Ray, throwing it back to Kevin. Ray never upstaged his employer.

'There, see what I mean?' said Kevin triumphantly. 'Thirteen, for God's sake. Mind you, when we'd got her out of hair and make-up she looked like seventeen or older, didn't she, Ray?' As usual, Kevin didn't wait for an answer. 'But I thought it was a bit much. She wasn't a happy camper, was she, Ray?'

Ray shook his head.

'No, I think she needed her mum. It's not right, is it? Still,' breezed Kevin as he put the last few rollers in Charlotte's hair, 'she'll be able to buy all the comics she wants on her wages.'

'But what about school?' asked Becks in between mouthfuls of Danish pastry. 'And why do they want a thirteen-year-old to look like a seventeen-year-old when they can get a seventeen-year-old to look like a seventeen-year-old?'

'Yeah,' said Tess. 'I mean, we're not talking wrinkles or saggy wotsits at seventeen, are we?'

'Oh, speak for yourself!' said Kevin with camp affectation. 'I looked middle-aged at ten.' He pulled his hair into a centre parting, pasted it to the side of his face with his hands and pulled a Shirley Temple pose. Everyone laughed.

'I think,' said Charlotte, 'that most men in the fashion industry are frightened of adult women. That's why they like little girls or women who look like little girls. Most of the photographers I've worked with talk about innocence and vulnerability like it's a treasured quality in modelling.'

Then, facing up to herself in the mirror, she added: 'I think there are a lot of grown women who don't value their own powers, so they behave like little girls to reassure the men in their lives that there's nothing to worry about.'

'Good call, Charlotte,' said Tess. 'You've been reading my mum's books, haven't you?'

Charlotte looked puzzled.

'You know,' persisted Tess, 'the "Help yourself to a life" kind of read. Really popular. My mum's got loads of them.'

'No,' said Charlotte carefully, 'but I'd like to. I've realized quite a bit about myself recently and there are certain things that I've decided to change about me and my life.'

'Glad to hear it, Charlotte,' said Trena, who had suddenly materialized. She checked her watch. 'Now, how about changing those clothes and putting on your first outfit?' She looked carefully at the model in front of her. 'You're looking thin, Charlotte. Have you been ill?'

But Trena didn't wait for an answer. She raised her voice above the din of camera technicians setting up behind her: 'Can we say everyone ready to go at half past?' She turned to check with the director. 'Pete, is that good for you?' Then, turning to her assistant, she said, 'Lara, you might have to pin the seams on some of Charlotte's jackets, she's lost weight.'

Soon the shoot was underway. As sessions went, it was simple for all three models. Simple but boring. There was much waiting around while the lighting was adjusted, white balances taken and framing discussed. Pete the director did not look at his subjects in the way that Petra had faced them previously, nor did he operate his camera – that was done by Dan. All Pete seemed to do was crouch in front of a small TV screen and call minor changes to his camera operator: 'Nice, Dan, but could you loosen the frame a touch?' Unlike photography, where the crop of the picture could present endless creative opportunities at post-production stage and almost be left until later, film required instant decisions in the studio. Once recorded, nothing could be removed from the corner of shot or added for extra headroom.

Charlotte, Tess and Becks replicated the pose that could be seen up and down the country in the first set of posters. Viewers watching the final cut would hear the words 'Hold yourself in Esteem,' spoken by a well-known actress. It depended of course on the voice-over fee, but Elle fancied that woman in the coffee advert.

Sparky, the assistant to the cameraman, unfolded a large silver disc about the size of a table. 'Nearer,' called Dan from behind the camera. 'I want the light to kick in from the right.' Sparky angled the disc so that it reflected light on to the face of each woman. 'OK, girls,' rallied Pete. 'Run up,' he instructed his team mate, 'and . . . action!'

Since each model did not have to do anything at all except hold the pose and smile while a wind machine lifted her hair gently off her face, there was much hilarity from Charlotte and Tess. Becks stayed quiet, preoccupied with the night ahead.

'You can't say "Action",' protested Tess. 'It's too daft, we're not doing anything.'

They tried over and over with Tess and Charlotte laughing and giggling at the sound of the word action. Becks wished she could join in.

'Can't you say something a bit more normal? Like "Go".'

'I'll say whatever you need to get this job done,' cautioned Pete. 'I've three to do before the light starts to change and you've got to get hair and make-up changes, so we haven't as much time as you think.'

And so the day went on, with each member of the team doing their thing to the best of their abilities. As the sun ripened and finally faded, Elle Cartwrite arrived unannounced. She carried three bouquets made from white lilies, delphiniums, sweet-smelling stocks and pampas grass.

'These are a small thank you to my models,' she said regally, standing on the sidelines. 'The poster is everything I'd hoped, and I'm sure this cinema ad will be also.'

'What's the matter, Becks?' whispered Charlotte under the synthesized music wafting from state-of-the-art speakers. She had felt Becks' body stiffen as the designer walked in.

'I'm not in the mood to speak to *her*. Look, I'll be fine,' she said. 'I'm not feeling that great these days. Maybe I'll head on home for an early night and –'

Then it happened.

There was a screech of tyres in the street below, accompanied almost instantly by shouting. To everyone in the studio it seemed that some poor driver might have had an accident. Trena was the first to the window, but stepped back with disinterest. 'It's some guy fresh out of a Duran Duran video,' she said flatly. 'He looks like he needs help to get back to the eighties.' Charlotte flushed as she realized it was Rick.

'Charlotte,' he called, 'I know you're there. I'm not going until you come down.'

The entire studio stood quietly.

Elle broke the silence. 'Let's clear up here, shall we? And leave Charlotte in peace to speak to the young man.'

Charlotte was at the window in an instant. The street was only one floor below and she could see Rick clearly. He had been drinking and his parking statement would not have earned him a test pass. 'Go away,' she hissed. 'I don't want you here. You are causing trouble.' She softened her voice. 'Rick, this doesn't look good for either of us. Please don't make a scene.'

'I'll make all the trouble I want,' he said defiantly. 'I'm not moving until you come down. And if you're up there with Mr Photographer, he's getting his face rearranged the minute he steps out of the door.'

Charlotte moved away from the window. She could still hear Rick, who had now resorted to detailed descriptions about which pieces of equipment he would like to stick up this photographer's arse. He was still expleting to his heart's content when Charlotte poured a large bucket of water on his head. Rick turned his fury to her and stormed back to the car, still shouting at the top of his voice as he sped off. Charlotte picked up her mobile.

'Police, please,' she instructed and waited for the connection to be made at the other end. 'Yes, I'd like to report a drunk driver.' When she had finished, the entire studio applauded.

'Hey,' said Trena pushing her glasses back up her nose, 'that guy was smashed *and* badly dressed. Personally, I know which I find more offensive.'

Charlotte was exhilarated. She had finally found something or someone inside herself.

'Now listen, pet,' said Kevin, every inch the actor and feigning fear, 'I know you might not have been happy with your hair, but Trena made me do it. Give me one more chance. Believe me, when I've finished with you, you're gonna look drop-dead gorgeous. Just don't –' he dropped down on one knee, wringing his hands and wailing – 'don't call the cops on me! Those prison cells are so dingy and you don't see a copy of *Hello!* for miles.'

Charlotte smiled. She wasn't really listening. She looked at the woman in the mirror. She seemed different somehow. The woman in the mirror smiled back and, for a moment, Charlotte thought she recognized the future.

18

'there are some people with no taste, but they are secure when they wear what is recognized as good taste.' **JEAN-PAUL GAULTIER**

$\mathcal{B}$ECKS padded from the bathroom to the bedroom with a towel wrapped tightly round her body. She dripped over the heap of clothes hastily removed just minutes before and stared distractedly at the pile of foliage on her bed. The flowers from Elle Cartwrite lay where she had thrown them; the air was perfumed with their presence.

She fussed ineffectively, drying occasional areas of flesh but missing others in her haste. There wasn't much time to get ready. Water trickled from her hair and down her back as she discarded the towel and stepped over it to reach the wardrobe. Standing by the open cupboard door, Becks snatched a turquoise dress from its hanger and bent to search for shoes. Yanking out one and foraging for its partner, she muttered angrily to herself.

At last the strappy sandal was forthcoming and, stepping into both simultaneously and without care, she wiggled her toes into the spaces while focusing on the next task. On her way to the mirror, Becks bent one leg to hook the tiny leather band over her heel, and, still walking, attempted to repeat the same procedure to secure the other. With one foot caught amongst her discarded clothes, Becks received a split-second warning of impending imbalance and hastily tried to restore the natural rhythm to her stride. But forward momentum dictated otherwise. With two fingers still hooked in the shoe, the reckless nymph lost balance and stumbled quite spectacularly, absorbing the full weight of the fall in one joint. It took a moment on the floor before Becks realized she had turned her ankle. The stabbing pain made her feel nauseous and sorry for herself. 'What am I doing?' she wailed.

It had been a long and tiring day and the last thing she wanted was to go back out. Maybe Jerry would understand if she told him how she felt. Becks hauled herself up and reached for the phone.

'Jerry . . . it's Becks.'

'Hi, Becks,' said Jerry evenly. He turned away from the phone and spoke to someone. 'Dave here was just saying how much he's looking forward to meeting you. I've shown him your picture and he's –'

'Well, that's the thing, Jerry,' said Becks. Her voice was not as confident as she would have liked and it betrayed her. 'It's just that . . . well, it's been a really difficult day today and . . .'

'Hey, Becks,' Jerry sounded firm but tolerant, 'take your time. Listen, I'll be round in about half an hour. It's all sorted. You can't let poor Dave down.' He lowered his voice slightly. 'There will be other girls there. We'll have ourselves a little party. Don't worry, it'll be fun – you'll see.'

'But, Jerry –' Becks was in no mood to humour Jerry right now – 'I've twisted my ankle and I really am feeling tired . . .'

'I don't think you understand me,' cautioned Jerry, his voice losing the veneer of paternal charm. 'I said it's all sorted. Now I know in half an hour you're gonna feel much better. Get some make-up on and wear a nice dress and I'll see you in thirty.' As if he felt the need to reassure her, he added with all the warmth he could muster: 'You'll have a lovely evening, trust me.'

Pretty girls were all the same – swore they were your friend when they needed a little H, but when it came to returning the favour they would try and wriggle out of it any way they could. Jerry put the phone down and turned to his friend.

Dave had been big in the early eighties as guitarist with one of the New Romantic bands. At forty, he was still a pull even though his devastatingly good looks were a touch raddled and his midriff visibly swollen after many years of professional inebriation. But tonight Dave was triumphant after a back-catalogue buyout which would enable the Baltic States to enjoy his music.

Jerry poured another glass of champagne. This was a contact he wanted to impress; famous people had no end of money to fritter and a whole load of famous friends to do it with. All it needed was a few celebs in his address book and Jerry could swing a new and lucrative career in party fixing.

Becks stared at her ankle: it was swelling up. She limped to the bathroom and turned on the cold tap, but the heat of the day had removed any chill from the water that now flowed over her aching limb. The ice box might do it. She hobbled to the kitchen. Becks wasn't organized enough to have a stack of ice cubes in dinky little metal trays, and the freezer compartment had long since frozen over. But a hammer – left by the last tenant – might just free enough chunks of frost for a compress. Moments later she had a plastic bag full of ice strapped to her ankle with a torn tea towel.

Moving very slowly so as not to disturb the makeshift ice pack, Becks returned to her mirror and began to gingerly apply make-up bought especially for the night ahead. She never wore any normally, and it was harder to apply than she realized. How did make-up artists get it so close to the eye without blinding the odd client? Becks decide to stay away from technical impossibilities and concentrate on the more likely exercise of colouring in her lips. Pleased with the result, she dabbed some blusher on her cheeks and spread a shiny highlighter around her cheekbones and below her eyebrows. Her hair was nearly dry as she ran fingers dipped in gel through her blonde strands and pulled it round her face as Karen the make-up artist had shown her. When the doorbell rang, she removed the compress and carefully pulled on the remaining shoe. The strap bit into swollen flesh.

'Becks,' beamed Jerry as she opened the door. A strong

whiff of aftershave almost overpowered her and, stepping back to avoid contamination, she was framed against the dark hallway. He ran his eyes over her appreciatively. 'You look younger,' he ventured. Apart from his recent mercy dash to administer a little medicine, he'd only ever seen her in full make-up or in pictures. A pang of guilt momentarily distracted him. His kid sister was only seventeen, and he wouldn't want some grubby bloke all over her. Still, this was business. And Dave liked 'em young – he'd said so.

'It's Dave's birthday tonight,' explained Jerry as they joined the others in the restaurant.

Becks was sandwiched between Jerry and Dave. 'Happy Birthday,' she said dutifully.

'Let's get some champagne in,' said Dave. He cast his eyes leisurely over Becks whilst raising his hand into the air and flicking his fingers in a gesture that might have been more willingly indulged all those years ago when he was at the top of the music charts, but now . . .

A young man Becks' age responded to the summons. Clearly he had no idea of the identity of this irritating customer, but professional subservience passed for attentive interest. 'My name is Gordon,' he said smoothly, 'how can I help?'

Soon glasses were in place and the bubbly brew flowed. 'Dave's been all over the world,' said Jerry as he passed drinks around the table.

'Where have you been, Dave?' Becks knew she had to feign adulation to keep Jerry sweet. They hadn't actually talked about her role, but clearly *something* was expected of her by both men. She would fulfil this favour to Jerry and make sure never to call on him again. She checked the large chrome clock on the wall directly behind Dave's head. By midnight, she'd be out of here.

'Well, honey,' said Dave, smiling at her, winking conspiratorially at Jerry – enjoying his own importance – 'I've been all the way.' He laughed at his own joke and Jerry joined in. Becks decided she, too, had better force a smile. The guy was an arsehole; still, she didn't have to like him. A seasoned actress in front of the camera, she could easily fake it for a few hours.

She watched Jerry hanging on Dave's every word. He had always seemed so worldly until now. He knew where all the best parties were, and seemed acquainted with enough grubby bouncer types to ensure entry into most of the West End clubs for free. But here he was, fawning like a pre-teen with an autograph book.

Seated around the table were an assortment of young women and older men. The male contingent talked loudly and occupied large spaces with their bodies and hand movements. A sparrow-like beauty with hard round breasts sat quietly next to Dave, who had lit a cigar and was happily polluting the entire restaurant. The girl gave a little cough, as if in protest. Becks thought she looked sad and weary.

Dave laughed and nudged the waif with his elbow. 'Come on, Avaline,' he said with empty jocularity. 'Don't put a damper on my birthday. Meet Becks here – you and she have got a lot in common.'

Avaline's eyes settled on Becks momentarily and she allowed a flutter of a smile to pass her lips, though it never made it to her eyes.

'Oh, forget it,' said Dave, turning his back on the haunted young woman. 'Drink your drink, do a bit of

Charlie in the toilets, and cheer up.' He turned his attention to Becks. 'Now then, I bet you aren't possessive with your boyfriends, are you?'

'Well, actually I'm not with anyone,' declared Becks, trying to catch Avaline's eye. She would much prefer to be talking to her.

'What, a pretty girl like you, not looking for a boyfriend?' queried Dave loudly. He was already on his third glass of champagne and clicked his fingers for more. 'While you're at it,' he yelled, 'bring something to eat.'

'But you and your guests haven't ordered yet, sir,' explained the young waiter.

Dave turned to Jerry. 'Fix it will you, Jerry? I don't want to spend half an hour reading some jumped-up cordon bleu dictionary. Go and stand at the bar and order enough for ten of us.'

Obediently Jerry moved from his seat.

'Oh, and Jerry,' called Dave, 'no seafood. I don't want anything nasty in a shell.' He turned to Becks. 'Nothing so low down the food chain that it eats its own shit. Oysters,' he exclaimed with distaste, 'why would anyone want to try them? What comes out of my nose after a cold is more tasty.'

Becks screwed up her own nose and resolved never to sample such gruesome dainties. Her eye caught the clock behind Dave's head as it registered the tiniest of changes. It was going to be a long night.

Waiters arrived with food and placed it in front of them. Jerry had ordered a variety of salads, pastas, fries and steaks. 'Is this organic?' queried one of the immaculately groomed hangers-on with a mid-Atlantic accent that sounded like a child whining.

'Nah,' said Dave as he pulled a plate towards him. The others followed suit as if taking guidance from their leader.

Becks helped herself to a plate of fresh pasta.

'Only, my nutritionist told me,' the woman continued, oblivious to the fact that her voice was capable of making enemies on the spot, 'that synthetic hormones in meat are upsetting my hormone balance.' She cast around the table for interest but none was forthcoming. 'You know, like you get a progesterone imbalance,' she prompted, 'and that makes your PMT worse. All restaurants should serve organic food. Even dairy products are riddled –'

'Tara,' barked Dave, 'you're full of shit.'

'I'm serious,' she said. 'None of us should be drinking cow's milk. Don't you know about the antibiotic residue? And then there's the bacteria. It's even been linked with Crohn's disease –'

'Tara,' snarled Dave, 'you stuff chemicals into your body like there's no fucking tomorrow and you think you've got a case against Daisy the cow. Who rattled your cage?'

'All I'm saying,' she said sulkily, 'is that some of the healthiest people on earth avoid milk. You know, the Japanese, the Chinese and other Pacific Rim people. And, anyway,' she added, 'pure heroin is much safer than alcohol. I could take controlled amounts for the next forty years and my body would only take six months to return to normal. If you continue drinking with the same enthusiasm, your liver will explode before you reach fifty. My nutritionist –'

'Did your nutritionist tell you how to avoid getting your face carved up?' said Dave, slipping into a hard North

London accent. 'Only, I've had enough of this. Who invited her?' He scanned the table accusingly.

'Dave,' soothed Jerry, 'eat your food.' He glared at Tara. 'It's Dave's birthday, for fuck sake. Give it –' his fingers mimed a mouth opening and closing – 'a fucking rest.'

'I'm all right, Jerry,' said Dave as he pushed his plate away. Very little food on the plate had been touched.

'Come on, Dave,' cajoled Jerry, 'eat something.'

'Nah,' said Dave, 'I'm off me food. Let's go. Oi –' he clicked his fingers at the waiter – 'garçon!'

Gordon appeared almost magically by Dave's side to relieve him of his credit card. 'No coffees, sir?' he asked, ever the professional. He looked around at the others, poised over their plates. 'Have your guests finished?'

'Yes,' retorted Dave. 'You can clear this lot.' He gestured at the table impatiently. 'Get rid of it.'

'Was there anything wrong with the food, sir?' persisted Gordon. A few plates were a handful of chipped potatoes lighter, and the odd steak was diminished in size, but most of the food remained uneaten.

Becks was still munching her way through a tasty dish, she sure was hungry. The others watched her as the restaurant staff began to clear from the other end of the table. Some of the untouched dishes had several cigarette butts parked unceremoniously in the centre. Becks looked at Jerry.

'Cocaine cuisine!' he joked.

Avaline allowed herself a small moment of mirth. She had not stopped smoking throughout the meal, her appetite satisfied by liberating a few olives from the side of an extravagantly compiled salad. Becks noticed how very tiny she was.

'Jerry, get some cabs,' ordered Dave. Becks glanced at

the clock. It was only ten forty-five – she'd never get away with disappearing now. Jerry would want some other favour to make up for it. Best to get this thing over and done with.

'Come on, Becks,' said Dave as they headed for the taxi. He put his arm round her proprietorially. Avaline walked alongside, clearly hoping for some attention from him. 'Let's go and party,' he said.

Jerry was the last to climb in. 'The Moonlighter,' he instructed the driver as they sped off.

The Moonlighter was Dave's favourite club. Built in an old church and situated on one of Soho's busiest junctions, its doors were forever blocked with queues of bodies. At the bottom of the steps, occupying a postage stamp of claret carpet, stood two security staff in black suits and dark glasses. Their faces were expressionless as they affected a self-conscious FBI kind of stance. On this tiny portion of pavement they were the 'Rulemakers'. All those wishing to enter had first to pass under the gaze of these two lofty sentinels.

Jerry approached one. 'Hi, Del,' he said expectantly.

'OK, Jerry,' replied the suit, barely moving his mouth. 'How many?'

'I got Dave Smethurst and his party with me.'

Del thought for a while. 'OK, man – I can only give you four VIPs for the top bar, the rest will have to chill downstairs.'

'Cheers, Del,' said Jerry. 'All right for gear?' He might as well ply a little trade while he was at it.

'Yeah, man,' said Del, his face still totally impassive as

he walked towards a youth in the crowd. 'No trainers, Jack!' he barked. 'OK, you –' he pointed to a pretty blonde with a generously arranged cleavage – 'you and your friend, come through.'

Once inside the club, Becks relaxed. She took a seat next to Avaline, who nursed a glass of pink liquid with an umbrella in it. 'I've seen you about haven't I?' she said.

'I don't think so,' the waif replied. 'I know you, though, from that poster.'

'It's just that you do look familiar . . .' Becks tried to concentrate. 'Do you model?'

'I'd like to do some proper modelling,' replied Avaline enthusiastically, 'but I haven't got the height, have I?' She was telling, not asking.

Becks observed her. Avaline was not much over five feet seven, it was true, but then neither was Kate Moss.

'Dave says he'll get me an agent soon,' said Avaline, slurping down the contents of her glass quickly.

'What sort of modelling do you do, then?'

'Well . . .' Avaline chose her words carefully, 'I don't do close-up work, but I do . . . you know . . . glamour stuff.' She said it self-consciously, but there was a level of pride in her voice. Close-up was a euphemism for hard porn involving full-on gynaecological styling. Becks had heard Paul talk about it once. A model he knew had resorted to close-up work to finance a heroin habit. Glamour modelling was the accepted way of describing topless photography. 'I've been told I'm very good,' ventured Avaline with a smile, her first of the evening, 'and when I'm ready, Dave is going to get me into films.'

'Dave is quite important to you, isn't he?' asked Becks puzzled.

'Yes,' replied Avaline, her face softening. 'He paid for me to get these done.'

So Avaline's rock-hard frontage was synthetic, after all.

'And I have regular plasmagel injections in my lips,' she announced proudly. 'We've been going together for about six months. He says I'm a long-term investment.' She lowered her eyes as Dave gatecrashed their conversation.

'My two favourite girls,' he said with a slur as he roped an arm round each and steered them towards the exit sign. 'Let's go.'

'But I haven't finished my drink, Dave,' whined Avaline.

'Then stay here, you silly cow,' he retorted, tightening his grip on Becks.

'And what about Tara and the others?' she wailed.

'Like I said,' spat Dave, 'stay here if you want.'

Avaline obviously thought better of relinquishing her hold on the drunken Adonis and followed without further protest. Becks looked around for Jerry; she wanted nothing more than an end to this evening. Perhaps she could wriggle free and be gone . . . but Dave had other ideas. He clutched at his prey, while Avaline followed obediently at her master's heel.

'Dave!' said Jerry, emerging from the shadows. It seemed he hadn't moved from his post by the door and would have caught Becks on the way out anyhow. 'Got you a cab waiting outside,' he said, pleased with himself. This new line of work was a whole heap better than wet-nursing addicts.

Jerry had been on the scene for years now and had witnessed a fast turnover of young and beautiful people as they flooded the city with hopes as big as their heads. They always thought they could crack it. They always thought of themselves as the chosen few. A bit of networking and they'd be on their way to career heaven. Of course, most of them would find out the hard way that dreams don't always come true.

All Jerry had to do was be patient and he could have his share of beautiful women. At first, they wouldn't want to know him, wouldn't want their stuck-up friends to see them with the likes of Jerry. Lord knows, he tried to be polite, and he looked after his body with regular visits to the gym. But he'd always get the same disinterested look, usually from a location directly above his head. He was short, but so what? A woman could always be relied upon to be incredibly judgemental about his lack of inches in the height department . . . until she wanted something – drugs, usually. Then, of course, she'd fawn over him like a bitch on heat.

Jerry would bide his time where Becks was concerned. She'd be his sooner or later, when the addiction was rampant and her skin was shot, but in the meantime she was a high-profile beauty, perfect for celebrity business like Dave. Jerry shook his head as he looked at Becks. Her complexion exhibited the pale, waxy glow that betrayed a heroin addict, and which, perversely, fashion photographers seemed to favour. Her limbs were long and lean and her cheekbones exquisitely accentuated. Heroin could cancel out appetite and remove hunger, making it a drug of choice for models. What Tara had said was true: a carefully managed heroin habit could go on for years and years with no real side effects. He'd read of an 84-year-old physician who'd used morphine for sixty years, and there was some surgeon who performed life-saving ops every day, all under the influence of H! Then there were 'the

259

Chippers' – City types who only took the drug at weekends. Jerry supplied dozens of them, but to see them in their grey suits and blue shirts crossing Waterloo Bridge in the rush-hour like droves of worker ants, no one – but no one – would guess.

Jerry shook his head again and smiled. Heroin management was a tricky business. H was not an easy horse to ride, and the likes of Becks with her erratic lifestyle and up and down moods would come a cropper sooner or later. When she became a fully-fledged junkie, then he'd have her. Jerry had made love to some beautiful women in his time. Sadly, most of them had been so stoned that they had neither cared nor noticed.

'Pay the man,' commanded Dave as the taxi stopped, depositing its human cargo on the street.

Jerry waited for his change and receipt, and watched as Dave tripped up the stairs with stereo babes, one each side. Avaline and Becks were assisting him with his unco-ordinated ascent and Jerry found himself wondering whether Dave ever managed the climb alone. Perhaps he just slept it off in the privet bush until morning. Just as he was about to follow, Becks turned and shot him a look as if to say, 'How much longer do I have to put up with this?' He hadn't told her everything about her obligations tonight, but she would find out in due course.

Once inside, Jerry busied himself at Dave's bar. The bloated band member had an enormous boat-shaped drinks cabinet at one end of his large pine-floored reception. A glass coffee table was flanked by two oversized black leather sofas, and pictures of Dave and his rock-star cronies adorned every wall, with large silver-framed discs dotted here and there. Against the near wall stood a reproduction dresser displaying bound copies of literary classics and lead crystal goblets. A vast black entertainment centre featuring a flat TV screen with matching speakers dominated the far wall.

Her imminent retreat forgotten, Becks stared in amazement at the amplifiers, decks, wall-to-wall vinyl records and compact discs. After all, it wasn't every day a girl got to hang out in a pop star's palace.

'Help yourself,' said Dave, gesturing magnanimously towards the sound system. 'Put on a little something that will help Avaline here to loosen up, and I'll make us a nice big spliff.' Avaline moved closer to Dave and tried to plant a sloppy kiss on his lips.

Becks turned her attention to the task in hand. She recognized none of the audio pleasure on offer in the record section: a gaggle of gaunt-faced, over made-up relics in tight trousers posed expectantly. Bauhaus, King, Belouis Some, DAF. What was it with those eighties guys and lip gloss? Becks wondered if Dave had ever worn ballet shoes and a quiff the size of the Eiffel Tower. She turned to scan the photographs on the wall nearest and was just homing in on some rather incriminating evidence when his voice pierced her thoughts.

'Get off me, you silly tart. Jerry, hurry up with the drinks – Avaline is getting on my nerves. I think she must be thirsty or something because she's trying to suck my face off.'

Becks swung round to see Avaline recoil from her boyfriend and run from the room in tears.

Dave smiled sheepishly. 'She'll be all right in the morning,' he said, lighting up a large joint. He drained the contents of his glass and immediately refilled it from the vodka bottle on the table. 'There's one for you, Becks,' he said, pointing to a large tumbler, 'and Jerry has a little something special over there.'

Becks recognized the familiar smoking tube. Jerry, helping himself first, held a flame under the silver foil while he concentrated all his efforts on inhaling the heavenly vapours. Becks walked over to Jerry as if in a trance. She had meant to skedaddle as soon as possible – but not without a little H for her troubles. It was so much harder than she had thought to control the dragon. Heroin was the ultimate short-term, live-for-the-moment drug. She knew that smoking it would decrease her chances of a swift breakout, but reason had vanished and in its place was a craving that grew with every impatient moment she waited for Jerry to pass her the gear.

'Come on, babe,' said a voice directly above her. 'Don't make me angry.' It was dark and Becks felt a heaviness on her chest. She forced her lungs to draw in air. Something was squashing her and anxiously she shifted her body in order to take her next breath more easily. She must have fallen asleep, but what was going on?

'Stop it,' warned the voice. It sounded distorted and slow. 'Hold still.'

The heaviness on her chest returned and she felt a sharp pain in her ribs, as if her ribcage were straining to prevent a ton weight from crushing her lungs.

'I can't breathe,' she said. 'Jerry, what are you doing?'

'Jerry went home a long time ago,' said the voice. 'There's only me here now.'

'Dave,' said Becks, almost relieved as she recognized the voice. 'Please, my chest . . . I can't breathe.'

'Then stop wriggling,' instructed her host as he occupied himself with the business of pulling her dress up.

Becks tried again to squeeze her body into a pocket of space beneath the drunken mass, and experienced the panic of knowing that survival in her current position was not an option. 'Dave, you're hurting me,' she gasped. The pain in her chest was unbearable and suffocation began to seem like a very real possibility.

Intent on freeing himself from his trousers, Dave concentrated all his efforts on his own clothing arrangements and ignored Becks as she pleaded for release. Girls like her were prick-teasers, prancing about in flimsy little dresses with their knickers on show. What the fuck did she think was going to happen, showing up in an outfit like that? He extricated one foot from his shoe and, using one arm and most of his body weight to secure his sport, he attempted to remove the other, inadvertently kicking her ankle.

Pain coursed through Becks' body. Her damaged joint was swollen and bruised, and nausea made it even harder to fight for breath. He couldn't have paralysed her more effectively if he had stamped on her stomach. Left with no more strength to struggle for the chance to inhale, she felt the crushing weight blot out her cares for the future.

'Please,' whispered Becks as she listened to her heartbeat thunder like a kettledrum, 'please . . .'

A sharp sting to the side of her face brought tears to her eyes.

'Shut the fuck up,' he snapped, shifting his bulk to gain better leverage. 'And don't make me hit you again.'

Mercifully, Becks could breathe now. She lay quietly, filling her lungs with life and waiting for the pain in her chest, ankle and face to subside.

'Don't lie there like a fucking corpse,' warned Dave, jerking his body. 'I can't fucking stand it when you do nothing.'

Becks used her free hand to stroke the back of his head. Silently she massaged his shoulder and traced a path down his spine. With every cell of her being she hated him, yet she would pretend otherwise.

'That's better, babes,' he cooed, lulled into a false sense of sensuality. 'There now, see how nice that is . . .' He jerked his body rhythmically on top of hers, and although the darkness masked his face, his contented rasps and grunts communicated pleasure.

Miraculously, Becks could feel nothing at all. Dave was clearly very drunk and it was possible that he was experiencing some confusion distinguishing between her body and the soft fleshy settee. Perhaps the cosy recess between the warm leather pillows beneath her was absorbing the full force of his ardour. She offered a silent prayer of thanks and allowed herself to relax slightly.

'Am I in?' he said, not waiting for an answer as he wrapped his arms round her hips and sank his hands into her buttocks. He groaned some more and continued to drive in and out of the firm leather upholstery with staccato tempo. 'You little slag,' he whimpered, snuggling into her neck and planting empty kisses round her throat. Becks did her best to sink into the padding and murmur intermittently. He must not discover that his mistress was in truth a mattress. The rapist urged himself on, reciting his mantra: 'You're all dirty little slags . . . all dirty . . . little . . .'

Becks continued to stroke his head. Getting this awful act over and done with was her first concern. Then she would wait until he was asleep and rip out his heart and stuff it down his throat. Or, better still, amputate his masculinity and make him smoke the fucker at knife point. She occupied herself with thoughts of surgical dismemberment until it was over.

'That's what you needed,' murmured Dave as he flopped on to Becks' shoulder. She knew she had to act quickly, otherwise she would be forced to spend the night pinned under his bulk.

'Dave,' she said as softly as she could manage, 'I've got to go to the bathroom.'

The spent conquistador didn't move.

She tried another tack. 'You didn't use a condom – and I don't want to get pregnant. I need to go to the bathroom.' Somewhere in the back of his mind, Dave must have considered the risk of a paternity suit and so when he lifted his body it was not out of concern for anyone but himself. As Becks stood over him, he settled on his back and began to snore very loudly. For a moment she toyed with the idea of actualizing one or two of her revenge fantasies as he lay in front of her, trousers round his ankles. He dribbled slightly and grunted before returning to a deep and peaceful slumber. Becks knew that a prison sentence would be hers not his. Heroin was to blame as much as this pathetic has-been in front of her. If she hadn't owed Jerry a favour, she wouldn't have been here in the first place. If she hadn't wanted, needed, craved heroin tonight, she could have walked out of the door earlier.

Becks gathered her things as the grey dawn began breaking at the curtainless windows. She found a marker pen on the kitchen worktop and stood over Dave one more time. On his forehead she spelled out the word RAPIST. So comatose was he that she was able to draw an outline of each letter and fill it in. The finished result was arresting and Becks almost smiled as she savoured the effect of the pop god's early-morning stumble to the newsagents for a packet of fags and some Alka Seltzer. Then, on a piece of paper torn from one of the precious leather-bound books, she wrote a letter to Avaline. Probably the young woman would take no notice. But maybe, just maybe she would consider her own future. Everyone had some choice in the life they elected to lead, and – as Becks had discovered tonight – the choices she had made since entering the world of fashion were not so clever after all.

19

'**dress** is an aspect of human life that involves strong feelings, some intensely pleasant, and others very disagreeable. It is no accident that many of our daydreams involve fine raiment; nor that one of the most common and disturbing human nightmares is of finding ourselves in public inappropriately and/or incompletely clothed.'

ALISON LURIE

*E*LLE Cartwrite checked a copy of the seating plan for the umpteenth time as she stood in an empty pavilion tent, surrounded by eight hundred gilt bentwood chairs. In a few hours this place would be full to bursting. The day of the show was finally here.

Elle and Trena had haggled over final details weeks before.

'What I want,' said Elle to her trusty show producer, 'is

women in a variety of ages and sizes up on that catwalk looking good in my clothes. The rest is up to you.'

'Glamour is our watchword,' said Trena, '*not* novelty. The press has got to see the look, the buyers, the potential. If you put anything over thirty-five up there, they'll be crucified – and you too. Remember the way they laid into Marianne?'

Marianne was a beautiful and fulsome fifty-something who had been reviled for daring to model some skimpy knitwear a few seasons ago.

'You've got to remember that you're showing your clothes to a bunch of angst-ridden pre-menopausal label queens – and that's just the guys. Don't stick your neck out here,' pleaded Trena. 'You've made your statement with Tess. She's larger than most. Now we've got to hit them with show-stopping, spine-tingling glamour.'

Two workers, one on a ladder, hoisted a large polystyrene letter M into place on the back wall of the catwalk to complete the word 'esteem'. A lighting director stood on the catwalk, which was still sheathed in a layer of protective wrap, yelling out instructions to the back of the room. Technicians adjusted computerized co-ordinates at a desk, and next to them a DJ tested his mixing equipment – live performance would add extra excitement.

Elle was feeling queasy. Soon the culmination of months of forward planning would be scrutinized by her peers. Would she be hauled over the metaphorical coals, ticked off by some vindictive journo with a superiority complex and a column to fill overnight, or, worse still, ignored in favour of the latest young stud and his cerebral ensemble? It was irritating that whilst women designed clothes in support of feminine lifestyle, their male contemporaries could be relied upon to ignore petty concerns for comfort in order to secure press attention and an invitation to design for a Parisian couture house. It was the same in other industries, too: women cooked, but men became chefs. Women painted; all the great masters, however, were men.

'Lucy,' she called, anxious to marshal her wayward PR, 'I want bottled water and programmes to go on all the seats. Only the first three rows get free gifts. They're in that box over there.'

Elle watched as Lucy stood jigging her three-month-old daughter up and down in a body pouch while issuing frenzied instructions to her staff. Power mums, thought Elle, save us from them.

But it had been Lucy's brainwave to have ylang ylang – a marvellously sensual and uplifting essence – decanted into small blue bottles carrying the Esteem label. Placed in a contrasting blue bag, and tied with the same cream ribbon used to secure the programmes, they were a tasteful accompaniment to the new collection and a clever way of making the dignitaries in the industry feel a little pampered.

'A good PR, especially one that is no longer extolling the virtues of fried placenta,' chuckled Elle, 'is worth her weight in gold.'

Lucy swung round as if she had heard. It was true she had wrestled her afterbirth from a horrified nursing official as it lay pulsing on the delivery bed. She insisted that cave mothers had consumed their placentas and all the hormones contained within as an intuitive antidote to postnatal depression. When Elle expressed her revulsion, Lucy had told her: 'You've lost touch with your primeval woman. And, anyway, there's no need to look so shocked – they all end up in face creams, along with amniotic fluid, animal thymus and spleen tissue. What do you think goes into all those expensive and totally ineffective anti-ageing concoctions?'

Elle had resolved never to put anything so unwholesome on her face again.

'Maddy, have the dogs been in yet?' she called.

'No,' came the reply.

'Well, what's good enough for Betty Jackson is good enough for me. Go over to the press office and get someone on it now.'

Day three of London Fashion Week and Global Defence had not yet shown themselves, but with the Western world's media eager to record any eco-warrior unsettlement, it was surely an opportunity not to be missed. And Elle had been receiving some strange calls. Nothing was said – on the contrary, it seemed she was being treated to some heavy breathing – but it had put her on edge.

'No one is going to rain on my parade, today of all days,' she grunted resolutely. The tension was causing her to feel downright ill. 'And where is Alicia,' she snapped, 'when I need her?'

'She's gone to get some flesh-coloured G-strings,' shouted Trena from the side of the stage, rolling her eyes. 'One of them has turned up in big school knickers.' She aimed her voice backstage. 'Everyone must wear a flesh-coloured G-string. I don't want to see any panty-lines, and definitely no pubic hair poking out of tights.' As if needing to impart something else, she disappeared backstage. A moment later she could be heard bellowing to her models: 'No piercings, either. If you've got anything hanging off intimate parts of your body, take it out and give it to your dresser.'

The announcement was met with a few groans from behind the catwalk.

Tess slipped into the crowd unnoticed. She had been waiting by the main gates for Simon to keep a promise she made at the beginning of their relationship. The backstage pass was now in his possession and would allow him the chance to come and go as he pleased.

'Hi, girl,' said Tess to another modelling acquaintance. 'Have you seen my rail?'

The woman pointed. 'It's next to mine. We're sharing the same dresser, I think. So don't be hogging her with one of your ridiculous outfits.'

They both laughed. The last time they worked together had been student fashion week in June. One fledgling designer had incarcerated Tess in an outfit with bandages and metal clips. After suffering the humiliation of parading down the runway with her arse hanging out of the damn thing, she'd had to wait helplessly as her dresser had cut her out, leaving seconds to change into the next flimsy garment.

'Oh, you can talk. No one's gonna forget your last appearance . . .' Her colleague rolled her eyes in memory of the monstrosity complete with translucent plastic panels that had made it to the front cover of some tacky fanzine.

'Hey, remember that dress last season that was full of spiders?' reminisced Tess. 'If that had been me, I'd've puked my guts up when I came off. They say the designer forgot to tell her she was wearing up-to-the-minute arachnids! She had them in her hair and down her knickers. Nasty . . . Still,' Tess looked around, 'nothing to worry about today.'

She looked for her rail. It had her picture taped to it and contained half a dozen outfits. During professional catwalk shows there were about thirty models to make a show of around twenty minutes. That way the changes were reasonably relaxed. Under the rail was a line of shoes. Each outfit required a different footwear look. Both women groaned at the size of them.

'Too small, as usual,' tutted the brown-skinned beauty.

'Hey, girl, count your blessings,' said her friend, depositing her belongings on a chair next to the rail. 'If shoe size is all there is to gripe about, we're laughing. I'll see you in make-up. I'm getting mine done before the rush.'

'Hi, Tess,' called Charlotte. 'Have you seen Becks? I'm a bit worried about her.'

'Wow, Charlotte,' said Tess turning to view her Esteem comrade, 'save it for yourself! Are you ill? You look thin.'

'I've had a stomach bug,' lied Charlotte. 'I couldn't eat a thing, but I'm fine now.'

'You want to get some good food inside you and *quick*,' urged Tess. 'There's sandwiches and crisps on the table over there.'

'Yeah,' said Charlotte, 'I know. Honestly, I'm fine now.'

Tess tutted to herself. It was well known that many models cut down before a round of catwalk shows. She knew of several modelling friends who had been sacked at the last moment for not fitting into show garments. One designer was renowned for cutting the catwalk samples extra tight, and then complaining loudly when a model with breasts or hips ruined the line of the garment. It was even rumoured that one of the top names had paid for her lower ribs to be surgically removed to enhance an already tubular waistline, and it was not uncommon to hear models complain how hungry they were during show-time. Charlotte had obviously taken it upon herself to lose a bit of pre-show flesh.

'It's Becks I'm worried about,' said Charlotte. 'Something's happened.'

'What do you mean?'

'I don't know for sure, but she hasn't returned my calls. And there was that stuff with her grandmother,' explained Charlotte. 'Becks has found out who she is, but . . . I get the feeling there's trouble. As far as I know, she hasn't contacted her.'

As if on cue, Tess noticed Becks at the other side of the backstage area. She was having her make-up applied.

'There she is,' announced Tess. 'She looks all right to me.'

Becks looked over and waved. She had a bottle of wine in her hand and tilted her head to enjoy its contents.

'Ah, well . . . maybe not,' said Tess.

'What is it?' said Charlotte as she reached the other side.

'Can you sit here?' asked a make-up artist, intercepting her. 'I can make a start on you now.'

'Sure,' said Charlotte. 'Becks, what's been going on?'

'Oh, nothing much,' muttered Becks. 'Everything's OK. Look, I don't want to talk right now.'

'Right, you're done,' said a woman with beautifully shaped eyebrows. 'Go and get your hair finished.'

Becks obliged and tilted alarmingly to one side as she left her seat.

'See that,' said Eyebrow Woman to her colleague. 'I'm sure she's drunk.'

It was true enough. Becks had indeed imbibed a considerable amount of alcohol. She had been trying to avoid her druggy friends and their various medications for days. Jerry had left a furious message telling Becks she was in Big Trouble and warning her not to go out alone. Now the bottle had become her saviour. It was also the only way she knew to nurse herself through the withdrawal symptoms of heroin and the unexpected anger upon learning of her grandmother's identity.

'Hey!' growled Becks at the peroxide blond who was now spraying her hair furiously. 'If I wanted to drink Pantene by the pint load, I'd empty it into a glass.'

'Ooh, keep your knickers on,' he replied. 'You're not getting this can. What would I do for a night-cap? Now, be off with you, you sassy young woman.'

'Becks,' cautioned Trena, stepping in, 'now is not the time to abuse your beauty support staff. And anyway,' she looked over in the direction of the hairstylist, who was chatting happily with another client, 'you're bigger than he is, so don't be a bully.'

The show producer walked off briskly and cornered her assistant Lara. 'I'm worried about that model over there,' she said under her breath, pointing discreetly to Charlotte. 'She's dropped too much weight for my liking. I know there are plenty of designers who'd have her, but . . .' Trena shook her head. 'She looks rough as far as I'm concerned.'

'But she's one of the Esteem girls on the poster, right?' exclaimed Lara, dismayed. 'She doesn't look that bad . . . I mean, you can't not use her . . .'

'I know that,' said Trena. 'All I'm saying is I want you to put a wrap or something with any outfit that shows off her body. She's too bony. Oh, and watch the other one . . . Becks – the blonde in the corner there.' Trena motioned with her eyebrows. 'She's not herself today, either. Honestly, they don't have to do much really except turn up and complain.' She rolled her eyes. 'Models! Where does it say in the contract that they've all got to have nervous breakdowns?'

The bespectacled woman clapped her hands and stood on a stool. 'OK, team, gather round.'

Like all good show producers, Trena always briefed her squad with a pep talk. Dozens of beautiful women in various states of undress slouched about like sporting players absorbing a bit of pre-match motivation from their coach.

'One: we will be starting on time. Or at least we will wait for Suzy Menkes of the *Herald Tribune* to take her seat and we will start ten seconds after that.' Trena looked around. 'So, no excuses, Kelly. In half an hour I want everyone ready in first outfits.

'Two – really simple stuff, ladies: hit the runway and keep to the right. One turn at the top and back down. Think Jil Sander, Helmut Lang.' She turned to one model. 'No hogging the flashbulbs, Lulu, or strange dancing. This isn't John Galliano time.

'Three: if anything falls off or down, don't play with it. Just pull it back up and carry on. Millie –' flashed Trena – 'I'm talking straps here, not knickers.

'Four: this is a classy show. Think cool glamour. No wiggles, no mucking about with photographers at the end of the catwalk. OK, everyone – clear? Right. Now, the wraps are being taken off the rails, so no smoking near the clothes. Oh, and finally,' rallied Trena, 'this collection is our only British sample range, so if I find fag-holes or wine stains, even nasty greasy make-up smears on anything . . . Jenny –' Trena wagged a finger in the direction of the usual suspect – 'I will hunt you down like a dog.'

The coach stepped down and adjusted her headset. She wore a large black transistor radio which allowed her to speak to the control desk at the back of the hall. 'Hi, guys,' she said, 'can you give me a picture on the monitor?'

The TV screen flashed into life. Now Trena could observe everything front of stage. Elle paced up and down by the side of an empty white catwalk. Camera crews had begun to set up their patch in the photographer's den and Lucy was directing the first few people to their seats.

'Guys,' radioed Trena, 'can someone bring Elle back-stage? She's looking lost out there. Let's get her back here and pour a glass of wine down her. And who is the jerk in the blue suit climbing on to the catwalk? Can security get him off now?'

Trena tutted to herself. TV crews were the worst, it was probably some jumped-up television presenter about to do a walking-talking piece to camera like it was an Oscar performance. Later on they'd be backstage asking the same three boring questions: 'Tell me about your hemlines . . .' 'Tell me about your colourways . . .' 'Tell me about your fabrics and textures . . .'

'Oh, my God – someone call the loser police!' Trena pulled her mouthpiece closer and spoke carefully. 'It's Mr Eighties, and that man is trouble.' She looked around for Charlotte – who was dressing, blissfully unaware of Rick's presence in the building – and turned back to the monitor. 'Get your biggest bouncer to eject him now. He's got a thing about one of our models and I don't want him any-where near her when the show starts. He'll probably try and propose or something. Yuk, hetero men,' said Trena down the mike to her male colleagues, 'need a lot of expen-sive therapy.'

Trena studied the monitor with satisfaction as her instructions were carried out. Nothing must go wrong today of all days. She watched Lucy welcoming guests to their seats. It was filling up now. The front row was still conspicuously empty, reserved for frock royalty. They would turn up at the last minute, having winged their way directly from another catwalk show in a different part of town. Some of the top fashion editors did nine or ten shows a day.

'Thank God I've only got to do one of these things

today,' she muttered and then turned to her cast. 'OK, everyone, this is your show producer speaking ... first outfits.'

There was a surge of activity as hairdressers released jets of sticky, sweet-smelling chemicals in the general direction of any free-flying hair.

'Tasty,' spluttered Tess, spitting out the gluey substance now coating her tongue as she bent down to allow a tiny make-up artist a final swipe with the blusher brush. 'If anyone drops a match in my hair I'll go up in seconds.'

'You can never be too careful, honey!' yelled the peroxide blond as he passed. 'It's hot back here; we don't want anything to wilt, do we?'

In the afternoon heat of a scorching September day, it was roasting at the front of stage too. Those that were seated had begun to fan themselves with programmes. A few had the real thing. Suddenly, with the previous show now finished, bodies streamed into the tent like a swarm of locusts. Each group made their way to the allotted area. Photographers and camera crews in multi-pocketed khaki waistcoats and boots with tractor tread, set down their ladders and silver cases at the foot of the catwalk. Whilst buyers – identifiable by their love of muted colours and showy jewellery – headed for one side of the catwalk, journalists and fashion editors attired in Mafia black and Japanese rucksacks flanked the remaining section. An army of PR staff in white Esteem T-shirts attempted to smooth away disputes about seat numbers and lost tickets as two set designers rolled away the plastic coating from the catwalk.

At last, all the air-kissing and general socializing gave way to a quiet hush as the audience looked expectantly towards the empty catwalk.

'We're ready out here,' signalled Lucy to Trena on her radio set.

Trena looked at her models. 'OK, go mode back here. Let's start this thing up. Boys, can you hear me?'

There was silence save a few electrical splutters and then came the reply from the desk at the back of the tent: 'OK, Trena, we have lift-off.'

The music fired into action and on her monitor Trena could see the darkness punctuated by one spotlight.

'OK, Candy, get out there and hold your position until lights are full glare. You're on your own. I'll send a group to join you on the music change.'

The blonde finished sucking the guts out of the last cigarette she would enjoy for twenty minutes or so and passed it to a willing taker. Climbing the stairs to a doorway leading to the front of stage, Candy disappeared through the brightly lit portal.

'OK – Kelly, Shelly, Amber and Saffron,' barked Trena, 'where are you? I need you here.'

Four bodies all perfectly accoutred in Esteem's new spring/summer collection sprinted up to their show producer and stood in line by the stairs. 'And Kisha, Natasha, Nadine and Kirsty, line up here behind them.'

On Trena's cue, each model carefully ascended the stairs. Once out, she would saunter serenely the length of the runway and back. Now Candy had completed her first lap, she moved out of the audience's sight and hurried downstairs, undoing her fastenings and kicking off her shoes as she went. Sprinting back to her rail, she stepped out of all remaining garments and waited starkers but for a minute pair of briefs as one of the dressers handed over a fresh piece of clothing and hung up the discarded designs.

Candy was soon fully attired in new colours and, as her dresser bent to tie her shoes, a hairdresser smoothed the disturbed locks and a make-up artist powdered her face once more. The race was on to reach the stairs before Trena began shouting her name.

Elle stood quietly in a corner watching with relief as each model wafted into her vision. Months of hard work were at last paying off and the collection looked fantastic. Soon the three Esteem models would appear wearing Alicia's specially designed catwalk outfits. Extravagant and extra-revealing, these were guaranteed to get the photographers snapping.

Trena looked at her running order and began organizing the next scene. 'Becks, Tess and Charlotte, where are you?' To Tess she yelled, 'You go out as a threesome. I'll give you your cue on the music change.'

'Tess,' screeched Charlotte, as they both stood in line waiting for their moment, 'where's Becks?'

'Becks,' stormed Trena, 'wherever you are, get your arse over here now!' Raising her voice as loud as she could, Trena barked at everyone in the room: 'Don't any of you dare miss your cues. Watch me and listen.'

There was a crashing sound as Becks made her way determinedly to the stairs, bypassing Trena's choreographed cue.

'Not yet!' yelled the fraught show producer, consumed with the business of salvaging her carefully composed presentation. 'Not yet.'

'Becks, no!' shouted Tess.

The music pounded from enormous speakers, drowning out everything except Becks' determination to reach the catwalk. Shakily, she launched herself towards the light, oblivious of the frantic wavings of her friends.

'Music change, now!' screamed Trena into her mouthpiece. 'I don't care if two others are still on. Start the new section and maybe we can save this.'

Everyone crowded round the monitor as Becks, adorned in full designer splendour and royally drunk, took centre stage.

'What's going on?' whined one of the models as she came off. 'You changed the music too soon.'

'Get into your next outfits,' barked Trena.

'She doesn't look well,' yelled the other, as she rushed to her rail.

They all watched with bated breath as the inebriated enchantress began to move. 'Oh, my God,' spat Trena. 'The bitch has got trouble written across her forehead, I can see it from here. OK, Tess and Charlotte,' she said, turning to the remainder of the trio. 'Your cue. Get out there and get her off safely.'

Charlotte and Tess climbed the stairs and stepped into the dazzling illumination. The heat hit them both. A thunderous symphony of tuneful mixing blotted out all chance of communication as they focused on the task in hand. But Becks had already begun a shaky walk and was tottering dangerously close to the edge of the runway.

'Oh, no,' said Tess under her breath, willing Becks to stay upright. 'Don't do it, don't . . .'

'No, no, no,' screamed Trena at the monitor. 'Don't even –'

But Becks could hear only the rushing of the sea in her ears. As Tess and Charlotte sprinted down the runway, she melted floorwards.

Gasps of horror echoed round the room as the beautiful young model nose-dived into the laps of several international fashion cognoscenti. A plethora of flashbulbs illuminated the scene and one or two adventurous lensmen broke free from their pen to focus more fully on the carnage.

As the house lights went up and the music stopped, Elle Cartwrite covered her face with her hands. A blast of flashbulbs ended her private frustration. Lucy was one of the crowd upon her.

'No photographs,' she yelled. 'Security, please remove the paparazzi from the premises. Elle, follow me.'

With her hopes for the future of Esteem in tatters, Elle Cartwrite obediently held on to Lucy and headed for the backstage area, passing a paramedic team on their way to administer eau de cologne to the casualties. Becks was amongst the human montage of laddered tights and orphaned Prada handbags, but Elle never wanted to see her again.

Lucy safely deposited her charge backstage, shut the door, and returned to the demolition scene. There was one member of the elite press corps who had been tipped upside down in her chair. Her expensive skirt had wrapped itself round her waist to reveal a Lycra gusset, effecting a fashion statement that no middle-aged sophisticate would be happy to convey. The hapless PR surveyed the bedraggled coven on the floor, knowing that all would require a considerable amount of encouragement and impossibly expensive gifts to deter them from submitting a scathing article about the day's events.

'What the hell happened?' thundered Elle as she got to Trena.

The house Tannoy system fired up. 'Ladies and gentlemen, we have an urgent announcement. Everyone must leave the premises immediately.'

But fashion folk, not known for their sense of priority, were only interested in getting a better look in the direction of the front row, where one well-known editor was taking a swing at a man with a camera.

'Ladies and gentlemen . . .' begged the voice behind the Tannoy. 'Ladies and gentlemen, this is a most serious request to leave the premises . . . We have a bomb threat. Now, please . . .'

The sound of stampede amplified by state-of-the-art speakers accompanied the uproarious departure of a glittering cast as chairs were thrust aside and scuffles broke out in the race to reach the outside world.

Backstage, Trena made frantic efforts to organize the preservation of her stock, while Elle stood transfixed amongst the debris of her career. Clothes had fallen off the rails and were being trampled underfoot.

'I am ruined,' said Elle to no one in particular. 'Whatever it was –' she looked skyward – 'that I did . . .'

Her soliloquy was interrupted by the noise of something small and animal-like. In a dark corner, wrapped up in a soft cotton shawl, was Cordelia, Lucy's baby, prematurely awake after an afternoon nap. The child's mother was nowhere to be seen, having been earlier swept out front of house with the hastily evacuated audience. Now her daughter howled for attention. Very gingerly, the designer bent down and gathered the infant up in her arms. Wiping away the hot sticky tears of a tiny human being that believed she'd been abandoned, Elle found a comfort denied to her nearly forty years before. Amidst the frantic noise and heat of a day gone mad, a woman rocked a child. 'There now,' she cooed as the desperate wails of the panic-stricken newborn subsided. Instinctively Elle pressed Cordelia close to her heart. 'It's all right,' she whispered, 'everything is going to be all right.'

'Dressers and models, pick up a rail between you and take it outside,' shouted Trena to a hopeless exodus of scantily clad models.

Elle suddenly fired into life. 'Trena,' she commanded, 'get out. It's only frocks.'

'But I've got to save the clothes,' protested her sidekick. 'This is our only . . .'

'Trena,' said Elle, taking her hand firmly as she cuddled the younger of her two charges, 'come with me now.'

As Elle, Cordelia and Trena stepped out into the bright sunshine they were greeted by an extraordinary sight. A crowd of extravagantly coiffed but nearly naked mannequins stood smoking to their hearts' content. Some had rushed out mid-change and huddled only slightly self-consciously in G-strings and jackets whilst sharing their cigarettes. One clasped a hastily grabbed Esteem skirt to her bare chest as she chatted away to her girlfriend. Dressers were busy peeling off spare items of their own clothing to distribute amongst their flock.

'This way, ladies,' urged a burly security man, herding his catch. He and his colleague had already removed their own jackets to restore the dignity of two in the crowd. 'We have to move well away from this area.'

As the entire British fashion industry poured out of the pavilion tents, Charlotte, who had managed to leave the premises in full attire, was amused by the visual incongruity of her world as it merged with real life on the pavement. Women with alarming headwear and fuchsia-coloured lips stood alongside men with ponytails and fans. Doll-like females with cantilevered breasts and orthopaedic footwear chatted to boyish nymphs with belly piercings and black nail varnish. And as the Esteem models in various states of undress gathered together in clannish familiarity, a member of the public tried hard to ignore her daughter's questions as she wheeled a pushchair through the scene. 'Mummy, why has that woman got a lampshade on her head?' the child seemed to be saying.

'Thank God,' gushed Lucy when she came upon Elle and Cordelia, who was now contentedly sucking on Elle's jacket lapel. 'I didn't know who had ... Oh, Cordelia ...' The young mother began to cry and Elle self-consciously hugged her as she returned the happy cherub.

'You stay here, Lucy,' said Elle. 'I'm just going to sort something out.' She turned to a young policeman. 'My sample collection is back there, officer. I need it for selling tomorrow. I have appointments with international buyers, you see. I wonder if you would be so kind as to ...'

'Everybody's possessions will be treated with due respect, madam,' promised the man in the uniform. 'But let's get things in proportion, shall we? We don't want anyone to get hurt while we wait for possible detonation of an explosive device, do we, madam?' He looked at her with the learned tolerance that a small boy might employ when addressing an institutionalized senior citizen. 'Now, move along, please.'

'There she is,' pointed a smartly dressed young woman holding a microphone. 'Elle Cartwrite, I'm Julie Johnson from CNN. We got some good shots of the clothes – if you'll talk about the bomb threat and why it took place in your show, we'll run what we got.'

The reporter turned to her camera for a breezy intro.

'Today, vigilante textile environmentalists threw London Fashion Week into chaos. Top British designer Elle Cartwrite was their chosen target. Ms Cartwrite –' the snappy hack flashed perfect teeth at Elle – 'how do you react to this attack?'

As Elle began her answer, she noticed a bevy of camera crews clamouring for an interview. Lucy was organizing the action. 'Sky next,' she called. 'CNN, I'm afraid I can only let you have one more question.'

This was more like it. Elle relaxed and smiled. Press was press.

⑥

'Charlotte!' called a voice from the crowd. 'Thank God you're safe. Look, I need to speak to you about the other day.' Rick stood in front of her in his favourite blue suit. He looked like a man out of touch with his advancing years; his newly applied blond lowlights and rolled-up suit sleeves didn't help. Charlotte wondered what she had ever seen in him.

'I would have apologized sooner about the other day, only I was pulled over by the police. Someone must have called them.' Rick looked around. 'I'd like to get my hands on whoever did that . . . I've got to go to court next month. But, anyway, I . . .'

'Rick,' said Charlotte, walking away, 'it really is over. I don't want to see you again.' She turned and almost collided with another body.

'Charlotte, it's me!' said the laughing brown-eyed man now standing in front of her. 'It's me – Guy. I was hoping to see you this week, although not under these circumstances. What's the matter?'

Charlotte could see there would be trouble and her face must have alerted Guy, but not in time to avoid completely the inevitable locking of horns with Rick Newman.

'So, you've been seeing him all the time, have you?' he jeered. 'You couldn't wait to see the back of me, could you?' He pulled himself up to full height and blocked Guy's way with his fists clenched. 'Are you the poncey little nobody that thinks he can move in on my girl?'

'No, I'm just a friend,' retorted Guy. 'But, hey, stylish behaviour, dude!' Guy turned his back on the blue suit. 'Charlotte, is this man bothering you?'

'Yes, he is,' confessed Charlotte, looking her ex-partner in the eye. 'But I know he's going to leave me alone now – aren't you, Rick?'

Rick thought about it and swung a fist in the general direction of his challenger's head.

'Guy, look out!' yelled Charlotte.

In an instant Guy had his assailant on the floor. With his foot wedged firmly in Rick's armpit, he bent the offending arm in an uncomfortable lock.

'Perhaps you would both like to come with me,' instructed a uniformed lawman. 'We can sort this little squabble out back at the station. And, madam –' he raised his eyebrows and beckoned Charlotte – 'I believe you were a witness. Would you be so kind?'

'Tess,' called Charlotte as she set off after the policeman, 'see if you can find Becks. Something is very wrong.'

'OK,' said Tess, distractedly, scanning the crowd for Simon. He was sure to be in the throng somewhere.

Everyone was still talking about the crazy model at the

Esteem fashion show as a security man finally gave the all clear to return.

Once backstage, the mood was sombre. 'Dressers,' called Trena deflatedly, 'I want a stock check. And any item of clothing that needs dry cleaning, give it to me.'

Elle was unruffled. 'You know, Trena, we can turn this thing around. I had more press out there today than ... than I've ever had. The campaign has worked well for us and I've got buying appointments all week. The clothes will look good enough after a clean.' Elle massaged her neck and waggled her shoulders. 'Everyone wanted to talk about the fact that Global Defence chose my show to bomb. It's ridiculous, I know that, but, after all ...' She fell silent, pondering some unspoken concept.

She helped herself to a glass of wine and handed one to her trusty aide. 'We work in a ridiculous industry. Two hours ago I thought I was finished. I thought that model had ruined everything. But she didn't.' The designer was incredulous. 'By some quirk of fate, those environmental terrorists saved the day for me. Can you believe it?' She beamed. 'I've asked Lucy to get on the blower and find out if Becks is OK. We'll send her some flowers – after all, she is an Esteem girl. I'm not saying she's not getting a blasting for that little stunt ...' Elle lit one of her slimline cigars and blew smoke into the air. 'But this will be the most talked-about show for a long time. I've already had a request to do Breakfast TV tomorrow.' The Crow chuckled. 'I've told Lucy to make sure Becks knows I want to see her after. We may need to investigate damage limitation here ... And we'll have to hope that the tabloids will find the bomb threat a more appealing story . . .'

'I can't believe you are taking this so calmly, Elle,' interrupted Trena. 'Months of hard work have been put into that fiasco back there. That was your chance to . . . to . . .'

'To what?' quizzed Elle with a strange look in her eye. 'To sell some more clothes. Sure, it's a business, but things will tick over like they always did.' The designer stared into the middle distance. 'There's more than this out there for me, Trena,' she said, reaching for a chair and sitting down. 'And I didn't know that until just now.'

'Are you all right, Elle?' asked Trena. 'Would you like some water?'

'I'm fine,' smiled Elle. She picked up a shoe from the floor by her foot and looked for its companion amidst the clutter. 'In fact, I've never felt better. Now,' she said, rising to her feet, 'let's get these clothes into the van and back to the studio. We've got some selling to do.'

As the designer and her show producer wheeled out their forlorn collection, Tess and Simon stood by the railings.

'I'm sorry you didn't make it in, but you didn't miss much catwalk.' Tess shrugged her shoulders. 'Still, that's a first. I've never had terrorist interest before.'

'Freedom fighters,' corrected Simon. 'It's all in the definition, you know. So, did the police find anything?' He offered Tess some water from his bottle. The sun was baking down on them both.

'I don't know,' replied Tess, blotting the perspiration from her top lip. 'But I think they took it seriously because the anonymous caller used some agreed code word. People could have been hurt!' she stormed. 'I could have been hurt.'

'I think there will be a fair bit of coverage in the papers, though,' chivvied Simon.

'God, what a way to earn a living,' groaned Tess, wiping the lipstick away from her mouth. 'This whole business . . . it's ridiculous.'

'Yeah, it is,' agreed Simon. 'I mean, some of those people back there . . . I've never seen such a bunch of bourgeois –'

'I was talking about these Global Defence idiots!'

'Oh, come on, Tess,' protested Simon. 'It looks to me like there's a lot of people who could do with a wake-up call in your world.'

'Meaning?' prompted Tess impatiently.

'The industry is riddled with fat-cat manufacturers making a fortune out of underpaid, undernourished children in the Third World. And what about the girls who are exploited over here? I've seen some of the stuff that gets passed off as art. It's nothing more than child pornography.'

'What are you talking about?'

'Young models, barely out of puberty, wearing sexually provocative clothes and appearing in cutting-edge magazines. That's what I'm talking about. I didn't think you would be so blind, Tess.'

'For God's sake, Simon. You sound like some old buffer. Lighten up, it's only fashion imagery.'

'Oh, yeah,' said Simon coldly. 'Then why is the Internet full of images like that? Paedophiles don't mind whether the pictures are shot by a top photographer or some tacky bloke in his living room, you know. I'm disappointed in you, Tess. Some things are worth fighting to change.'

'Listen,' flashed Tess, 'I'm not saying it's squeaky clean

out there. And, as a Black model in a world of blue-eyed blondes, I think I know what I'm talking about. But every industry has its seedier side. Don't tell me the music industry doesn't have a drug problem any more, or the sports world a steroid issue. Or the electronic world . . .' Tess looked at Simon accusingly. 'Your telly was probably assembled in Taiwan by a factory full of badly paid women. Does that mean it's OK to set fire to a Tandy store? The fashion industry is . . . well, it's one way to earn a living and it's full of decent people too. People,' she said crossly, 'who don't think it's OK to maim others. Anyway,' Tess folded her arms, 'how come you know so much about the fashion world all of a sudden? Unless . . .'

Simon's face was distant. Suddenly it was all beginning to fall into place. The night she had met him, he had seemed so . . . passionate about animal rights, and pollution of the Rhine, and a hundred other things. She was at that anti-fur party: a perfect place for someone who wanted to connect with the world of fashion and the odd dippy model . . . Of course! Tess realized with growing humiliation that she was just a pawn. She didn't know where he worked or the names of any of his friends. Come to think of it, she didn't even know where he lived.

'Simon, I trusted you,' said Tess quietly. 'I thought you were . . . I thought you wanted to be with me. I thought we were . . .'

Simon was already taking a few steps back. 'Tess,' he said gently, 'what we had was special, but . . . well, I can't get involved. I don't think it's a good idea if we see each other again . . . Look,' he mumbled, 'I've got to go.'

'When were you going to tell me, Simon?' asked Tess.

Simon bent his head. Although he was still standing in front of her, Tess could see that he had already gone.

'I'll ring you some time,' he said as he turned.

Tess watched him walk down the road. 'Don't bother,' she called. The men she cared about had a habit of disappearing abruptly from her life. 'And don't send me a postcard, either,' she said quietly, as she turned away to wipe the tears from her eyes.

In another part of London, Rebecca Cotton closed her front door. Dropping the keys on the chair, she went straight to the tap for water. The day had been a total disaster. It had been ages since her last fix and the desire to blot everything out was strong. She could make a phone call and get some medicine, but that would undo all the hard work she'd already put in. Seven days' cold turkey would be wasted. 'If I can just sleep to the end of the week,' pledged Becks quietly, 'then I'll be all right. I'll have kicked this thing once and for all.'

'Howdit go?' asked Marcia, now suntanned and covered in henna patterns the length of her arms. She and Lal had returned from their travels the previous night.

'Dreadful, Marce,' confessed Becks. 'I totally screwed up. And I feel awful, you know. Like ill, really ill. I've made a mess of it all.'

'You don't look well,' said Marcia with concern. 'You know, Becks, you look like you should see a doctor . . .'

'I drank too much today, Marce,' said Becks, 'that's all. I . . . drank too much. Did I ever tell you my mother was an alcoholic? No? Well, I'm using a little family method of blotting out the world. It's too complicated out there.' Becks stepped out of her clothes and flopped on to the couch. 'I've got to get into bed and sleep,' she said, pulling a coloured blanket over her body. 'Did I ever tell you,' she mumbled as she closed her eyes, 'my grandmother . . .' She lost her train of thought. 'Everything will be all right when I've slept this thing off . . .'

'By the way,' said Marcia, 'there was some guy round today. He was sitting on your doorstep when I came by earlier. Said his name was Paul, I think. He reckoned you were going to put him up while he was in London. He's coming back this evening . . . Becks, did you hear me?'

As if she had imbibed a storybook sleeping draught, the girl in the bed snored gently. The wine she had poured into her body earlier in the day was working its magic like a dream.

20

'I think that I am fat on my body and thighs. I could be a lot slimmer.'

LONDON SCHOOLGIRL, AGE FIFTEEN

'DON'T ever do that to me again, Rick,' stormed Charlotte as they stepped out of the police station. Rick had been given a caution and bound over to keep the peace for one month.

Rick held his jacket in his hand. He looked tired and limp. Guy had gone on home; maybe he wouldn't call Charlotte again. The thought of some neurotic ex-lover trailing her every move, like a dog abandoned by its owner, was possibly too off-putting for words.

'I've made a fool of myself one too many times, haven't I?' said Rick as they stood in the street. His eyes were watery and pale. 'I can't seem to get it into my thick skull that you don't want to be with me any more.' He shook his head and looked upwards as if waiting for some special sign. The trees were still and lifeless and the sun peeked through a canopy of leaves from its westerly post in the sky.

'I thought I had everything – you, a place to live, a direction – but I took it for granted. I know I did. I thought ... well, I thought ... we'd always end up together. I had everything I wanted, and I couldn't see that you didn't.' Rick seemed to be gulping at air. 'I mean, I never hit you or anything, did I? My dad used to knock my mum about and I hated it. I . . .'

'You never told me that before,' said Charlotte watching the face of the man she knew best of all.

Rick was still struggling for an explanation. 'I congratulated myself on doing better ... I thought I was better than he was . . .'

'And you are, Rick,' said Charlotte quietly, 'but you've got a lot to learn and so have I.' She reached out and touched his hand gently. 'I don't want to see you again for a good while, I . . .'

'Charlotte,' said Rick carefully, 'I know what you want and I won't bother you again, but there is something I want to ask.'

'Yes,' said Charlotte warily.

He took a breath and looked her in the eye. 'I want you to get help ... professional help. I know that's really something, coming from me, but ... well, I know what you're doing. You probably thought I didn't hear you in the bathroom late at night, but I did. I didn't say anything – I didn't know how to –'

'I don't do that any more, Rick,' said Charlotte stonily.

'Then perhaps you aren't eating enough,' said Rick

gently. 'When I saw you today I was kind of surprised . . . You look . . . well, too thin.'

'Rick, let me remind you that my career has taken off because I've lost weight. In fact,' she said proudly, 'I've never had so much work.'

Rick lowered his eyes and took two steps backwards. 'I know it's always been my way to pretend I have all the answers, but the truth is I don't. I don't know why I stopped showing you I cared, and I don't know why all those idiots think you look better like that.' He lifted his head and looked straight into her eyes. 'The thing is, Charlotte, for all the lying I did, I never lied to you about one thing.' He kept his eyes firmly locked on hers. 'You are a beautiful woman. And you had a beautiful body. You had the best body I ever saw and I loved it. I know I didn't love it enough.' He corrected himself: 'I didn't love *you* enough. But, Charlotte, you've lost something. That beautiful body is disappearing in front of my eyes. You don't have any of those lovely curves any more.'

'It was fat,' she said, 'and now I've got rid of it and I'm having the time of my career.'

'Some things don't make sense do they, Charlotte? Goodbye, beautiful woman,' he said as he turned. 'Have a nice life.'

Charlotte fixed her eyes on the blue suit and watched it disappear. She would walk all the way home tonight, that would burn off a few calories and earn her a good meal.

'He said I was too thin,' she said indignantly as she stood in front of the mirror later that evening.

'Well, you are,' agreed her companion. 'Haven't you

noticed how your bones ache when you get out of bed? Or how cold you are even when it's hot out there. Do you still have periods, or have they stopped too?'

'Listen,' said Charlotte, 'I shut up your friend in the kitchen the other day and I can do it to you too; all it takes is a hammer.'

'If you do that,' said the woman in the mirror, 'you are truly on your own. You need me, Charlotte. I am the voice you dare not allow yourself. If you shut me up, you lose yourself.'

'You live,' said Charlotte, 'because I let you, but you are trapped in that frame, and the only time you come to life is when I visit you.'

'And what about the trap you've set yourself, Charlotte? If you eat and enjoy your food, you're damned. But if you don't, if you starve yourself, or flush all food out of your system with laxatives, or by sticking your finger down your throat, or exercise it all away . . . you are also damned. Is this what you want, Charlotte? Muscle eating away at itself, stomach ulcerating under acidic attack? And how long do you think you can keep it up?' The woman in the mirror locked eyes with her listener. 'Until your bones begin to weaken with lack of calcium and osteoporosis sets in, or until your hair gets thin and lifeless and your teeth loosen in your head? What sort of damage do you want to inflict on your body? And why do you torture yourself this way?'

'It's not torture,' snarled Charlotte, 'it's discipline. I happen to believe in achieving the best I can and it's a competitive world out there. I've got to work hard, really hard, and that means not giving in, not ever giving in to . . .'

'Not ever giving in to who?' asked the mirror. 'Who forbids you to seek pleasure and sensuality? Who has imprisoned you in a cycle of self-loathing and revulsion?'

'I don't know,' confessed Charlotte. 'Me, I suppose. I say when I can give up.'

'Loving yourself isn't giving up. It's not the end of something, Charlotte. Loving yourself is the beginning. It's the start of everything.'

'But I don't deserve to be loved. I'm fat and I'm ugly and my body is bursting out all over the place. It's always trying to ruin my life.'

'Let me show you someone,' said the voice. 'She's just a child, and she lives this side of the mirror with me.'

Charlotte watched the little girl sitting forlornly on the other side of the glass frame. Her thick black hair was clipped at either side of her face. She waited quietly, her hands clutching her frilly dress.

'Who is she?' whispered Charlotte. 'She looks so sad and lonely.'

'Perhaps you will recognize her,' said the voice. 'There are hundreds, even thousands, just like her back here.'

'But why?'

'They get left behind, stuck in a time warp. I've seen it over and over from this side. They turn up in their school uniforms, their muddy jeans, their nurses' uniforms with sick dollies in their arms. We get all kinds. They don't come often at first, just now and then, popping their lovely little heads through the door with eyes alive and bright. They're far too busy running, jumping and skipping, exploring their world. But they start spending longer and longer periods here, preoccupied and thoughtful. Then something happens – for some it's sooner, for others it doesn't take place till much later. They step in here and they can't get back. They are locked in. Locked into a time frame that holds them fast. They can see themselves on the other side as they stare back through the mirror, but they can't free themselves. For every year that passes they stay the same while their reflection grows up in the real world.'

'What does the woman in the real world see when she looks in the mirror?' asked Charlotte.

'When the grown woman looks in the mirror, she does not see herself, she sees the child she once was. She has made time stand still, and in the mirror she can visit the past. When her reflection visits the mirror, the captive shrieks with panic, waving her arms. "I'm here, but I've got to move on." At first she waits expectantly by the doorway, ready to leap out and throw herself back into life when the chance arises ... But they wait so long. I've seen some give up altogether.'

'That's so sad,' said Charlotte.

'Yes it is,' agreed the voice, 'and the saddest thing of all is that the woman on the other side of the mirror has locked away a little girl who feasts on fun, who is greedy for life and who nourishes herself on freedom and spontaneity, stuffing herself full of experience and knowledge. The woman on the other side has locked away all her hopes and dreams, and her belief in an ability to own the future on her own terms.'

'Why are you telling me this?' quizzed Charlotte.

'Because growth is what every woman must seek,' said the voice.

21

'when we slip on our best jacket and we see our deplorably unimpressive shoulders artfully magnified and idealized, we do, for a moment, rise in our own esteem.' **QUENTIN BELL**

*E*LLE Cartwrite sat at her desk surrounded by the day's news. She'd hardly slept the night before: a combination of nerves and the fact that in order to lounge on a pastel-coloured sofa with a synthetic presenter for a Breakfast Television appearance, she'd had to rise at some unearthly hour. She flicked through the papers restlessly. Fortunately all but one seemed to focus on the bomb scare. There was a large and rather humorous group picture of her models on the front page of the *Guardian*, with the caption: 'Show Stopper'. Others had reported more conservatively on their inside pages. 'No way could I have got front page of a quality read,' said Elle, pleased. 'Now that's the kind of advertising no one can afford.' Her show was mentioned in glowing terms, but the main thrust of the article was devoted to Global Defence. The authorities were convinced that someone within the industry had planted the bomb because it had appeared after the sniffer dogs had done the rounds. So someone must have witnessed the police search, slipped out and slithered back in with the deadly package.

Maddy stepped into the room with a steaming mug of coffee. 'There are two bunches of flowers for you in reception,' she said, like a nurse talking to a convalescing patient. 'I thought you'd like to know that. And I've sent a car to pick up Becks. How did your interview go this morning?'

'Very well, Maddy,' said Elle, 'if you count talking about bombs, boobs and big hair with an overly made-up talk-show hostess at seven o'clock in the morning as a plus.'

'Well,' said her secretary, 'Lucy has been on the line. You've been inundated with interview requests, and *London Live*, *News at Five* and *Capital Week* would like to come and film at some point today. I'd say,' she said with a twinkle, 'that things are panning out very well, considering.'

'And I'd say you are right.' Elle smiled. 'Maddy,' she said shaking her head, 'isn't life strange. Do you ever think that?' She took a sip of the steaming beverage that Maddy had set down in front of her. 'I did a lot of thinking last night and I'm going to set something in motion today that will make a big difference to my life.' Elle stood up and walked over to the window. 'I've been working too hard,' she said decisively. 'I've been working too hard for about thirty-five years and I haven't stopped to enjoy the life I've made. There are people out there –' Elle scanned the streets below as she spoke – 'that I don't even know.'

'It's a big city,' said Maddy awkwardly. 'Elle, are you all right? You know, it was a traumatic thing that happened yesterday and maybe you need some time to . . .'

'Actually, Maddy, I've never felt better,' declared Elle, turning away from the window and folding her arms. 'I learned something yesterday and I learned it from a child . . . a tiny baby.' Elle stared thoughtfully at her shoes.

'What do you mean, Elle?' queried Maddy, concerned that the pressure was beginning to tell.

'I'm going to step back from this business and hand it over to Alicia,' announced Elle decisively. 'She's earned it. She designed all the best garments in that show.' Elle shook her head. 'Sadly, no one got to see them properly, but they will.' She walked over to her secretary. 'And you . . . I've been hard on you, too. I've been angry about . . . well, about the marriage . . . you know.' Elle put her hand out to touch Maddy's shoulder. 'I was like a jealous old witch. I thought I'd lost you, Maddy. I thought that because you wanted to get married, you were throwing away your life. I was angry with you for leaving me . . .'

'But I haven't left you, Elle,' said Maddy reassuringly.

'I know that now,' said Elle, 'and even if you *did* go . . . you know, for another job, or to have children . . . All I'm trying to say, Maddy, is . . . I know you have a family already, but you are very special to me . . .' Elle put her arm round her surrogate daughter and smiled. 'I do want to design the dress, you know,' she laughed. 'And all your bridesmaids' frocks.'

Maddy's eyes misted. 'Elle,' she said, 'that would be the icing on the cake.'

'Cake,' said Trena as she passed the office, 'is just what we need. I don't know about you, but I'm ravenous today and I can't manage another moment without a decent breakfast. I'm going to visit the bagelry – anyone want supplies?'

The office was filling up as Maddy returned to her desk to take a call. 'Tom,' she said excitedly, 'you'll never guess what . . .'

Elle surveyed the office. This place had been her world, and her desk her kingdom, but once she retired, as she inevitably would, there would be nothing. The family she had created for herself was little more than a business arrangement. Her staff out there returned to their real families every night, and as for her paper daughters . . .

Trena returned with her cream cheese and smoked salmon banquet and headed for the showroom up the corridor. Soon a gaggle of buyers from Germany, Italy, Belgium, Holland, Japan and America would descend on the premises. It would be a long and arduous few days, but this was where the real business was done. Designers didn't actually need to send their clothes down the runway at all. Half a dozen models – new ones without previous catwalk commitments – would soon parade the freshly dry-cleaned designs in the showroom to each buying group and the trading would follow.

Elle took the two bouquets into her favourite show producer, who was lovingly laying out the collection. 'Here's one bunch for you, Trena. Thank you . . . for everything you did yesterday.' She cut the second bouquet from its wrapping and dropped the flowers into a large cream vase. 'No one could have prevented Becks launching herself into orbit,' lamented Elle as she stepped back to view her floral arrangement. 'From what I'm hearing, she was an accident waiting to happen. I wonder if her mother knows about the lifestyle her daughter leads.' The designer shook her head. 'I don't think we should be too hard on her, Trena.

302

The agency will have already dealt with it, I'm sure. Now, did we get food and drink ordered for today?'

'Elle,' said Trena, 'I'm wondering about security. It's not that I want to worry you, but we did have a terrorist with an explosive device in our midst yesterday and I think it would be a good idea to post someone outside our front door to check buyers off the list. I mean, we've got a lot of visitors coming today and anyone could stroll in, couldn't they?'

'Good point,' agreed Elle. 'I'll get Maddy to draw up a list of callers and then get on to MA. Their people are the best. Nothing must be allowed to go wrong. I've got a feeling that today will be a memorable day. How do you feel about working more closely with Alicia?'

'What do you mean?' said Trena as she spaced the stock evenly on each rail. The collection was divided into colour themes.

'I mean,' said Elle, drawing breath, 'you and her as managing directors of Esteem. Trena, you are far more than an ordinary show producer: you're my creative director and Esteem needs you. I'm going to step down, and I want you and Alicia to run the company from now on. I'm going to tell her in a minute. I shall be around, of course, but I . . . I want something different.'

Elle walked over to the large studio window. It was one of her favourite spots and offered an almost panoramic view of the world below. She could see the British Telecom tower in the distance and an Esteem poster across the road. Three beautiful women smiled a smile that would last for an eternity, or until replaced by another poster. 'There is someone out there,' she mumbled, 'who I need to find.'

'Are you looking for somebody in particular?'

'Yes, Trena, I am,' declared Elle with conviction as she

watched a mother bend down to rescue her child. The toddler had tripped on an uneven paving stone and lay stretched out like a human starfish. 'I lost her a long time ago and I don't really know where to begin to try and trace her. But I do know that I won't ever find her if I don't try . . .'

'Elle,' said Maddy as she stood at the door, 'I'm sorry to interrupt, but Becks is waiting in your office.'

Elle and Trena exchanged looks. 'In the meantime,' said the Crow, fluffing up her feathers as she walked towards the door, 'duty calls.'

'She doesn't look well,' confided Maddy as they walked back down the corridor. She opened the door and waited for Elle to enter the room. 'Would you like coffee?' she said as she prepared to shut the door.

'Yes please, Maddy,' said Elle. 'I think we both would, unless . . . Becks, would you prefer Coke or juice?'

The sulky teenager was slouched in a leather chair opposite the desk of her employer. She took a breath and spoke. 'Coke, please.'

'Now look, Becks,' said Elle firmly, 'I'm not about to shout at you. But I feel I deserve to know what went on yesterday. You cost me tens of thousands of pounds, and you could have cost me my reputation . . . and my business. As it is, I think I can save things, so I'm . . .'

'It's all you care about, isn't it?' sneered Becks.

'I don't think you are in a position to mock me, young woman,' said the Crow stiffening. 'I have a business to run and I employed you to help me. I didn't,' she said banging her hand on the table and raising her voice, 'expect to be so thoroughly humiliated in front of every top journalist in the entire fashion industry.' Elle tried to control her voice as she continued: 'Now, I'm willing to try and under-

304

stand what happened yesterday and I'm willing to accept an apology . . .' Maddy entered the room with drinks on a tray. 'Thanks, Mad,' Elle said gratefully as she sat back in her chair.

'You've got an appointment in ten minutes,' said Maddy cautiously as she registered the tension in the room. 'I'll let you know when they arrive.'

As Maddy closed the door behind her, Elle returned her gaze to Becks. She poured out a glass of brown fizzy liquid and set it down on the table in front of her visitor. 'Now, Becks, I'll ask you again: what was going on yesterday and why were you so drunk?' Elle surveyed the bedraggled blonde in front of her. 'You look like you hurt yourself,' she said pointing to the bandage on Becks' sprained wrist, 'and you don't appear to be at all well. Does your mother . . . ?'

'None of your business,' snarled Becks. 'My mother doesn't know anything about me . . .' She looked Elle in the eye and then leaned back in the chair. 'From what I've learned,' she grunted, 'that's the way with a lot of mothers.'

'Well,' said Elle, becoming more irritated by the minute, 'I think she has a right to know . . .'

'Oh, do you?' snapped Becks. 'You're very clear on the rights of mothers, aren't you? And what rights do you think their children have?'

'Oh, Becks, this is ridiculous,' dismissed Elle. 'I can't see the point of having this conversation. You are a very angry young woman and I'm not going to fight with you.'

She walked over to the window. The Esteem poster looked like some surreal moment in time. Three happy faces, three happy lives. What a ridiculous lie. One of its members was a long way from knowing the meaning of cheerful; worse still, she was sitting in the office behaving like the antichrist. And there were rumours that another was ill with an eating disorder.

Elle turned back to face the sullen young woman. 'Whatever happened between you and your mother is none of my business, but . . .'

'You mean you don't want it to be.'

'I'm sorry, Becks, but I've had enough. I'm getting nowhere here. I thought you might want to apologize to me at the very least, but I see I was wrong. Now I've got an appointment which . . .'

'And I thought you might apologize to me!' shouted Becks as she got up to leave. 'You think you're so untouchable in your big ivory tower, but I know who you are . . .' Becks shook as she spoke. Her anger was filling the room and Elle began to feel uneasy.

'Right, that's it,' she snapped in an effort to regain control of the situation. 'I shan't be working with you again, Becks. I don't want anything more to do with you.'

'Oh, you made sure of that a long time ago,' replied Becks coldly as she reached for the door handle. 'You think you can get rid of people if they get in your way, don't you?' she jeered as she exited.

Maddy almost bumped into Becks on her way to collect the designer for her first buying appointment of the day. 'Are you all right? Do you need any help?' she said with concern.

'No, only the loo,' said Becks quietly.

'It's up the corridor next to the showroom.' Maddy had long since got used to the English way of talking about the restrooms, although at times it still made her smile. She pushed open the door and popped her head round. 'That nice man from Tokyo is waiting in the studio for you, Elle.' The designer looked shaken.

'OK, I'm ready. Where did that model go, Maddy?'

'Oh, she went to the "loo", you know like you English do, and then she said she was going.'

Elle grunted. 'I've half a mind to see her off the premises myself. Will you make sure she leaves?'

'Of course,' said Maddy. 'What on earth happened between you two? She seemed upset.'

'I fired her,' said Elle flatly as she walked up the corridor to meet her appointment. 'She is no longer one of the family . . . Ah, Mr Kiwunabe, how lovely to see you again.'

And I never was, thought Becks to herself as she rinsed her hands and face. She could hear voices outside in the corridor. Everyone was going about their business. Phones trilled in the background and doors opened and closed. Becks stood in the brightly lit room with its mirrored tiles and considered her options. She'd really blown it. The old woman didn't want to know her; maybe she'd even convinced herself that the child she'd given birth to all those years ago no longer existed. People could do that, couldn't they? Her grandfather had done it; he had blotted out the part he had played in her creation. Her grandfather had ruined lives, and that old woman out there was no different.

Becks remembered the cleansing flames she had invoked to punish the old man. Just as he had poisoned her world, she had gleefully annihilated his by setting fire to his bible. Memories of the satisfying crackles filled Becks' head as she recalled the demise of her grandfather's beloved holy book. All the worn pages, thin as tissue, with tiny pencil scribblngs marking the spot of his favourite psalm or story.

The scribbled notes at the back and the collection of letters in a different hand, all faded and tied up with an old ruby red ribbon. She knew how to exact revenge all right, and why should Elle Cartwrite not get what was coming to her? What was it that Elle valued over and above anything else? What did she have that Becks could take away? She knew in an instant. The answer was in the very next room – the collection, of course! The clothes all freshly pressed and hung in the studio would be the perfect tinder for an angry spark. Becks reached for her lighter and flicked it with her thumb. A beautiful flame danced before her eyes. Mesmerizing and melancholy, the silky yellow and purple slash cavorted with carefree abandon. Becks remembered the joy of feeding the flame and watching it grow.

She snapped the lighter shut. Best not to run the gas down. Ignition would have to be swift. There was probably a sprinkler system, so no one would be hurt. It was the clothes. She wanted to destroy the precious clothes. She wouldn't wait to watch the fire; she'd turn and run, leaving this hellhole for good. Start up another life, maybe in New York. Somewhere where she could choose her family. Her hands were clammy and her skin itched. The need for a little more medicine was strong. Heroin was her enemy, but it was also her friend. Thoughts of a heavenly sleep filled her head. Just a small dose would see her through. Becks ran the cold water tap into the basin and shoved her head in the cooling pool. Her scalp tingled and her eyes stung. Throwing her shoulders back she sprayed droplets of water across the room. A stream trickled from her crown and down her neck into her T-shirt. With a hand towel she blotted the excess and reached for her lighter. Elle and Maddy were talking in the corridor once more. Instinctively Becks hid in a cubicle, locking the door as she crouched on the toilet. Above her was a feng shui teaching, instructing users to close the toilet lid and help the company prosper.

'She must have gone,' called Maddy as she popped her head round the door. 'Now . . .'

Becks listened to Maddy detail the day's appointments as her voice grew fainter with each step further down the hall. So there was twenty minutes until the next buyer was due to arrive.

'Get some coffee on,' yelled Trena in the distance.

Now was her chance, the room was empty and the corridor was quiet. Becks slithered off her post and deftly slipped out into the hallway. Unnoticed, she entered the showroom and hurried to the rails of pastel designs as they waited for the attentions of their creator. Tiny dust particles drifted lazily in and out of the sunlight and around the elegant gowns that Tess and Charlotte had worn the day before. Uneven satin hemlines skimmed the floor and fluttered in a delicate breeze. Becks reached for her lighter and turned up the petroleum-saturated wick as high as it would go. Then, sparking the flame, she placed the tiny metal container on the bleached wooden flooring under a deliciously flammable organza skirt. Without waiting to bask in the glow of extinction, Becks turned and walked out of the door, shutting it quietly to remove any possibility of early discovery. The bonfire in the buying room must be allowed to live.

Becks had made herself invisible all her life and today she would retreat from the Esteem offices without anyone even noticing. Head down, she glided past Kirsty on the front desk. Within moments she was out in the bright sunshine once again. Heart racing. Skin crawling. Across the road the Esteem poster caught her attention. A shiny, smiley woman looked her straight in the eye. 'You're not me,' spat Becks as she snarled at an image of herself from across the street. 'You've got nothing in common with me. You're some nasty Frankenstein creation from that bitch up there. That's what she does, she goes around creating people and then dumps them or kills them off when she's had enough.' Becks walked towards the hoarding. 'She'll tear you down when she's finished with you,' she warned. 'All of you. I know.'

Becks dived down a backstreet and headed for the underground. She would pack up her stuff and leave. No one would know where she was. As she walked, Becks could feel dampness around her shoulders. Behind her ears where her hair was still wet, the air cooled her neck. The sun beat down on the top of her head and she put her hand to her crown to feel the heat. She had dressed hurriedly this morning and wore baggy army fatigues and a crumpled top. She hadn't even cleaned her face of yesterday's make-up and traces of mascara smudged underneath her eyes.

People filled the streets with their movements. Journeys big and small were being undertaken right in front of her. The scent of sun lotion combined with car fumes wafted up her nostrils. London had been her refuge for a short while. It was where she had spent the happiest times. In this dirty, smelly city she had re-invented herself. She was no longer Rebecca, quiet and mousy, but Becks: a whole person with expectations and desires. This was where she would have lived if her mother hadn't been sent away at birth. This was her home. The desire to stay and fight for her right to be was overwhelming.

Becks sat on a bench in the shade. If only she could have told Elle the truth and given her a chance. She had been so angry that she hadn't made sense. Now she had killed all chances of any reunion with her grandmother. Unless . . . Unless she could pluck up the courage to go back in there and tell her the whole story. But then a fire engine raced past and Becks remembered the blaze that she had gleefully initiated as a parting gift.

'Oh, my God,' wailed the agitated blonde as she sat bolt upright on the wooden seat. A woman stared hard as she passed; London was full of weirdoes these days. 'Oh, my God. What have I done?' cried Becks, covering her head with her hands. 'What have I done?'

'What's going on?' barked Elle as she raced down the corridor to her showroom, leaving behind a gaggle of immaculately accessorized buyers. The sprinkler system had emptied its tanks of life-saving water and rained all liquid floorward upon first detection of smoke. Now water seeped out from the crack under the door and advanced ominously towards the elegant crowd who waited in expensively crafted shoes to commence the day's business.

Elle pushed hard at the door and stumbled through, stepping in a pond of brown water as she did so. 'Oh, Jesus H!' she howled as she surveyed the smoke-blackened corner. 'We've had a fire,' she called to Trena, 'and the sprinklers have covered everything in filthy . . . Oh, it goes from bad to worse.' She turned to apologize to her customers, who were preoccupied with evacuation, and thought better of it. First things first.

With her shoes drenched, Elle paddled into the room in the vain hope of saving her clothes. The sprinkler showed no sign of letting up as it spluttered and choked out yet

311

more bilge. The system was probably as old as the building itself and the pipes were aged and rusty. Years of silt and stagnation spewed over everything in the room, including those brave enough to enter.

'Get this water turned off now,' screamed Elle above the sound of hissing emissions, 'and get all hands in here with buckets and mops. We've got stock downstairs and it's going to go straight through these floorboards. Oh, why,' she implored, her face turned skywards, 'couldn't I have chosen a tasteless deep-pile shag that would have soaked up all this shit?'

Insurance would cover losses, but she could never make up for the lost time. Elle caught sight of herself in the mirror with slime-spattered tailoring and hair in disarray. 'Somebody is trying to tell me something,' she muttered as she removed her jacket and laid it on a wet table. Even the vase of fresh flowers so optimistically arranged a few hours earlier was full to the brim with muddy rain.

It wouldn't have mattered if she had wept for all she was worth – or not now, as the case may turn out to be – no one would have been able to tell the difference. Elle Cartwrite was drenched to the skin. The Esteem poster mounted at the end of the showroom was wrinkled and warped, and her business was in ruins.

'Oh, Elle,' gasped Trena as she arrived with a mop in her hand, 'how could any one have got past security? I don't understand why Global Defence has got it in for you.'

'I've called the police,' called Maddy from the doorway, 'and I've rung the buildings manager. He's sending someone round to get into the loft to turn it off.' Realizing that there was nothing for it but to join the salvage operation, Maddy entered the room. 'Yuck,' she said as she removed

312

her shoes and placed them on the table next to Elle's sodden jacket. Alicia followed with several studio assistants in tow, and they formed a chain, passing each item of clothing not yet ruined out into the dry corridor and hanging them from the metal window frames that lined the wall on one side.

Soon the downpour began to ease up. Either the reserves had run dry or a handyman had managed to stem the flow. 'What really winds me up,' snapped Elle, 'is that the next bugger who has a fire will get clean water coming out of those things.' She jerked her head in the direction of the ceiling and then bent to pick up a garment from the floor. It looked like a piece of rugby kit worn for the duration of the match on a muddy pitch. 'I don't think we could have ruined these clothes or our chances of success this season more thoroughly if we had tried,' she tutted.

22

'**clothes** are inevitable, they are nothing less than the furniture of the mind.'

JAMES LAVER

'*T*ESSA Collins?' said the policeman. He looked like a school leaver and his smooth chin bore testament to the fact that he probably was. 'Would you come down to the station, please.'

'But why?' groaned Tess. It was too early in the morning for anything as stressful as a visit from a humourless civil servant in a navy safari pantsuit. Besides, she wasn't long up and had promised herself an extensive period under the power shower before breakfast. 'All my parking fines are up to date. I've paid my council tax regularly since the first court summons and . . .'

'I would be obliged if you would dress and accompany me down to the station, madam,' repeated the policeman flatly. 'We require your assistance with our inquiries concerning a fire at the offices of Elle Cartwrite.' He spoke like a man in need of adenoid removal and his eyes were empty and lifeless.

'What on earth are you talking about?' she said panicking. 'I've been nowhere near the Esteem offices.'

'Do you have anyone who could testify as to your whereabouts yesterday, madam?' enquired the officious young man.

Tess had spent the day in the flat moping, lamenting Simon's departure theatrically and tearfully, and playing Bob Marley records very loudly.

'No, I don't,' she said irritated. 'When I'm trying to get over a broken romance, I usually do as much sobbing as I can in private.'

'Ah,' said the boyish man.

Tess surveyed her caller. He probably hadn't got much further than the odd crush, so he'd have no idea what she meant. Then she looked down to see a wedding ring on his left hand. Wow, people got married young these days. Mind you, it was probably all part of the job, like never dropping litter and only crossing the road when the little green person said you could.

'I'll be five minutes,' she said testily. 'I need to clean my teeth and select suitable attire.'

The teenage husband did not answer.

'So,' said a plainclothes officer at the station as they sat in a room, he one side of the table, she the other, 'you side with the likes of John Wallis and his merry men, do you?'

'Who the hell is he?' demanded Tess. 'As far as I know, I'm helping you with your inquiries, not being implicated in them.'

'John Wallis,' continued the drab-looking man in front of her who had earlier introduced himself as Detective Constable Harris, 'or should I say, *Simon* –' he emphasized the name with camp delivery – 'is well known to us all round here. We believe he and a little circle of earnest international friends are the ones behind Global Defence. Does that name mean anything to you, Miss Collins?'

'Yes, of course,' answered Tess. 'Everyone in the fashion industry knows who they are. Or knows of them.' She corrected herself, suddenly feeling that whatever she said was about to be taken down and used in evidence . . . or however it went when they said that kind of thing on *Prime Suspect*.

'And what do you know about Global Defence?'

'Nothing . . . I mean . . . what is there to know?' She knew she was stammering and that was probably a dead giveaway.

'Did you know, for instance, that we observed the ring leader, John Wallis himself, coming out of your house on several different occasions in the run-up to the bombing attempt? Mind you,' he allowed himself a little titter, 'why he chose your employer, Elle Cartwrite, I don't know. Hardly top-quality kit, is it?' DC Harris assumed the role of man in the street in order to deliver his thoughts. 'Yes, I'd say designers have got very strange ideas about what the general public likes to wear. From what I've seen,' he paused to inject a small amount of gravitas into his discourse, 'most of it is aimed at prostitutes. Certainly not the sort of thing a respectable member of the community like my missus would wear. Very flimsy, I'd say. Do you

317

like wearing very flimsy clothes, Miss Collins?' questioned her inquisitor salaciously.

'Hey, what is this – some sort of accessories offence?' protested Tess. 'I mean, don't you think you could concentrate on something a little more critical, like the amount of racism that some of your *lads*' – now it was her turn to emphasize a word – 'seem to get away with?'

'No, I'd like to concentrate on accessories, Miss Collins,' came the reply. 'Let's talk about the fact that we could charge you with being an accessory to attempted murder. That wasn't some little firework that was planted at your employer's show, you know.' His voice was oozing with sarcasm. 'And now that we can add arson to your repertoire,' he sniffed and watched her carefully, 'I'd say we're looking at a few years behind bars – and not the sort where you can order a poncey drink.'

'I did have a relationship with Simon,' confessed Tess, 'but I had no idea . . .'

'We weren't born yesterday, Tess,' said her interrogator impatiently. He had a haircut that looked like it needed a lot of attention and dandruff on his shoulders. 'You were at an anti-fur party when you met him – you are a supporter, I take it? Do you think,' he leaned closer to her, 'that these poor defenceless animals deserve a pension plan and a nice little cottage by the sea?' He laughed at his own humour. 'They are farmed for their fur,' he snorted. 'Some of them live a lot more comfortably than battery hens, but no one gets their knickers in a twist about that.'

'Look,' said Tess angrily, 'I've told you that I know nothing about the fire. I did . . .' she faltered, 'I did get Simon an invitation to the catwalk show . . . I didn't know anything about his other life. I didn't ask that many questions.'

'Pretty girls like you can afford to be more choosy,' he said, eyeing her up and down. 'I mean, a man like that could get you banged up,' he allowed himself another little snigger, 'if you know what I mean. Now then,' he said, straightening his shirt, 'let's get a statement from you. Oh, and if you don't have any legal, now is a good time to think about it.' He swept out of the room and returned moments later. 'When she's done that –' he didn't bother to look at Tess – 'she can go, but tell her not to leave the country.'

Tess fidgeted uncomfortably on her plastic chair. As a child, she had grown up on an estate where a family's worth was measured by the fewest visits from the local law enforcement division. Her mother had prided herself that the police had never come knocking on her door. She hoped this brief episode of perceived criminality would not find its way back to her mother.

Once outside, Tess tried dialling a variety of mobile numbers. None of her friends were taking calls yet. Fashion Week was a full-on party opportunity in every direction and most of the people she knew would only recently have made it to bed. No one would be picking up any messages for hours. Then it came to her: Becks! She could vouch for the fact that Tess had been home yesterday morning, because they had spoken briefly on the phone. Becks had seemed rather disorientated and had been cut off, but at least she could confirm Tess's story. Charlotte would have her number – they hung out, didn't they? Tess dialled and hoped for life at the other end. Disappointment must have registered in her voice as she spoke. 'Yeah, Charlotte, it's me – Tess. I was hoping to speak to you . . . It's . . . well, I need Becks' number urgently. Give me a call when you can. I'll be on the mobile. Bye.'

Charlotte preferred to listen to Tess as she spoke on the answer machine. Sometimes it was so much easier to hear life taking place and not have to do any thing about it. Actually, having a life was exhausting. Tess was one of those women who always seemed to breeze through everything. A woman like her had no idea how messy it could all be sometimes. Charlotte hated mess, but her world was full of it and she was always trying to tidy it away. If only she could get dressed.

'I feel so empty and worthless,' she confessed to her friend in the mirror. 'None of it –' she motioned with her hand to the window and the world outside – 'means anything any more. I don't know what I need to do to feel alive again. I thought I needed a relationship, however bad it was. Then I thought I needed a busy career, but now I've got it . . .' Her voice trailed off. 'I used to know what I wanted . . . but that was a long time ago.'

'Why don't you know any more?' asked the woman in the mirror.

Charlotte sat on the floor and rolled herself into a tight ball. 'I think I learned that what I needed wasn't important.' Charlotte looked into the mirror to see a small girl standing stiffly in a pristine pinafore dress and remembered the times she had returned to the house as filthy as her two brothers. Neither would ever receive a scolding, but Charlotte knew her fate would be different. Mrs Davis couldn't tolerate dirty little girls. Her face only had to twist unattractively and her daughter felt instantly naughty. She hated her mother's mood swings and couldn't escape them like her father and brothers, who had long since given up trying to please Jennifer Davis.

While the men of the house would set up camp for the weekend in some faraway muddy wood and fish for trout, Charlotte kept her mother company. Over the years, she had learned what to do in order to keep the day on an even keel. 'We're having a girls' weekend,' her mother would coo. 'No horrid smelly maggots for us.'

Charlotte longed for the freedom to run wild in the boggy undergrowth with worms in her pockets and twigs in her matted hair, but that was a boy's privilege. The feminine equivalent involved shopping trips and tea in town. And at the end of the day, during a gentle walk through the local park, Mrs Davis would categorize her friends' daughters as monstrous trollops or bitchy young madams; all destined – unless they learned to make the best of themselves – to a life of miserable spinsterhood. Making the best of oneself was the only feminine sport on offer. On rare days, Charlotte would be invited into the bedroom (normally out of bounds) to sit on the fluffy lilac eiderdown and review her own performance.

Occasionally – perhaps before her father was due home – Mrs Davis would sit at the mirror and allow Charlotte to witness the magical process of beautifying. The potions and liniments that lined the top of the dresser all had different functions. Charlotte would gaze apprentice-like at the impressive number of bottles and containers required by one woman, bewildered at the amount there was to know about being female.

Some balms would be employed quite casually; others, like the ones in the smaller, rather exquisite-looking jars still in their protective packaging, seemed to invoke hushed exclamations of reverence from the elder. The bedroom would become a confidential and intimate space for mother and daughter to collude – one passing on a timeless knowledge, the other poised in silent appreciation. Then, handling them like collector's items, the beautiful maiden would begin to concoct a spell. Humming sweetly, she would carefully unseal the amulets and apply small amounts to different parts of her body – her face, her wrists, her neck, her hands, between her breasts, even her legs. The room would be heavy with incense as transformation took place: the enchantress lost in incantation as the protégé watched and learned.

Charlotte understood the power was in the vessels at the shrine. And worship should take place daily. She revelled in the intimacy she shared with her mother as they sat in front of the mirror. Sometimes she would sneak into the room and run her fingers over the matching silver brush and hand mirror that lay on the glass surface, wondering whether she, too, could summon the spirits in the same way.

'What did you need back then, Charlotte?' asked the woman in the mirror.

'I needed to be loved for who I was.'

'And what do you need now, Charlotte?' encouraged her confidante.

'I really need to get better,' said Charlotte almost inaudibly. She lifted her eyes to take in the reflection in front of her. 'I've spent a lifetime trying to fulfil somebody else's expectations of me and it's making me ill.'

'You must get help,' said the woman. 'Ring the doctor now.'

'But I can't – what shall I say?' she exclaimed, horrified.

'Tell them that you need help.'

'Hi, Sara,' said Tess as she stood in the hot sun outside the police station. 'I'm in trouble.'

'I know,' said her agent. 'We've had some press agency on the phone wanting your picture and they gave us an appetizer. Said you'd been arrested. Tess, what's going on? You're far too sensible to get tangled up with the police.' Sara's younger models were in and out of her office with their complicated little lives. Abortion, boyfriend bust-ups and an addiction to slimming pills: these were some of the things she'd had to deal with in the past week. But Tess – she was rock solid.

'I've been accused of starting some fire,' relayed Tess, 'and it seems they think I had something to do with that bomb the other day.'

'But that's ridiculous!' squealed her agent incredulously.

'Look, I didn't want to say anything, but it turns out that guy I was seeing – you know, Simon – well, he's something to do with Global Defence. I haven't seen him since the show . . . We split up.'

As if the deception he'd practised wasn't bad enough, Simon or whatever his name was had given her a leaving present. 'The bastard,' she snarled under her breath. As far as being shat upon from a great height went, this was a contender for the big one. 'I'm worried, Sara,' confided Tess.

'Look, we can sort something out. I'll speak with the

company's solicitors,' soothed Sara. 'But whatever you do, don't talk to anyone in the media. You know how quickly news gets round. Stay low. Once they've got the sniff of another story – you know, some footballer thumping his wife, that kind of thing – they'll be out of your hair.'

'I'm going to try and track Becks down,' announced Tess decisively. 'She could prove to be the only alibi I have at this stage. I know she lives east, so I'm going over that way. Can you get the address from her agency?'

'Yes,' said Sara, 'but Tess – is it wise?'

'Oh, she's harmless, a bit of an airhead, but if I can get her to give them a statement, then I'm cleared. Speak to you later.'

'Can I see Doctor Bolton?' asked Charlotte. A fulsome-cheeked receptionist with silvery hair swung round.

'Doctor Bolton is on holiday,' replied Mrs Dora Bridgwater. She had a name badge on her floral blouse and smelled of freesias. 'Do you have an appointment?'

'No,' stammered Charlotte, 'but I need to see someone urgently.' She had run from her house to the community surgery and stood exhausted and breathless in front of the matronly official.

'What's the matter with you, dear?' breezed Dora, not bothering to hide the disinterest in her voice.

'I'm . . . I'm not eating enough,' blurted Charlotte. 'It's just that . . . well, I can't eat.' She tried to keep the conversation as private as she could, given that she was in a large waiting room full of people with visible ailments. Youths with an assortment of heroic plaster casts, children with skin complaints, old people with dressings on ulcerated skin. The harassed receptionist swept her eyes up and down Charlotte's body.

'Is it a stomach bug?' she asked.

'No, it's . . .'

'Are you in pain, dear?'

'No, I . . .'

'Well then,' said the silvery official, 'I'm afraid you'll have to make an appointment for next week. We've got two doctors on holiday and we're very short.'

'But I'm desperate,' began Charlotte. 'I've . . . I think I've got an eating disorder.' There, she had said it at last.

'Look, dear,' said the receptionist briskly, 'if you are worried about your weight, go home and eat.' She looked at her colleague for support. 'I certainly wish I had your problem.' She took a breath and then relented. 'What I can do is make an appointment in the diary on Wednesday next to see Doctor Redmond. If it's cleared up by that time, ring to cancel it, would you. Goodbye now.'

Charlotte was crestfallen. Back home in front of her mirror she shed tears of frustration.

'You can beat this,' said the mirror. 'Think of the overflowing reservoirs of discipline and determination you have. At the moment you use them exclusively to punish yourself. Your body is not your enemy, Charlotte.'

'But it is . . . it's . . .'

'It's a fine body. It has served you well for the last twenty-nine years, even though you haven't always made it easy. It could be a powerful body if you let it. Women can be big and strong too, Charlotte. Long ago, women were.'

'What do you mean?' asked Charlotte. The tears had made shiny tracks on her cheeks. She pushed hair out of her eyes.

'They fought battles, they were warriors, they captained armies . . .'

'You're making it up,' dismissed Charlotte. 'I never leaned that at school.'

'Women have done a lot more than is reported in school history books,' said her teacher knowingly.

'Why didn't we learn the truth?' quizzed the student, her interest ignited.

'Because if a prisoner finds the key to her own cell, she will use it to set herself free.'

'So where are these warriors now?'

The woman in the mirror looked Charlotte in the eye. 'They are out there,' she said, 'but maybe, like you, they are fighting the wrong enemy.'

'Becks, wake up girl!' Paul stood outside the front door with his bags. He had been buzzing the intercom for all he was worth. Her friend had said she'd be back, so why couldn't Becks shift her butt and open this damn door? He'd had to sleep on a floor last night and he was in no mood to do it again tonight. 'Becks,' he called, 'it's Party Paul. I've come to stay.' He leaned on the doorbell. It rang with head-splitting determination.

'All right, all right, all right,' shouted Becks as she fumbled with the Chubb lock before finally wrenching the door open. 'Paul,' she squeaked, like a startled animal.

'What,' yelled Paul dramatically, 'am I an alien today?'

'I wasn't expecting you,' confessed Becks, trying hard to conceal her irritation. This was all she needed.

'I wrote you,' he said accusingly. 'You said you'd put me up over Fashion Week. I know I missed some, but I got here in time for the finale. Hey,' he said as he eased past her with his bags, 'this is a poky little place you got ya'self here. Still . . . Any coffee for your old friend?'

'Look,' said Becks, 'things have been a bit up and down recently, and I . . . I don't feel like going out, that's all.' It annoyed her that she had been woken before lunch-time when there was no good reason to get up. She busied herself with the task of liberating the congealed dregs of brown powder from the bottom of the coffee tin. She hadn't shopped in ages and the flat was a tip. She never noticed it normally. God, why had she made such a promise?

'I know how to make this place seem a little more homely,' said Paul to himself as he began to turn out the contents of his backpack. He was looking for something specific. 'So what's your problem, girl?' he called.

'Problems,' corrected Becks as she walked into the living room with a steaming cup. 'I'm not cut out for modelling. I . . . Well, I only did one show this time and I fucked up.'

'What are you talking about, girl?' Paul took the cup. 'Any cookies?'

'And I don't do drugs now,' she said carefully.

Paul looked at his hostess with dismay. She wasn't the girl he had thought, and she wasn't very well connected either. It was going to be harder to get tickets for parties and shows now. 'Well, you're a regular little party pooper,' he said, affronted. 'Like, first you drag me out to East London. I mean – Hackney! It's like going to Queens or something.' Halfway down his bag, he came to his Marlboros. Pulling out the soft pack he tossed a cigarette into his mouth with obvious dissatisfaction. 'I've come all the way to see ya, girl,' he said as he reached for his lighter, 'and I thought we'd be partying all night. You can't leave me to go on my lonesome.'

'Paul, I really don't know those kind of people anyway,' explained Becks. 'I never said I did.'

'No, but you were very happy to hang with my buddies,' countered Paul crossly. He blew jets of smoke out in between his words and flapped his hands to disperse the cloud. 'Like, it was great to go to the free clubs I got you into, and drink the free drinks I bought you – oh, and take the free drugs I gave you.' Paul's voice had taken on a whingeing quality. Becks noticed for the first time how pockmarked his skin was. 'Now it's payback time,' he grumbled, 'you don't want to know.' He smoked rapidly like someone hoping to beat a personal best.

'Look, it's not that . . .'

'Oh, save it,' sneered Paul. 'I can find other people. I didn't come all this way to hang out in Hack-nee.' He emphasized the word like it was some kind of affliction and sucked even harder on his rapidly diminishing comforter. 'Look, I'm beat. I'm gonna crash out and then I'll make some calls and find out where the party people are. Where there's heroin,' he said, emboldened, 'there's always a net-work. Besides –' he looked at his bag – 'I got to get more supplies. Where's your bed, girl?'

Becks pointed. 'In there,' she said, hopeful that Paul was going to be out of her hair soon. This was the world she was trying to escape and it had tracked her down once more. Paul kicked off his trainers and headed for the bedroom. His presence could best be likened to a debt collector back for settlement later. Her thoughts turned to Elle and Esteem and she knew she needed to speak to her grandmother urgently. She'd sort this thing out once and for all. She'd apologize. She'd make up. Becks had stayed yesterday and she hadn't seen a fire break out, none of the staff had even ended up on the pavement, so the flames must have been caught fairly early on. Thank goodness. After she'd explained everything, she'd start all over again. For an instant, Becks felt glad to be alive. There was a world of possibilities from today on. And not a moment to lose. She picked up the phone.

'Hello . . . is that Maddy? Oh, Kirsty, OK.' Becks could feel her heart racing. She had to speak to Elle. This was the woman who could sort it out. She would do whatever it took to convince Elle that she was a granddaughter worth having. 'Could I speak to Elle Cartwrite, please?'

Then the doorbell chorused again. Someone was thumping the door with such force that it sounded like it might cave in. 'Becks!' yelled a female voice. 'Open the frigging door!'

'Jeezus,' complained Paul loudly, 'let's have a little peace and quiet, there's a jetlagged New Yorker trying to get some sleep here, and we're not nice when we're crabby.'

'Open this door!' came the demand from the outside world again. 'I've got to speak to you now. I know you're in there.' The thumping, together with the electric buzz that filled the room in short blasts, made it impossible to think.

'Becks,' yelled Paul, 'get the goddamn door!'

All hell had been let loose in the house and she slammed the phone down. A reunion with her long-lost grandmother would have to wait. Striding over to tackle the source of this unbearable din, Becks prepared herself for a showdown. No one but no one was coming in, and if it was one of Paul's associates they would get a tongue-lashing that would prevent them from ever abusing someone's home like that again.

'What?' bellowed Becks as she threw open the door. 'What?'

'Becks, I've got to speak to you now,' shrieked Tess. She practically leapt into her friend's arms as she spoke. 'It's urgent and I'm in deep water. There was a fire yesterday. You've got to vouch for me!'

'What do you mean?' queried Becks.

'The police are talking about me being an accessory . . . You know that bomb the other day?' Tess was racing through the conversation, forsaking the finer details for hasty recall of the whole event. 'Then the fire – they're saying I could be behind bars. I've got to prove I wasn't at the Esteem offices yesterday, and you are the only one I had a conversation with all day. Do you remember?' she chivvied, confident that this ordeal would shortly be over.

'Police?' repeated Becks in a daze. 'Prison?'

'Well, obviously I didn't do it,' said Tess, beginning to relax. 'But you've got to tell them.'

'But it couldn't have been that big,' blurted Becks. 'I know.'

'How so?' said Tess.

'Well, I mean, I don't know for sure. But . . .' Becks took a deep breath. 'What I mean is . . . I was there. I had an appointment with the old bag . . . because of that business with the show.' She smirked sheepishly. 'I didn't hear about any fire.'

'Well, it must have happened after you left,' continued Tess. 'The whole collection was ruined, apparently . . . Anyway, for some ridiculous reason, they think I could have done it and I need you to come down the station with me and tell that arsehole . . .'

'Was anyone hurt?' snapped Becks.

'Not that I know of,' replied Tess.

'Thank God,' breathed Becks. 'Look, Tess, I can't do that.'

'What do you mean?' fumed Tess. 'Becks, I'm not asking a favour here, I'm in real trouble. Do you understand?'

'Tess,' confided Becks quietly, 'I've got something to tell you.'

Elle Cartwrite opened a case and put it on the bed. She had a CD playing gently in the background: the strains of Grieg's *Peer Gynt* soothed her as she picked out clothes and folded them neatly into squares. She never took much with her when she visited her little country hideaway. Sheep shit and sheep, these were the only things she encountered when she arrived. There wasn't even a phone or a television in the house, let alone a fax or a video; simply an old stereo, on which she played all her vinyl records, and a radio. When her friends came to visit, they inevitably got fed up with the lack of facilities and made excuses to go early. When Elle went somewhere to rest, she didn't want to take media London with her.

'Ah, Maddy,' she said as she sandwiched a portable phone between her chin and her shoulder, 'I've briefed Alicia and Trena. We'll sell from whatever stock is remaining and the footage we have from the show. Buyers know the situation; we did enough sales before the show to keep things ticking over – just. Alicia is working up samples again. I trust them both. I'll ring you from the village when I get there, but after that I'm going to have a few days to myself. Nothing to do with hemlines for at least seventy-two hours, maybe a week.' She chuckled. 'Don't worry, Mad, they don't call me the Crow for nothing. I'm a tough old bird.'

Buyers, thought Elle to herself as she put down the

phone. They never bought the exciting pieces anyway and some had taken to redesigning the pieces on the hanger. Actually, she could have more fun chewing a limb off without anaesthetic. It was fantastic not to be there for once, and maybe in some strange kind of way this was meant to be. She would never have stepped down so soon if it hadn't been for the last couple of days. Yes, a week or so communing with nature in her cottage by the sea would set her right, and then she'd begin hunting for the child she gave up thirty-seven years ago.

Elle hoped that in one respect at least her daughter would not take after her: forgiveness had never been her strong point.

'Don't you see?' cried Becks. 'I've ruined everything. She'll hate me and I'll never have the chance to make it better.' She stalked the room. 'I can't believe I've ruined her collection and probably her business. And now I'm a criminal!' Becks threw her hands up in the air. 'I'll go to prison for sure. My mother will disown me. I'll have no one . . .'

'Becks,' prodded Tess gently, 'this can all be sorted out, you know.' Against her better judgement, she cuddled her friend; a slap might have been more effective. 'I know it doesn't seem so simple right now, but the only way is up. Believe me, once you decide to talk to her and tell her the truth, things will improve.'

'I was trying to get her on the phone before you turned up,' sniffed Becks accusingly. 'But that was before I realized that I really did trash her collection. Oh no –' she put her hands to her head – 'I can't believe I could have been so selfish. She's the person I most want to impress right now,

332

and it couldn't be worse if I'd planned it. I mean, what if I've ruined it all? My life is totally out of control.'

You got that right, thought Tess as she attempted to propel her only witness toward the stand. 'Look,' she soothed, 'this will all blow over and, who knows, you could have a brand-new life. But for now you've got to face up to things. The first step is to get me off the hook, and then I'll help you talk to Elle. We could visit her together, if you like.'

Becks was transfixed. 'I can't,' she stammered. 'I can't. What if they throw me in prison and I don't get a chance to . . .' Suddenly she was overcome with panic. 'Tess, I've got to speak to Elle first, I've got to.'

'Here's the phone – just do it,' encouraged Tess, keen for any kind of progress. As days went, this one was a complete turkey.

'Hello, Kirsty? It's Becks. Can I speak to Elle, please . . .'

There was an unbearable silence as both women waited, their eyes doing the talking as each looked hopefully at the other.

Maddy came on the line. 'Hi, Becks,' she said. 'How are you today?'

'I'm fine, Maddy,' replied Becks as coolly as she knew how. Her hands were clammy and she could feel the telephone sliding out of her grip. 'I need . . . I would really like to speak to Elle, please . . .'

'Oh, Becks, you missed her, I'm afraid. She's taken a few days maybe a week off and she's not contactable.'

'Surely there's a number she can be reached on?' pleaded Becks. The desperation in her voice was surfacing. 'Only it's really urgent that I speak to her.'

Maddy was impenetrable. 'Sorry, Becks, she's had a dreadful time of it recently, as you know,' her voice was slightly accusatory. 'And yesterday we had a fire that completely ruined all the stock, save a few items, and well . . . she needs some time to herself.'

'Maddy, this is really important,' pleaded Becks. 'I've got to speak to her.'

'Well, can I help?' asked Maddy.

Becks hesitated. How could she drop a clanger like: *Well, I torched the collection yesterday and, while we're at it, I'm her long-lost granddaughter, so I'm hoping my new credentials will save me from prosecution. What do you think my chances are?* Becks kept her voice as level as she could. 'Could you tell her that it's really urgent. Perhaps if I give you my number . . .' Becks put the phone down and turned to Tess. 'Look, I'm sorry, I can't do anything until I square it with her first.'

'OK, Becks, I understand. This is all kind of wild, isn't it – I mean, you being related to Elle Cartwrite, and she doesn't even know. It's a bit spooky, if you ask me . . .' Tess gathered her things and headed for the door. 'Can you ring me as soon as you get through, then?' she said hopefully. 'Only, I'm slightly stuck until you do.'

Becks closed the door and leaned against it. If she could only stay with it . . . She was so close to doing the right thing. Fantasies of forgiveness and family bliss filled her head. The flat really was a mess and there was nothing in the fridge. Maybe she should pop out and get some milk and bread. Even a paper – perhaps there would be a report on the fire damage. After all, if they thought it was a Global Defence attack . . . She grabbed her keys and slammed the door shut. She didn't hear the phone in her flat fire into life as she crossed the road with hope in her heart that this mess would soon be sorted out.

'Becks, are you there?' called Maddy down the line. 'No? OK, well, I've spoken to Elle and she's leaving her house soon for the country. She says you can call her there, but she'll be gone in an hour or two. Becks,' cautioned Maddy, 'she's had a difficult few days, what with one thing or another. She has agreed to speak to you because I told her you were very sorry about yesterday . . . You know, I said you wanted to apologize for being rude. But I really don't think you should push it any further than that. Anyway, this is the number to ring,' she reeled off a few digits and prepared to sign off. 'Good luck,' she said cheerily.

'Well, Maddy, thank you very much, darlin',' said Paul to the answer machine as he stood over it with a smile on his mouth. He replayed the message and scribbled down the number. The machine reset. Paul had listened to the whole story when Becks poured out her heart to Tess. He'd feigned sleep when she put her head round the door, but leapt up swiftly to enjoy the following conversation. Little Miss Squeaky Clean wasn't so pure after all!

Paul was a man who enjoyed the struggles of others. Some might call him a rainy-day friend, others a user. The fact was that he could only relate to people when they, like him, were sinking up to their armpits in emotional marshland. His reluctant landlady was a more interesting prospect now. A top British designer, a fire and a secret adoption . . . Poor little Becky deserved her break, and she would meet her precious grandmother in the end – but not before he'd squeezed a little cash out of the old girl. Work had been a bit scarce recently on account of the occasional bout of excessive partying, and his debts were beginning to mount up. People were so uptight these days. He heard the key in the lock and moved away from the phone.

'Paul,' said Becks as she shut the door, 'you're up already. Have you had enough sleep?' She didn't wait to hear the answer and looked in the direction of the telephone. 'Any calls?' she asked, trying to sound casual.

'Well, I didn't hear anything, and there's nothing on the machine,' said Paul, equally nonchalantly.

'Only I'm hoping for a really important one,' explained Becks on her way to the kitchen. She took a deep breath and continued, more for her own benefit than by way of explanation: 'I'm going to sort out my life once and for all.'

'Oh, yeah,' said Paul innocently. 'Like, how?'

There was silence until Becks reappeared with coffee cups in her hand. 'I got myself into a mess back there and I've worked out a way to put things right.'

'Good,' said Paul with practised pretence. He watched Becks disappear into the kitchen again and raised his voice above the clanging of spoons. 'You've got to sort yourself out, girl. I'm trying to do the same thing myself, you know.'

'Oh, really?' said Becks as she returned with two steaming cups of brown liquid and a packet of chocolate-chip cookies.

'Yeah,' he continued, watching her from the corner of his eye. 'I really want to give up the Harry now. Too many missed opportunities.' He took a breath and let out a theatrical sigh. 'Yep, too many people hurt,' he said as he reached for a biscuit.

'Oh, Paul, I know what you mean. It's not worth it, is it?' Becks felt comfortable with her house guest for the first time since he had arrived. 'The last two months have been like some strange dream for me, what with learning about my mum and . . . and . . .' Becks checked herself. Oh, what the hell, she thought, he doesn't know anything about my life and he's a foreigner. What harm can he do?

For the second time that day, Becks reviewed her life with another. But this time she was careful to leave out any connection with Elle Cartwrite and also her own part in the fire. But talking about her childhood, her mother and her grandfather, Becks felt a weight float away from her body. Paul was silent.

'Everybody's got a story,' he said quietly when she finished. 'Everyone who uses wants to escape from something.' He was lost for a while in a childhood not dissimilar to his own. He had watched his father drink himself to an early grave and when his mother followed, leaving her three sons to the care of a relative, Paul had tried his best to hold the family together. But the nocturnal visits from his uncle were too much to take and he left one night, never to return. He didn't know where either of his younger brothers were right now, but he hoped they were happier than he was. He assuaged his guilt with whatever medication he could find. First it had been large quantities of alcohol, later trippy high-as-a-kite pills, and finally heroin. There was nothing like a little Harry to blot out the world, and he'd been searching for that initial euphoria ever since.

'So, do you know where your grandmother is? I mean . . . is she alive?' he asked, already knowing the answer thanks to the conversation he had stumbled upon previously.

'Yeah, I do,' said Becks, 'and I'm hoping to speak to her soon to explain everything.' She checked the little alarm clock perched on top of the television. 'If she'll let me.'

Paul calculated how much time he had left before Elle Cartwrite left for her little country mansion. He hated himself, but business was business. 'I'm just gonna split for some ciggies and candy,' he announced, patting the crumpled piece of paper in his pocket inscribed with Elle Cartwrite's private number. 'Then I'm gonna make a few calls when I get back, see if I can't find me another place to stay.' Becks didn't fight him, although it would have been nice, he thought as he let himself out, if she had. Still, it made things easier.

Once inside a public callbox he plied his trade. 'Hello,' he said, exaggerating the Brooklyn accent he had long ago left behind, 'I can save you a lot of social embarrassments, Ms Cartwrite . . . but it is going to cost you some money.'

23

'keep a pair of high-heeled slippers in your bath-room.'
BRITT EKLAND

*E*LLE had told no one about the call, which was why – a few hours after receiving the blackmailer's invitation – she sat alone in her car outside a dingy flat in East London waiting to meet an anonymous American. All to buy some control over her life. The clock on her dashboard was fast and she was early, so there was time to kill.

In the heat of the sun Elle Cartwrite shifted with clammy discomfort and reviewed her world. It had been more or less orderly until last week. For years she had motored along, prioritizing fiscal management, social satisfaction and the right to read the Sunday papers from cover to cover without interruption as she sipped a good claret. In those very publications she had read about women who juggled their world to fit in stressful jobs, fractious children and the demands of a self-centred husband. There was always some issue to do with child care, glass ceilings, or relationships on the skids. From what she could see, nineties living made nineties women ill. Women weren't out there *having* it all; they were out there *doing* it all. Elle had made choices, and had avoided a life full of guilt and recrimination. She had made room in her life for her life, hadn't she? The Crow nodded to herself.

So why then had everything reached such an unsatisfactory climax on this muggy September evening? In less than seven days her world had collapsed. A dog squatted determinedly on the pavement by her door. 'That's all I need,' she remarked to the flame-haired Jack Russell as it carried out the most basic of animal functions right before her. 'My business may have gone down the toilet, I'm on the run from terrorists with a penchant for traditionally designed middle-market clothes, and I'm being blackmailed.' She instinctively reached for the money she had packed into her pocket. The caller had demanded five thousand pounds, and Elle had rushed to her local bank then waited with bated breath while the cashier confirmed that cash funds were available. 'And as if that's not enough,' she continued to address her furry companion, oblivious to the fact that older women would always be judged more harshly for muttering to themselves in public, 'you are depositing a little something to further soil me as I attempt to cleanse myself of this foul week.'

Elle scanned the streets for an owner with a plastic bag or a pooper-scooper. If an earnest dog lover materialized this very minute and removed the steaming pile from her path then everything would be all right. Like some kind of sign from above, this act of human conscientiousness would signify the beginning of something better.

'I'll give it five minutes,' she muttered under her breath, looking at her watch. Although she felt like a wilting vine in a greenhouse, she really didn't want to get out of the car. This was her world and it was safe. Out there it was a jungle, and there were animal droppings all over the place to prove it.

When Elle had taken the call, she'd been incredulous at the suggestion that she might have plenty to hide from the tabloids. But the caller had put a very convincing case. Did she know that one of her models was a junkie (they'd love that); another had been arrested earlier today in connection with Global Defence activities; oh, and hadn't one of them engaged in some dubious glamour-modelling early on in her career? And then there was the fact that Elle had sacked one for ruining the catwalk show. What kind of message did she think she was sending to ordinary women out there?

Elle could see the potential for a gratuitous attack using her as the frock world's equivalent of Reggie Kray. The British media loved to knock its own fashion industry. Designers did not rank as highly as their European mainland counterparts. On top of everything that had happened recently, she wondered if the business would survive its creator receiving such a character assassination. But giving in to a low-life seemed the greater of two evils. 'Let the tabloids do their worst,' she had said. Then the caller deliberately called her 'Elsa' and suggested that she might also want to know a little about the people from her past. It was at that point that Elle decided to pursue things. If this person had some sort of proof and a contact number that would lead her to her daughter, then she would hand over the money. After all, some people paid private detectives and waited years before they got any kind of result. Elle wasn't prepared to dally that long.

She checked her watch and observed the pub across the road. Reassuringly ordinary groups of drinkers sat outside embracing honest pints surrounded by old barrels and large pots of pink petunias. The wooden furniture had seen better days, but the place looked welcoming. It was a safe enough venue for a clandestine meeting. Elle was just preparing to open the car door, mindful of the assault course that awaited her clean shoes, when she noticed a familiar blonde step out of a house further up the road. It was Becks.

'So, you're behind this, are you – you little minx!' burst Elle in disbelief. Of course, how else could the extortionist have acquired her private number in the first place? This model was big trouble.

'You are one major pain in the arse,' mumbled Elle in disbelief. Her words did not reach Becks, who stood twenty-five metres away. The ex-Esteem model briefly chatted to a neighbour or a friend with cropped blond hair, unaware of any cussing in her direction. Elle fumed. 'So you think you can get me back for sacking you, do you?' She hoped that her anger could be communicated long distance. Becks shivered a little in the breeze and hugged her arms to her body as she looked up and down the street. 'Well, you won't be working in this town again.' Without further thought, Elle turned the keys in the ignition and pushed her foot down on the clutch. First gear did not happen with any ease and the engine grated loudly as she struggled to leave her parking space. 'Wait a minute . . .' Elle turned off the engine. There was the question of her daughter . . . How could Becks have learned her real name? She had to know.

Elle relaxed momentarily as Becks disappeared back into the house. Now she turned her attention to the neighbour as he set off down the road. Her pulse quickened when he disappeared into the public house and returned outside moments later with a Coke. He chose a table at the corner of the concrete patio and sat alone. So what, thought Elle, trying hard to reassure herself. He could be having a drink, like Englishmen did. Her liaison could be with someone completely different.

Ten minutes later no other lone gentleman had arrived on the scene. The blond neighbour was looking decidedly twitchy as he checked his watch every thirty seconds. His glass was empty but he didn't move. Elle cursed the fact that she had never been enticed by any of the mobile phone campaigns enough to own one. The phone across the road would have to do.

Directory Enquiries furnished her with the number of The George and she dialled, feeling a touch pleased with herself.

'Hello, I'm sorry to bother you, but I'm late for a meeting with a colleague. He's one of your customers and it's very important that I speak to him . . . Yes, a blond gentleman. I believe he'll be outside . . . Thank you so much.' Elle watched as the blond man followed a member of staff back into the public house.

'Yeah,' said the voice, not yet revealing any incriminating accent.

'Are you who I think you are?' asked Elle.

'Honey, I'm whoever you want me to be,' came the reply. 'Who is this?'

Elle was satisfied. It was unmistakably the same voice she had heard a few hours ago. Clearly he and Becks had hatched a plot for some easy cash. No doubt it would be

343

spent on dubious substances. Elle sighed, but, realizing the need to get back to her car and out of the area before being spotted, the devious grandmother summoned her best Angela Lansbury strategy and continued.

'I'm coming to see you now,' she instructed coolly. 'Stay at the bar and order me tonic water and Angostura bitters.' That would keep him occupied for long enough. Barmen could never seem to find the little bottle of non-alcoholic seasoning. Elle put the phone down and returned to her getaway vehicle. In a few seconds she would be out of this town, five thousand pounds richer and well shot of Bonnie and Clyde. Elle would find her daughter all right, but it would be without interference from a witless model and her boyfriend. Becks needed teaching a lesson and Elle would make sure she knew never to contact her again. Reaching for her bag she pulled out a large diary containing everything but a spare pair of tights. A folded note and envelope was exactly what she needed.

When the doorbell rang, Becks went to answer it. Paul had no doubt got himself fixed up with a livelier crowd and had come for his things. She rolled off the sofa, hopeful that life was about to improve, and padded towards the noise. Once he had gone she would clean up her act completely. She was practically off heroin now and all she needed was some time to get herself together. Soon she'd have spoken to Elle and life would be different. Oh, so very different. Out of her own flat and across worn grey carpet into the communal hallway, Becks focused on the front door where normally the frosted glass revealed the outline of any visitor. There was no one, only a white square on the threadbare mat beneath the letterbox. She bent to retrieve it and scanned the front. Neat hand-writing addressed to her provided no clues as to the caller's identity.

Paul had waited and waited at the bar. But after half an hour, he became agitated and stepped out into the last of the evening's sunshine. He scanned the human traffic in the area for an aged contact. The old girl had set him up. Why hadn't she come into the bar and why was she playing so hard to get? The thought of all that cash nestling in her handbag had briefly made him feel that life once again held opportunities, and could be lived – for the next month at least – in relative comfort. Professionally, Paul was all washed up these days and the price of a Caribbean package holiday with plenty of party-filled nights was hard to come by. Sure, he could sell the story to a tabloid, but Elsa Crabtree alias Elle Cartwrite was hardly A-list material. Even if he really juiced it up *National Enquirer*-style, a deal would probably not yield much more than a couple of thousand bucks. Still, it would be better than zero.

Paul looked at his watch. An appointment to procure a large amount of heroin, which he knew he could sell on for a better price, was imminent – but, without the money, pointless. So he was forced to sell this story. What other choice did he have? Paul looked around once more and crossed the road to catch the 38 bus into Soho. Half an hour with some sleaze-bag hack would be the easiest money he would make this week. Then on to do a little business. Paul walked tall; how clever he was today.

I know everything and you are lucky I have chosen not to involve the police. If you ever contact me again, I will.

Elle Cartwrite

Becks had read the letter in disbelief. In fact, she had retraced the elegantly written words over and over again until they made shapes in front of her eyes. Her world had silently crashed about her ears and the hopes she'd had for reconciliation and a new beginning were now vaporizing into the atmosphere.

'Maybe it was Tess,' murmured Becks to the walls. 'She's the only one I told. Now Elle knows I trashed the collection.' She put her hands to her head. 'And she knows who I am . . .' The tension caused by the realization that an unwelcome visit by the police was only a phone call away – and the fact that her grandmother had chosen to dump her – was partly relieved by aiming an iron at the TV. The satisfying tinkle of glass was a start and Becks looked around for another missile.

With the anger successfully vented and her exterior world suitably rearranged, Becks considered her interior requirements. Her throat was dry and tight as she reached for a warm can of beer stationed amongst a pile of magazines, Rizzla papers, coffee cups and a brimming ashtray. Tipping the contents into her mouth with speed, as if the act of choking back the flat ale really fast might salvage the situation, Becks didn't stop until she had finished the can. Then she closed her fist round the aluminium container, enjoying its demise. She rooted through Paul's bag for another, released the ring pull, and gulped back the bitter remedy to a day that needed a swift end. More supplies would be essential.

After a visit to the off-licence, Becks settled into her chair and prepared to submerge her sorrows in a time-honoured family way. 'In our family, we women like a little tipple now and again,' slurred the angry blonde as she toasted a lifeless television set. She was still drinking resolutely when her temporary flatmate bounced into the room a few hours later. The new arrangements made little impact. With a smile on his face as he helped himself to refreshment, Paul announced his presence to the furniture. 'Stand back, girls,' he laughed, merry at the thought of imminent oblivion, 'the party has arrived.'

'Charlotte,' said Guy, 'I'm so glad you came.' He opened the door of his studio and welcomed her in. 'I'm just clearing up here before I go to Canada for a few weeks. I've got relatives out there and I thought I might take my portfolio about.' He cleared a space for her to sit. 'I just wanted to see you before I went. How are you?'

It was late and Charlotte was pushed for time. Her mother would be over shortly, but Guy had been in her thoughts since way before that fateful episode with Rick. 'I'm fine,' she replied automatically.

'Will you have a cup of tea?'

'Yes, please,' said Charlotte, distracted by the imagery that adorned the walls. She had never seen such a collection of pictures before.

'Oh, Eleanor is just getting ready for an exhibition,' explained Guy as he filled the kettle.

Charlotte registered fleeting disappointment: was Eleanor his love interest?

'She's my sister,' said Guy, sensing the question.

Charlotte blushed. How embarrassing. She attempted to deflect attention back to Eleanor's forthcoming show. 'When is it?' she asked as casually as she could.

'In a fortnight's time,' answered Guy, peeking out of the kitchen area. 'I wish I could be here, but, well ... hey, what do you make of the pictures?'

'They're ... they're ...' Charlotte stumbled for an answer. 'They are actually quite beautiful.' She heard the surprise in her voice.

'Aren't they,' agreed Guy, directing the flow of scalding water on to the tea bags in two identical mugs.

'Who are they?'

'Eleanor works at a Women's Centre,' he said, opening the fridge and reaching for the milk. 'The women you see here have all been through some kind of life-changing experience. As part of their ongoing recovery, they set themselves a project. That's when Eleanor involved me and the studio. That's Kath –' he pointed to a portrait – 'she was left for dead by a hit-and-run motorist. And that woman – Cecilia, her name is –' he stopped at a picture of an elderly white-haired woman – 'was institutionalized seventy years ago for giving birth to a mixed-race baby out of wedlock.' He shook his head. 'She was forced to undergo some kind of primitive electric shock treatment. Eleanor will tell you the story. Anyway,' he said, surveying the prints arranged about the room, 'all these women are survivors and they wanted to photograph survival. You know: What does a survivor look like? They decided that survival was the most basic human need and so they elected to photograph themselves in the most basic state – naked.' His eyes shone. 'Don't they look incredible? Of course, I wasn't here. No one was actually in the studio while they took their own pictures, I just set it all up.'

Charlotte examined each print and looked deep into the eyes of each face. Then she gazed at each body. Cecilia sat proudly on a cushion, the love of three or four generations etched into her cheeks and round her eyes. She drew her legs up in front of her, fine fingers and wrists entwined themselves round her knees while her feet, the skin hardened by life's physical journey, stretched out in front. Kath sat wistful but triumphant, sideways on to the camera, displaying red weals that tracked the length of one leg and across her back. Her expansive hips and curved round thighs were made more beautiful by the fleshy railway line puckering across her body. Another jumped for joy, and it was only after close inspection that the discerning viewer could see a prosthetic limb.

Charlotte was lost in silent admiration. Individually, each woman appeared so very different in physique from the next; the antithesis, in fact, of the clone-like, lifeless uniformity exhibited by her modelling colleagues. Here was beauty and here was victory. She dwelt a while before a beautiful blonde who faced the camera squarely, one breast perfectly sited, the other now a memory and in its place a large scar. Charlotte examined every crevice, every fold of skin. She beheld the symmetry of such strong shoulders, admired the smoothness of the collarbone, and allowed her eyes to travel all the way up the sitter's elegant neck until she established eye contact. Unlike most studios she had known, where technicians – intent upon moulding, squeezing and kneading femininity into sanitized packages – prohibited any departure from perfection, this antechamber was an oasis of sanity, of reality and ... magnificence.

'That last portrait was my idea,' explained Guy as Charlotte stepped in front of an empty frame.

'But there's no one there,' said Charlotte, puzzled.
'Yes there is . . .' Guy smiled. 'Look harder.'

'Darling,' cooed Jennifer Davis as she flopped into an easy chair, loosening her jacket and peeling it from her body, 'I never liked him anyway.'

Charlotte's mother was talking about Rick, although she might as well have been discussing her own husband, for she had left him again. Mrs Davis did it every couple of years – 'Simply to give him a bit of a scare,' she confided, wrinkling her nose as she kicked off her shoes.

'I thought I'd stay here for a few days, Charlotte, dear. I know it's a bit of an inconvenience for you, what with your busy life and your friends . . .'

This would normally be a cue for Charlotte to offer large amounts of reassurance. Of course it was perfectly OK to drop in unannounced and go on at length about what a monster her father was. She chose silence.

Jennifer noticed it. 'I haven't got anywhere else,' she apologized, slightly miffed. 'I was going to stay at your Aunt Jacqueline's, but she's . . . well, her marriage isn't up to it these days.'

Charlotte placed two cups of tea on the table. 'Does Dad know you are here?' she asked hopefully.

'Well, I haven't told your brothers anything, but I expect they'll work it out,' said her mother confidently. 'Honestly, men . . .' She shook her head and her cleavage wobbled in agreement. 'Now, tell me how you've been. And what happened between you and Rick?' Jennifer Davis deposited two saccharine tablets into her tea from a tiny container she carried with her at all times and settled back, looking

350

forward to some time spent criticizing the opposite sex.

'I don't really want to talk about it, Mum,' replied Charlotte as she opened a window and shut the door to the kitchen. Her mother's presence always made her feel less sure of her own adult world and she instinctively tried to control it. 'I shouldn't have been with him. He wasn't doing me any good and so I finished it. End of story.'

'Oh, God, I know what you mean,' agreed her mother. 'I don't know why I stick with your father, I really don't . . .'

'Why do you, Mum?' said Charlotte as she sat on the sofa opposite. 'I mean, ever since I can remember you've been furious with him for one thing or another. He's not a bad man, is he? Couldn't you be happier on your own or maybe with someone else?'

'Oh, that would be far too simple,' dismissed Mrs Davis. 'Thirty years down the drain as easy as that. And do you think,' she said, turning to her daughter with a look of intensity that Charlotte had never seen before, 'do you think that at my age I'd find someone else? Oh, he would – let's be clear about that,' she stormed, slamming her teacup back down on the saucer. 'He'd find a woman half his age in an instant, but no one wants this –' she gestured angrily at her own body. 'He's had the best of me, and because of me,' she spat, 'he has three children. *Three* – I was the one!' Jennifer's voice was infused with rage and injustice. 'I was the one who bore the physical burden. Do you know what having three children does to a body?' She didn't wait for an answer. 'I was the one that made all the sacrifices so he could go on having life exactly the same. If I go out there looking for another man, I'm competing with women half my age – women with neat figures and wrinkle-free faces. This –' she practically hit herself as she spoke – 'is all I have and it's not enough any more.' Jennifer Davis did not attempt to conceal her disgust.

'Was it ever enough?' asked Charlotte gently, seeing the future with a clarity she had never known before.

'Oh, I was a good catch, you know,' retorted her mother. 'I never had trouble getting any man's interest.' Bolstered by the memory of better days, the portly matron basked briefly in bygone triumphs. 'I prided myself on my legs. I wasn't modelling standard like you . . .' Jennifer Davis self-consciously smoothed away her thighs. 'Not tall enough. But I was . . .' She struggled to find a description that fitted. 'I was somebody. I was the only girl in our office to have had her picture in the *Gazette* twice in a row, one summer after another. When your father met me, I could have had any man . . . but I chose him. It's not like I haven't tried over the years to keep myself looking young for him. I have.' Jennifer Davis sighed. 'I don't know what he wants any more, and now I find this.' She held a crumpled batch of letters. 'I know he's seeing someone.' She dropped them back into her bag and reached for a tissue. 'She's bound to be young and gorgeous. He's a handsome man, your father. I mean –' Charlotte's mother dabbed her eyes – 'what chance have I got now?'

Charlotte sighed. In so many ways her mother was a fighter. Not a warrior in full battledress like historical women written out of history so very long ago, but a fighter just the same. Her generation required women to use their girlish bodies to secure a partner for life. Being a wife and mother left no time for education or careers, and so, in a struggle to keep husband and home – because one invariably went with the other – women like her mother used the only weapon they felt they had. Bodies were a battleground, where internal skirmishes with need, desire and sensuality were fought daily to maintain an external front of perfection.

Ever since she could remember, Charlotte had watched her mother attack herself verbally for needing more. More love, more reassurance, more support. Jennifer Davis had grown up believing that only if she were pretty enough, perfect enough, *deserving* enough, would she get the things she needed. Since she had not achieved happiness of a storybook nature, it must be her fault – or, more specifically, her body's fault. Unwittingly she had taught her daughter to believe the same. For the first time, Charlotte could see beyond the empty crusade for physical perfection. It only existed in the minds of the soldiers who chose to persecute themselves.

Later that night, with her mother safely tucked up in bed, Charlotte stood in front of the mirror. The older woman had commented on her daughter's willowy appearance but had been reassured to hear that a virulent stomach bug was the cause. 'I wish I could lose weight like you,' she had said enviously before turning in.

Slowly Charlotte removed her clothes and stared dispassionately at the fleshless frame in front of her. All the magazines she had ever read featured 'lose weight fast' articles with complementary pictures of thin, happy, carefree women. All her life she had believed that a perfect body was a thin body. Indeed, most women talked about weight loss like it was the key to eternal fulfilment. 'Big and strong' was not a description ever applied to women as a compliment. In fact, women were punished for committing the offence of daring to take up more than a sliver of space by a fashion industry which branded them 'Out-size'. Food was something to be viewed with deep sus-picion, for fear it would make you grow large and robust; enjoyment of it was seen as tantamount to insatiable glut-tony. A feminine woman must deny herself such pleasure. Charlotte had always assumed that the recognition for strict adherence to the path would be forthcoming, but when? Had her mother ever known contentment? Char-lotte swept her eyes over her body again. If this was perfec-tion, where was her reward?

'Is this really me?' she asked the mirror.

'Yes,' said the voice, 'it is you.'

'Am I hurting myself?'

'Yes,' said the voice, 'you are. Can you feel any pain yet?'

'No,' replied Charlotte.

'Then maybe you've become used to the torment,' came the reply.

'Am I alone?' asked Charlotte.

'Women restrict their pleasures in so many ways,' replied the woman in the mirror. 'Some cram their lives into rigid social rituals stifling every bit of creativity they produce, others sabotage their power with destructive displays of helpless femininity. One might force her feet into shoes that pinch and squeeze. Another will incarcerate her body in tight uncomfortable clothes. The punishment we choose for ourselves isn't so very different from yours. We are all our own jailers in the end.'

'The thing that really hurts,' confessed Tess as she nestled in the old leather-bound armchair nursing a coffee with

354

three sugars, 'is that I was so taken with everything he said. You know, like not what he did but what he said he did.'

'Isn't that the same?' asked Belle, her brow furrowing. She was slouched widthways across a long sofa, having surrendered the comfiest seat in the flat to her heartbroken friend. The room glowed with the soft light of scented candles and, from his post by the window, Bob Marley did his very best to soothe the melancholy woman. Belle reached for her hot chocolate. 'I mean, what's the difference?'

'The difference is huge,' replied Tess, peering into her cup. 'He talked a good relationship and nothing more. All those fine and noble ideas about equality and racial harmony ... It was all image. God,' she groaned – a touch theatrically, Belle thought. An idea was forming in her thoughts; she'd speak to Henrietta on Monday morning. She could stitch this guy up for her friend and make a great story to boot! Belle returned her attention to Tess, who was still beating her breast.

'I can't believe I fell for it again. All he did,' she cursed, 'was use me. It's not like I haven't been used in my time, but at least . . .' Tess scratched her head. 'I knew I was being used.'

'What, and that made it all right then?' teased Belle incredulously.

'I didn't see this coming and I feel like a fool,' confessed Tess. 'All the codes were right on the outside and that's all I saw. I didn't look beyond the packaging.'

'Ah, the Dom Perignon has arrived,' declared Elle as she sat at a table with her friends. Delaying going to the country by a day had been necessary due to an impromptu sojourn east earlier in the afternoon. But now, wrapped in the bosom of her professional family, Elle was glad to be in London. Specifically her favourite Soho restaurant.

'To Esteem,' toasted Maddy gaily as she raised a glass. Her handsome husband-to-be joined her; he tipped his head in the direction of his future wife's employer.

'And all who seek it,' added Trena, who sat happily holding hands with Rowena, her girlfriend of five years.

'I'll drink to that,' agreed Alicia as she replenished her own and Elle's glass.

'Now,' said Elle turning to the happy couple, 'may this be the first of many toasts to come your way. Please, everyone . . .' She paused, waiting for Kirsty to tear herself away from the waiter with Brad Pitt eyes. Esteem's front-desk operator was celebrating an offer from a busy magazine: soon she would have a much larger biking community at her disposal. Elle drew herself up. 'I would like to say how very pleased I –' she checked herself – '*we* are for you both. It goes without saying that we all wish you a fairytale wedding and a happy-ever-after ending.'

Maddy beamed while Tom got to his feet and rather stiffly though endearingly toasted his fiancée. Turning to his audience he raised his glass again. 'Is this the bit where I thank the bridesmaids?' he asked hopefully. 'I'm so nervous, I wish this was it now and I could get it done.'

'You'll be fine, Tom,' calmed Maddy. 'Sit down and have some food.'

'Are your parents excited, Tom?' asked Elle, keen to make the lone male feel more comfortable . . . for Maddy's sake.

'Yes, they are,' answered Tom. 'A bit too excited, I think. My mother has gone into overdrive, what with all the arrangements. Half the county is coming. She's helping Maddy, you see,' he added by way of explanation, 'because her parents are . . . well, they're in America and . . .'

'And have you got your speech sorted?' quizzed Trena.

'That's the bit that's keeping me awake at night,' he said, rubbing his hand anxiously across the back of his neck. 'You see, I'm not very good at that sort of thing and it's not done, is it, for a chap to make a mess of it all?'

Maddy squeezed Tom's arm. 'He gets as emotional as I do. Thank goodness all I have to do is look good.'

'Yeah, there are some advantages to being a girl, aren't there?' Trena laughed. 'Ro and I have decided that if we ever tie the knot – you know, romantically speaking – we'll both have to do a speech or none at all.'

'Do you think you ever would?' asked Alicia. 'I mean, it's different for two women, isn't it?'

'Yes and no,' replied Rowena, a spiky brown-haired enchantress with impossibly perfect bow lips. 'I mean, we can't benefit from it for tax reasons or anything, but, well, I'd still get a bucket-load of earache from my mother as to where it should be, who should be invited, and had I got a reputable florist. God, she's such a snob.' Rowena giggled. 'And then of course there would be the dress and the bridesmaids' dresses . . .'

'I'd get off lightly by comparison,' announced Trena. 'My parents can't even bring themselves to say the word "lesbian". They both hope it's a phase I'll grow out of one of these days in time to supply them with grandchildren. I think they'd simply send a telegram and stay well out of it.'

'My mother thinks I'll end my days as an old maid,' confided Alicia. 'She puts it down to the fact that I don't make enough of myself. Of course,' smirked the beautiful brunette with a twinkle in her eye, 'if I could get into a size twelve dress, the old bat is convinced the problem would vanish because men would be throwing themselves at me with proposals. For her, it's only about exteriors – you know, what it looks like on the outside. "What will the neighbours think?" "What will people think?" I've never actually told her that I don't intend to become someone's wife.' Alicia laughed. 'To her, spinsterhood is what happens to women who aren't pretty enough to attract a man.'

'It's amazing what impact parents can have on their children's lives,' piped Tom. 'I think the only reason I'm getting so nervous is that I'm worried I'll cry in front of my dad. It's not done, is it? Don't get me wrong, it's not like I don't want him there, but . . . well, I'm conscious of trying to do things the way he would want me to.'

'Maybe when you have children,' said Elle gently, 'you can allow your child the chance to be the person he or she needs to be.'

'Why didn't you have children, Elle?' asked Rowena matter-of-factly. The others watched their leader for signs of unease and waited to hear the answer.

Elle carefully considered the response she might give before opening her mouth. 'I had the chance to be a mother a long time ago,' she said, 'but I didn't think I would make a good enough job back then. I had been taught to believe that I wasn't capable on my own.' She picked up her glass and raised it again. 'I've learned differently now, of course.'

'Would you have liked to have children?' pursued Rowena, oblivious to the consternation travelling round the table. The others believed their no-nonsense chief wouldn't tolerate such an intrusion into her private life.

'I did have one,' confessed Elle wistfully. 'I just didn't bring her up. Perhaps she's better for it, I don't know.'

'Elle, that's incredible!' gushed Maddy. 'Where is she now? Do you know anything about her?'

'Nothing,' answered Elle with a determined look in her eye. 'Nothing yet.'

Becks hitched herself out of the chair and on to her feet. Paul was snoozing in the chair next to her. Had she consumed all of those cans or had he helped?

'Who cares?' she mumbled as she made her way shakily to the bathroom. 'Even if I drink a bathtub full it wouldn't be enough tonight.'

Becks stared at her face in the mirror. 'I know I'm drunk,' she announced, 'because I'm talking to myself and I only ever do that when I'm drunk.' She collapsed on the toilet seat and steadied herself by holding on to the sink. 'I know I'm drunk,' she said again, 'because I've wet myself and I only ever do that when I'm drunk.' She stared hard at the woman in the mirror. 'Things are never all they are cracked up to be,' she told her reflection.

After a lengthy session of staring at the towel rail, Becks pulled herself up and lurched back into the living room. It was dark and depressing and she knew eight hours would take a lifetime to pass with no more drink to keep her company now that the off-licence was shut. She spied Paul's little pharmacopoeia laid out on the table. He too injected now. Becks knew this because he had fallen asleep with the needle sticking out of his vein. Realizing there would be no more conversation from Paul for a good while, and no chance of waking him even if she tried her hardest, Becks was crestfallen. Heroin made people into zombies in the end, that was why she had stopped taking it, wasn't it? Becks removed the syringe from her flatmate's arm and transferred her concentration to the table. There was some powder left. Excitedly she picked up the bag and watched the grains shift temptingly before her eyes. Becks glanced at Paul and considered her own options. In a few moments she could be out of this body, all of her problems gone. She cursed herself; the memory of heroin was stirring a passion in her veins. Like a beguiling lover, she knew that one more kiss from those beautiful lips could cost her her sanity.

Then there was option number two: don't take it. Sit in the dark and wait for dawn to come. The latter paled into insignificance beside the former. One more fix would see her through. Tomorrow would be a fresh start.

It was a dirty syringe, but now that the addict in Becks was awake, she could no longer hold on to reason. Becks retrieved Paul's lighter and set to work. No warning signal sounded as she processed the amount of powder she was used to taking. Had Paul been awake, he might have warned her that her tolerance was now much lower through abstinence and she should cook up less. Hey, didn't she know that over half of all accidental overdoses were down to addicts misjudging their tolerance? He might even have pointed out that the alcohol in her system now saturating her judgement and obliterating her resolve would greatly increase the chance of overdose.

Even if Paul had awoken after the strawberry blonde had injected his heaven, his morning fix, into her body, he could have spotted the shallow breathing or pinpoint pupils and called an ambulance. But as the woman in the darkened room yielded to a journey familiar only by her choice of travelling equipment, her guide slept on.

24

'We are all old; for some of us it doesn't yet show.'
WENDY CHAPKIS

ELLE stared at the newspaper in disbelief. She'd been about to leave for the country, suitably empowered by yesterday's powwow, when Maddy had rung. After the call Elle raced to her local newsagent.

So the two of them had done it anyway. 'Well, Becks,' huffed Elle, 'you're really showing your true colours. How wrong I was about you.' It was ironic, thought Elle as she stared out of her kitchen window and into the garden, that the troublesome teenager had been her own choice. Trena and Petra had both plumped for a russet-haired Dane, while Alicia had fought hard in favour of Helena Christensen. But Elle pulled rank and insisted on Becks . . . There was something about those eyes.

The Crow waited for the kettle to boil and poured the

scalding water on to a mountain of coffee granules. She applied herself to the article now in her hand entitled 'designer in drugs shock', an 'exclusive' penned by a vitriolic hack called Nora Einstein. 'Sadly, you aren't one, dear,' said Elle to herself, 'or you could conceive a title with a little more creativity. But top marks for spelling the long words correctly.' She sipped her coffee and reached for more sugar. It was good for the system in a crisis.

The strap line was the real nail in the coffin: 'Elle Cartwrite, owner of Esteem, seeks to boost ailing company with mischievous models.' To accompany the damning report someone had spitefully selected a rather unflattering shot, garnered no doubt from last year's British Fashion Awards. It was unnerving to think that while she had played the convivial *bonne vivante* last night, a Fleet Street minion had scoured the picture library for her likeness so that Voodoo Dora, or was it Nora, could glue the print to a wax effigy and stick pins in her. At least there was no mention of her private life and the past. Elle shuddered. Perhaps they were saving that for tomorrow's issue.

The poster campaign photograph had a whole page to itself with each of the models singled out in type. 'Drug Addict', proclaimed one caption. 'Global Defence Mistress', avowed another. Charlotte has escaped lightly, thought Elle. Topless waitressing was hardly illegal, was it? Elle cursed herself. She was as bad as the rest. What on earth was she doing reading the rubbish in front of her? She scanned the picture one more time. It really should have been a great campaign. She never thought it would end up in a rag like this.

'But why would you do this to yourself, Becks?' asked Elle as she contemplated the blonde practically obliterated by the charge that had been stamped across her body in

18-pt Helvetica. She shook her head. 'Something is not quite right here.' She picked up the phone. 'Maddy, get Harold on to the Press Complaints Commission. But before you do that, fish out Becks' number again, will you?'

'Don't get involved, Elle,' warned Maddy.

'I already am,' said Elle oddly. Something about the strawberry blonde teenager had worked its way under her skin. It was impossible to explain, but Elle was convinced that Becks knew much more than she let on. When she had been in Elle's office a few days ago, the sullen model had unleashed a passionate tirade. It was personal, all right. Then there was the American. He had called Elle by her real name and no one, not even Maddy, knew that. Her secretary returned to the phone and recited the number. Elle scribbled it down on the blotter and quickly dialled. Then she replaced the handset. Better still, she'd go round there.

The curtains were drawn and all was quiet at the flat. Perhaps they were still in bed. There was a row of off-white doorbells, each greying with the filmy grime of a thousand fingerprints. She flattened her palm against the appropriate button and left it there for some time. A head popped out from the apartment above.

'There's no one home, love,' yelled a woman, her head a mass of tight pincurls. Elle couldn't see her shoulders. The dismembered appendage opened its mouth again. 'Are you a reporter?'

'No,' said Elle craning her neck to answer.

'I know you . . . You're that woman in the paper, aren't

you,' accused the head. 'Are you looking for the model?'

'Yes,' said Elle.

'She's not here. There was an ambulance in the night. Really bright lights, there were. Anyway,' said the head, 'she went to hospital on a stretcher. Overdose, I expect. You know what young people are like. She hung around with some funny-looking people. That's what I told the reporter, and that's all I'm telling you. Goodbye now.' The head vanished.

Elle circled her own head on her neck to ease a cramped muscle. She stepped on to the pavement and scanned the brick-fronted building for an open window. 'Hello there,' she called hopefully, 'do you know which one? Hello . . .' Elle raised her voice enough, she hoped, to ensure the return of Mrs Head. 'Which hospital was it?'

Charlotte woke up early. She felt something in her stomach. But it wasn't the usual gnawing hunger. It was something different. She swung her legs out of bed and sat on the edge of the mattress inspecting the socks on her feet. Poor circulation made her feet cold.

There it was again! A faint . . . she couldn't put her finger on it. She stood slowly, and after stretching, padded to the window. Battersea Park was filled with flowers. She'd never noticed such colours before. An ice-cream van floated past, on its way, no doubt, to a prime site filled with high-spirited children proffering coins and expectant faces. Dogs greeted each other warmly and intimately with their owners in tow; while helmeted youths sailed nonchalantly by on boards and skates. Today was going to be a beautiful day, she could feel it in her . . . Suddenly Charlotte was filled with the joyful sensation of fluttery butterfly wings dancing in her belly.

She left the spare room and bounced downstairs into the kitchen where the groceries procured for her mother from the late-night store lay on the table. There was fruit, eggs, butter and a sealed polythene bag of bakery goods. The smell of mouth-watering ripe plums filled the room with a delicious fragrance of meadows and wild honeysuckle. For the first time in what seemed like an eternity, Charlotte felt a sense of hope and optimism. Only she could undo her bindings. She threw open the windows and sucked in great lungfuls of air. There was a whole world out there and it was hers too. Hope made her feel hungry for life. And life was the sweetest-tasting experience of all. As Charlotte sank her teeth into a buttery croissant, flakes of pastry melted in her mouth like laughter.

At the table, after a second and equally delicious jam-filled doughy delight, and as the watery sun shone through the window, Charlotte hatched a plan. She would meet her father for lunch and lay it on the line. 'Yes,' said Charlotte to her reflection in the cooker, 'I'm going to take responsibility for my life, and others will have to follow suit.' It sure felt good. She would take her mother breakfast and slip away after that.

'Love changes,' explained her father as, surrounded by leafy plants and well-dressed diners, they sipped iced tea in a glass conservatory. He dabbed a crumb from his mouth with a starched linen napkin. They had shared a special conversation about life, exchanging for the first time intimate details about themselves. Now James Davis would attempt to be honest with his daughter. 'I loved your mother for the first fifteen years of our marriage,' he said quietly. 'Being a father was the best thing that ever happened to me and I'll always be grateful to Jen ... your mother ... for so much.' James Davis struggled with what he was about to say. 'For the last fifteen years, we haven't really had any kind of marriage. Jennifer has been so ... angry with me. I don't know why. Maybe it was something I did. God knows I'm not perfect. But ...'

A waiter who had hovered nearby for the last half-hour removed their plates and topped up glasses of iced water. ''Scuse me, miss, are you the lady in the fashion campaign?'

'I am,' replied Charlotte gracefully.

'Well, it's nice to meet you. Is everything all right? Would you like anything else?'

'Not for me,' answered Charlotte. 'Dad, what about you?'

'I'll have an espresso and the bill,' instructed James Davis. He turned to Charlotte and, smiling paternally, said, 'Are you sure you don't fancy a little chocolate torte? It's really very nice here.' He patted his stomach. 'I've got to be careful, but you don't look like you need to worry.'

'OK then,' laughed Charlotte, 'chocolate torte it is.' Her father smiled as his daughter licked her lips in playful anticipation.

'When I saw you,' he said carefully, 'I was worried. You look too thin, Charlotte. I know I wasn't the best father ... but I'm here now ... If you want to talk about it.'

She plucked up courage to ask the question that had been bothering her. 'Mum says you're seeing someone else. Is she right?'

'Yes, Charlotte, she is,' confessed her father. 'I'm sorry. I couldn't make the marriage last on my own.'

'Mum says you stopped loving her a long time ago and that you want someone younger.'

James Davis leaned across the table and gazed into his daughter's green eyes. 'I never stopped loving her,' he said with disarming sincerity. 'But it's very hard to love someone who doesn't love herself. When she saw you growing into the beautiful woman that you are now, she was proud, but it hurt her too. She saw her own allure slipping away. It became the only thing we seemed to discuss. I tried to encourage her to develop interests and make friends, but she wouldn't bring other women into the house for fear that I might find them more pleasing than her. We had so many arguments because she felt I couldn't possibly find her attractive any longer. And the truth is, I didn't.' He swept his hair out of his face. 'It had nothing to do with how much, or little, she spent on cosmetics, liposuction, and designer labels. Although I'm not saying that I'm not attracted to beauty, but . . . well, Jen seemed to . . . to lose the appetite for living itself.'

Her father sat back in his chair. His face was serious. 'The person I have begun to spend time with is two years older than Jen. She has grey hair and two grown-up children of her own. She doesn't worry about what she looks like because she doesn't have time. That's the part,' he said with simple conviction, 'I like about her most.'

'I'll have him for everything he's got,' snarled Jennifer Davis.

'He said you could have it all,' reported Charlotte.

'Oh, did he?' flashed the now unattached woman as she paced the bleached floorboards. 'Well, I want none of it.

If he thinks he can throw money at it then he's got another think coming. I'm not giving him a divorce.'

'I don't think he wants one.'

'Then what the hell does he want?' demanded her mother. 'And what is he doing with an old witch who can't even put a rinse through her hair?' In her book, a much bigger crime had been perpetrated than mere adultery with a younger woman. Here was a member of the female race who had let herself go, and her husband wanted an association! 'I bet she doesn't bleach her top lip,' snorted Jennifer Davis. 'Worse still, she's probably got a moustache and hairs growing out of warts. She won't even know what a pair of tweezers looks like! I don't know why I bothered all these years,' she said, shaking her head, 'I really don't.'

'He says he wants you to be happy too,' reported Charlotte.

'Happy!' shrieked Jennifer Davis incredulously. 'Happy is not something that happens to women my age. Where,' she demanded, hands on hips and eyes ablaze, 'am I going to find happiness at this hour?'

'You find it inside *yourself*,' said Charlotte, replying as much for her own benefit as her mother's. 'You find it inside yourself,' she repeated slowly.

The hospital was clean, bright and enormous. Dozens of people, some in wheelchairs, others leaning on crutches or sticks, criss-crossed in front of Elle as she headed for the information desk.

'New admissions. Emergency, was it?' asked the kindly official. 'Second floor. Yes, madam?' He beamed, welcoming the next customer. 'Proctology department, you say?'

Elle headed for the lift. Hospitals made her feel a bit queasy at the best of times. So far, touch wood, she had managed to avoid them. And the uniforms were such an eyesore. The starched cotton A-line shifts looked neither comfortable nor practical. Trousers and tunics would be far better suited to leaning over beds and lifting patients. Elle was reminded of an incident years ago in Milan when she had been stuck in a lift with a well-known male fashion editor. For two hours he had moaned and groaned. 'I can't breathe,' was all he could say over and over, flapping his hands. 'I can't breathe, I can't breathe.' The fire brigade eventually arrived and forced a comforting shaft of light and air between the metal doors. While others, anticipating freedom, stood up and brushed themselves down, an assistant excitedly relayed details of their rescuers' vital statistics and physical attributes to his superior. Close to expiration, a little voice in the corner resumed command: 'I can't hold on much longer,' he snapped, 'just tell me, what are they wearing?'

'Take your time, dear,' said a grey-haired daughter to her elderly mother as they shuffled forward. Elle held the doors open. 'Now, Mum,' fussed the younger women, herself a pensioner of some years, 'don't go getting yourself all upset. Doctor Carver said there was nothing to worry about.'

The doors slid open and Elle slipped out. Would anyone fret over her in thirty years' time? Would her daughter even want to make contact? Becks seemed to have some answers, but perhaps it was too late. Elle shuddered at the thought of the lonely model making a decision to take her own life; she resolved to give her all the help she needed to return to health. There could never be a good reason for anyone to sacrifice themselves to a poisonous needle in the dead of night.

She spotted Becks asleep in a bed by the window.

'Are you family?' asked an official, eyeing her floral gift with suspicion. The NHS was stretched to the limit dealing with genuinely needy cases, but self-inflicted harm with drugs . . . well, that was plain attention-seeking. Now she'd have to look for a vase. 'Only family allowed, I'm afraid.'

'I'm not family, but please . . .'

'It's all right,' said a voice with a West Country burr. The speaker walked into view. 'I know this person.'

Elle turned to see a woman who looked to be about forty. She wore a mask of struggle etched across her face. Elle decided she was probably younger. The jeans and sweatshirt she wore had lost colour through repeated machine washing. They were almost obsessively pressed. Small gold earrings and a cross and chain finished the look.

'You must be Elle Cartwrite. I'm Patricia Cotton . . .' She smiled politely. 'Rebecca's mum. She talked a lot about you the last time she visited me. Said you had given her a big break. She was so excited.'

'What happened?' asked Elle as they walked towards the bed.

'She's sleeping now,' said her mother as she stroked Becks' forehead, her fingertips brushing the faint scar she had inflicted in a drunken accident when Becks was a child. She was quiet for a moment before continuing: 'They think she overdosed accidentally . . . Heroin.'

'How did they find her in the middle of the night?' quizzed Elle.

'There was someone in the flat with her who called an ambulance and told the medics what she had taken, but he's disappeared. Do you know who it might have been?'

Patricia's eyes blurred with tears. 'I'd like to thank him for saving her life. Her breathing was very shallow when they got to her. He must have known she was close . . .'

'Will she be all right? I mean . . .' Elle felt somehow responsible; her letter, delivered in anger a few hours before, could not have helped things at all.

'There's no brain damage,' replied the mother quietly. She shook her head. 'It's taken this . . . for me to finally wake up to being a mother.' She looked at Elle. 'I wasn't a very good one, you see.'

'Don't be so hard on yourself,' soothed Elle. 'It's very easy to look at other people and think that they are doing it all so much better.'

'I was never there for her,' continued Patricia. 'When she ran away, for months I didn't even know where she had gone. It was only your poster . . . I went into the city one day – it's got a big shopping centre – and there was my Rebecca smiling at me. She looked so happy, so lovely. Anyway, I took a photograph of it and sent it to a London modelling agency. One of the bookers there was very sweet; she tracked Rebecca's agency down.' Patricia Cotton smiled. 'You got us back together again. If it weren't for your poster, I would never have been able to find her.'

Elle enjoyed a small moment of pleasure. Reunion between this mother and daughter might be the nearest she would get.

'It hurts to think that she didn't want anything to do with me,' continued Patricia, 'but I've got to face up to the fact that I wasn't worth knowing back then.' She glanced at Elle. 'I spent all of her childhood with a bottle in my hand. She's not had much from me, but I want to make it up to her now.'

'Are you staying with relatives?' asked Elle.

'No – I haven't got any. I'm in a bed and breakfast in Paddington. It's where I got off the train.'

'Would you consider staying with me? I'm nearer to the hospital ... I have plenty of room, and I'd like to do something to make your stay more comfortable.'

'I've paid two nights in advance,' said Patricia, as if contracted to stay put. 'But I must admit, it's not very homely there. If you're sure I wouldn't be any trouble ... I haven't got much stuff.' She smiled and reached to pat her daughter's hand. Rebecca Cotton slept on with cherubic serenity. 'It would be nice to have some company after today. I'll come back later this evening and help her home.'

There were few nursing staff around. Becks would be encouraged to leave as soon as possible. 'I'll be back this evening,' she said to a passing uniform before leaving.

'Do you have children?' asked Patricia as they travelled westwards in a taxi to retrieve her overnight luggage. The sun was slowly sinking behind the concrete hills ahead.

'Yes, I do,' confessed Elle. 'A daughter. But, like you, I wasn't around when she was growing up.'

'I expect you see more of her now, though?' said Patricia. She sat neatly with her hands folded in her lap.

'No, I lost touch with her a long time ago. But I think about her often.'

'I'm sure you'll find each other again – that is, if you both want to.' Patricia's expression was warm and encouraging.

'I do,' said Elle thoughtfully, 'but I don't know if she ...' Elle felt a small stinging at the back of her eyes. 'I worry that I might be too late. I mean, it's been so long since I ...'

'It's never too late,' opined her travelling companion. 'I know.'

'I'd like to do an exposé,' said Belle as she stood in her editor's office. Henrietta Hargrieves was the fashion world's equivalent of a pedigree lurcher. All legs and concave stomach.

'Let's get on board with this Global Defence thing,' enthused Belle. 'Think of the controversy – the fashion industry does have some rather intriguing skeletons in the closet . . . It would be good for the paper.'

'And what did you have in mind?' quizzed Henrietta as she sucked on a pair of promotional Gianfranco Ferre sunglasses.

'Let's carry an interview with the leader of the group. He's English – and I know someone who has access to him.' Belle twinkled ever so slightly. This last bit was a slight exaggeration, but Belle was not to be deterred by a technicality.

'And why would we want to do that?' asked her superior reaching into her bag – a stunning panelled leather and tapestry affair – also a free gift, for her cigarettes.

'Because we are a competitive publication, and if we don't someone else will . . .'

'That is an excellent reason,' agreed Henrietta, 'but not enough of one to upset the entire fashion industry.'

'Who cares about upsetting them? We could lead the way with contentious issues. You know, shake things up a bit. After all, there is an underbelly to any industry.'

'There is also a considerable amount of kiss-arse to any industry,' reprimanded Henrietta. 'Mr Global Defence is probably some bearded vegetarian with a decidedly unsexy line in sound bites. He won't look good in a David Bailey portrait, no matter how much we restyle him, and he's never going to say anything that will appeal to our advertisers.'

'But what about our readers?' retorted Belle.

'I don't give a monkey's cuss about our readers!' said her editor indignantly. 'They'll read what we give them. A nice cosy designer profile with a special offer is all they're good for. I've got a whole series lined up to take us to Christmas. Designers love it and . . . well, didn't you notice what good seats we had at the shows?'

Belle had been about to protest and her face must have signalled attack. Henrietta nipped dissent in the bud.

'Advertising,' she corrected, 'is our goal, not cutting-edge editorial. If we don't get the revenue, we don't have a fashion supplement.' She lit a cocktail cigarette with an expensive and monogrammed lighter. Belle guessed it to be another gift. 'Sycophancy . . .' instructed Henrietta pausing for breath and an inhalation of nicotine, 'keeps the frock-makers sweet and the PRs happy. We get a chunk of advertising budget, plenty of free gifts and samples to boot, *and*' – she nodded towards the ceiling – 'it keeps the suits upstairs quiet. And at the end of the day, as long as I can avoid a rollicking from some badly dressed publisher in a Moss Bros two-piece, things are tickety-boo. I'm surprised at you, Belle,' she said stiffly. 'I had you down for a smart cookie. We all know it's a sham. But fashion editors have to prioritize toadying before anything else. I didn't get where I am today by slagging off my best advertiser's catwalk collections. So I'm sure you can understand why I'm not particularly keen on allowing an earnest hippie in Jesus sandals the chance to criticize production procedures. Now then, that's given me an idea . . .' She drew her chair up to the desk.

'I can guess,' said Belle. ' "How to look good in Green!" We ring round the designers and see who works in recycled yarn, uses both sides of their Xerox paper, and gets two cups of tea out of one tea bag.'

'Excellent suggestion, but no,' corrected Henrietta. 'I want you to ring a few PRs and tell them we need cocktail attire ASAP for a shoot we're doing over the weekend. And I'd like a good choice of designers.'

'But, Henrietta,' wailed Belle, 'I've already made plans for Saturday.' If credible journalism required spontaneous donation of weekends at the drop of a Philip Treacy hat, then philanthropy sucked. 'Anyway, how does a little black dress figure in the grand scheme of environmental awareness?'

'It doesn't,' stated Henrietta Hargrieves as she got up to tweak at her hair in the mirror specially positioned by the window. 'I've got some dreary perfume launch to attend tonight and nothing to wear.'

'If there are other women out there like me, how will I know them?' enquired Charlotte, peering into the glass oracle and waiting for an answer.

The reflection tutted. 'You won't. Each has her own way of *fitting* in. Women are brought up to edit their needs, they become so very good at shrinking their lives to *fit* the world . . . you know, tailoring their bodies to *fit* the clothes.'

'But that's about practicality,' protested Charlotte.

'Yes, trimming oneself down . . . It's the way we've been

taught to behave for thousands of years. We must always reduce our expectations, mustn't we? Reduce our lives. Reduce our bodies. But what is so wrong with passion, expansion and voracion? What is so very wrong with living as large a life as possible? Tell me that if you can. Did you know that millions of women were burned as witches all over Europe? Why? Because they had *big* ideas, because they were *powerful* women. Female scholars were imprisoned and tortured because they had *large* intellects and *big* dreams.'

It was all falling into place for Charlotte. Still today, a medieval witch-hunt was in progress and women were punished for daring to grow too big and strong. First there was the fashion industry which outlawed all who did not fit an antiquated sizing system and catered for them so scantly – even going so far as to publicly humiliate its own stars for adding an inch or two to their own gaunt frames. Then there was the diet industry: a multi-million pound empire founded on the anxieties of ordinary consumers. Big strong women were repeatedly told they were over-weight by an industry that had a vested interest in securing new custom.

The voice continued, 'Only the woman in the mirror can really know the truth. The woman in the mirror knows the real you. *You* are the woman in the mirror, Charlotte. You can be anything and everything.'

'Does everyone have someone like you? I mean –' Charlotte lowered her voice; her mother might return home at any minute – 'if there is a woman in the mirror for us all, then . . .'

'Expectations make a lot of noise,' explained the voice. 'Not just our own, but those of our parents and the people around us. The woman in the mirror can't always make herself heard. When she does get through, she is frequently discredited. We don't really value what the woman in the mirror has to say, do we, Charlotte?'

'But you talk so much sense,' protested Charlotte.

'I'm glad you can hear me,' smiled the beautiful brunette. 'I think that, now we understand each other, my job is done.'

The door downstairs opened and shut. Charlotte heard her mother walk past the stairway and into the kitchen. 'Did my mother ever see the woman in the mirror?' she asked swiftly, anticipating the impending departure of her glassy companion. 'Did she?'

'Your mother never looked,' replied the reflection.

'What do you mean?' whispered Charlotte; she could hear her mother busying herself at the sink. The kettle would no doubt be on and the coffee pot ready and waiting. 'My mother was always at the mirror. She had a lovely dressing table with a chair . . .'

'Charlotte,' trilled her mother up the stairs, 'fancy a coffee?'

Charlotte strained to catch the answer supplied by the mirror. The woman in the glass frame was beginning to look so very familiar.

'Your mother never looked *for* herself,' came the distant reply. The magic was wearing off. The woman in the mirror seemed to melt into fog, revealing a sight Charlotte had seen a thousand times before. Her words hung in the air as the green-eyed woman checked her reflection and turned to leave the room.

'Does your friend want a cup?' asked her mother, tea towel in hand. She was pleased to see her daughter, and had lots to report. As a result of a conversation they had had last night, Jennifer Davis had secured herself a small flat in London. Theatreland beckoned, and who knows what else.

'There's no one here, Mum,' explained Charlotte as she helped herself to a biscuit with her drink.

'Then who were you talking to?' enquired her mother, slightly bemused. 'I could hear you. There were two voices, I'm sure – unless, of course, I'm going mad.'

'I was talking to myself,' declared Charlotte, exhilarated. The simplicity of life today made her feel positively ravenous. There was a whole world out there for the taking and she could just eat it up if she so wished. 'I was talking to myself,' she said again, enjoying the satisfying vibration of her voice, full of hope and joy. 'You should try it some time.'

'Promise me you'll never do that again, Rebecca.' Patricia Cotton had her back to her daughter. 'I thought I'd lost you.' She turned to face her child. 'No mother should ever have to feel such emptiness. Lord knows, I deserved it though.'

Becks pulled herself up on her elbows. Her throat was dry and sore, the stomach pump – an unnecessary procedure but one that served as medically approved chastisement – had been roughly inserted and she still felt groggy. One nurse had acted as if she were a waste of time and money, and had spoken harshly when Becks called out for water. Had she just enjoyed the democratic apportionment of stretched services, or did street people with drug habits get treated even less sympathetically?

From her hospital bed, Becks could see a variety of horizontal bodies. Were they in for similar medical misdemeanours? she wondered. A large bunch of flowers, hand-tied and wrapped in green tissue paper, posed elegantly at the foot of the bed. 'You didn't, Mum,' she said hoarsely, slightly distracted by the foliage.

'No, they're from Elle Cartwrite,' replied her mother. 'She's told me everything, Rebecca. She feels very unhappy about the whole thing and hopes to talk when you are feeling better. I'm staying with her, you know. She's really very . . .'

Becks was not listening. What plan had that heinous old witch brewed now?

'Mum,' interrupted Becks, 'what exactly has she told you?' Did Patricia Cotton know that she was the daughter of that bitch? Surely not.

Patricia stroked her daughter's arm. 'We both think you got in with a bad crowd. I saw that women – Marcia – when I went to your flat to get your overnight things. She was posting a note through your letter box. She looks like trouble to me. When I told her what had happened, she wanted to come and visit you, but I said I didn't think you were ready . . .' She thought for a while. 'You're well out of it, Rebecca. I really think . . .'

'You don't know the first thing!' flashed Becks. 'For a start, Marcia is a trained librarian. She works in a women's bookshop and every weekend she does a stint at Shelter – you know, voluntary work. Marcia is my friend. And as for that *woman* – Elle Cartwrite is a . . .' Becks struggled to find the words.

'There's no need to be so protective, Rebecca,' said her mother gently. 'Addicts can hold down responsible jobs. I know, I've been talking to one of the staff.'

'No, Mum. You don't get it, do you?' Becks was actually laughing. 'Marcia doesn't use heroin. You think that just because of the way she looks . . .' She rolled her eyes. 'Mum, you can't write someone off for wearing beads in their hair.' Becks shook her head. What would her strait-laced mother make of Lal, who had collected several more piercings around his eyes and mouth since his first near brush with hep-B? 'Do you think I look like a heroin addict?' she challenged.

'No, of course not,' retorted Patricia.

'Well, I am one. And does Elle Cartwrite look like a vicious old cow? No? Well, she is one.'

'Rebecca,' calmed her mother, 'Elle told me that you and a friend tried to blackmail her. She didn't call the police, and I think that, at the very least . . . we owe her an apology. Now, I know that drug addicts will do anything to get the money for a . . . a fix,' Patricia Cotton had obviously received a crash course in street-speak.

Beck sneered. 'That's a lie. That's an outright lie. There, you see what I mean? She's an evil old bat. You've got to move out of there. She's turning you against me.'

'Rebecca, stay calm,' soothed her mother. She had been reading some leaflets and spoke with borrowed authority. 'This is to be expected, you know, and there are organiza-tions that can help you through this. They say there can be all sorts of complications during withdrawal. Each person handles it differently. That's why I want you to come home. You know, to remove all the . . .' Patricia thought for a minute. 'That's it, to remove the triggers – the people and places that remind you of heroin.'

'Mum, I was off it before,' protested Becks. 'This is a bloody nightmare.' Whatever had she seen in Elle Cartwrite?

'Elle also wants to ask you something about a woman called Elsa Crabtree. She said that your American friend told her he could help her find her daughter.'

'But Elle *is* Elsa Crabtree. She knows that. That's her real name, Mum.'

'Well, Elle wants to find out how much you know. She's trying to trace her daughter, you see.'

'But she knows,' said Becks, exasperated. 'She wrote it in the letter.'

'She told me about the letter. She feels dreadful about it, but your friend who went to the papers and tried to blackmail her . . .'

So Paul must have overheard her conversation with Tess. He said there had been no calls. It was becoming clearer by the nanosecond. What a lying toad he was – and after she'd put him up and everything! Becks was fuming. Patricia watched her own daughter's face and mistook her angry silence for obstinate refusal.

'Oh, Rebecca,' she pleaded, 'Elle's had a terrible time recently. Did you know that a group called Global Defence sneaked into her studio and tried to burn it down? We've had long chats; I've never met anyone like her. She's so exciting and . . . well, anyway, I'd really like to help her.' Patricia brightened. 'I told her that I was adopted, too. I've never told anyone that before.'

'So you don't know then?'

'What?' asked Patricia Cotton.

'Well, for a start, that *I* set fire to the studio.'

'Oh, Rebecca,' her mother looked around nervously, as if someone might act on such an outlandish admission and cart her daughter off. 'You don't know what you're saying, do you? You must feel very distressed. I'll call a doctor, dear.'

'Mum, it was me,' persisted Becks. 'I did it.' She sat upright. 'I was trying to tell Elle about you, and she wouldn't listen.'

'What were you trying to tell her about me?' quizzed Patricia Cotton, exasperated. 'Rebecca, I don't know what you mean.'

'So you really don't know? And Elle Cartwrite . . . she doesn't know either!' Becks almost laughed out loud at the simplicity of it. Neither party had any idea of their connection.

'What are you talking about, Rebecca? What is going on?'

'Hello, Patricia. Hello, Becks,' said Elle. Her hair was tied back and she wore a loose linen pantsuit. Without the harsh tailoring, Elle Cartwrite appeared so much more approachable. 'I got here as fast as I could,' she said slightly breathlessly. 'Is everything all right?'

'Yes,' said Becks, holding court from her bed, 'everything is all right.' She took a deep breath. Should she admit to destroying Elle's collection, or announce the good news first? An excitement gripped her by the throat. 'I've got something to tell you both,' she blurted, settling for the latter and looking from one to the other. They returned her gaze with expectant expressions.

'She's been like this since I phoned,' explained Patricia to her new friend. 'Says she's got something really important for us both.' She lowered her voice. 'I'm sorry for dragging you out like this, but she's been so excitable, like a dog with a bone.'

'Could someone pull the curtain round the bed?' instructed Becks mysteriously.

'I don't believe it,' exclaimed one voice. Onlookers, were there any actually awake in the ward, would have noticed a pastel-coloured drape circling two sets of feet. One set casually attired in trainers and jeans; the other more formally presented in cream trousers and Patrick Cox footwear. The legs stood facing each other. Neither set moved. There was stunned silence.

'Becks,' pleaded the voice, 'stop playing games.' And then, anger creeping in: 'Heroin is a dreadful thing. If it's money you're trying to . . . I'll not be part of this!'

'But, Mum,' replied the accused, 'I'm telling the truth – I've got proof. Ask her what her real name is . . . I found her for you. I found her in an old book of births registered in 1962.'

'I changed my name,' confirmed a third voice hesitantly, 'when I started up in business. I had to – Crabtree is hardly . . . but no one knows that, no one knows my name . . . But it's there on the birth certificate . . .' The legs headed for the bed, disappearing as the speaker took the weight off her feet. '. . . in 1962.'

'Are you all right, Elle?' asked the first voice. 'Would you like a glass of water?'

There was a pause. 'I didn't want to give her away.'

The remaining legs paced the small corridor of space between the bed and curtain; there was restless movement. 'Honestly, Becks, I don't know why you want to go getting everyone so upset like this. Haven't you done enough?' Patricia Cotton threw back the curtains. 'I always tidy when I'm under pressure,' she explained, looking at the visitor carefully and securing one length of fabric neatly to its post.

Elle nodded her head in agreement. 'So do I,' she said quietly. 'So do I.'

25

> 'since you are like no other being ever created since the beginning of time, you are incomparable.'
>
> **BRENDA UELAND**

*I*T would soon be Christmas. Good gracious, how time flew. Elle sifted through the things on her desk. She paused momentarily at a framed picture of Trish and Becks. She kept it close by at all times. Elle had been in shock for weeks after she learned the real identity of one of her house models, and Patricia had taken even longer to come round to the idea of Elle Cartwrite as family. They all had some adjusting to do. Elle found it hard to forgive herself for delivering her daughter into the hands of a – what was the word the counsellor had used? – 'dysfunctional family'. The midwife's words – 'decent couple, respected members of the parish' – reverberated in her head. The authorities had been seduced by appearances. Once again Elle considered the power of image. He may have seemed to be a 'God-fearing man', but he had committed child abuse. And his 'respectable' wife was, in private, nothing more than a hopeless old soak. The bitter irony of learning that, as a single mother, she would have made a better parent than her successors, would always haunt her on wet October nights.

But her first Christmas with her family – now that was an exciting thought. For years Elle had fantasized: log fires, sherry, dogs, carollers, children and loved ones to share the crisp December day. Each year she would accept the generosity of friends, sharing the turkey, their family and all the trimmings. This year she could do it herself. Trena and Rowena would be there and Maddy and her new husband. Elle enjoyed a deep and satisfying yawn as she leaned back in her chair and stretched. Only another week until the Christmas holidays and, with the office party tonight, there was so much to look forward to. The phone burst into life.

'Trena is on line three,' said Maddy with renewed efficiency.

Her right-hand woman was back on the case. The wedding had been a dream and Elle had cried heartily as she dispensed confetti petals and horseshoes over the happy couple.

'Thanks, Mad, put her on.' As the result of a timely deal with a Japanese company intent on capitalizing upon the Englishness of Esteem and producing it in quantity for their still buoyant domestic market, Esteem had relocated to new premises in Clerkenwell. There was now enough room for both Elle's lieutenants to luxuriate in their own offices.

'Thought you might like to have a look at the diffusion samples,' Trena said excitedly. 'Alicia has really pulled it out of the bag. We're going to do some shots in the New Year, so if there's anything you want to tweak . . .'

'Everything will look great, I know it,' said Elle with conviction. The diffusion range would be launched next season on the catwalk. It would be labelled 'Esteem too'. It was just a play on words: most designers titled their second collections numerically, but Esteem 2 had quickly been nicknamed Esteem too – and there it had stuck. Alongside this cheaper line was an accessories range produced in Italy, and Elle would shortly be discussing a new range of make-up with her inscrutable partners. 'Self-Esteem' was to be a brand-new concept in cosmetics manufacture and would be produced both sides of the Atlantic.

Elle had meant to retreat into cosy retirement, but long walks in the country ad infinitum weren't all they were cracked up to be. She couldn't stay away from the hustle and bustle of frocks. After all, it was what she knew and, hey, she didn't want to overdose on peace and quiet, did she?

'Trena,' said Elle mischievously, 'how about a little meeting before we party tonight?'

'Do you mean one that takes place in a wine bar and has absolutely no agenda at all?' replied Trena with roguish glee. 'Because if you do, we're all on.'

The Wharf Studios boasted large hangar-like spaces where heavyweight pop bands and musicians, Oscar-winning actors, distinguished writers, and just about every beautiful person in the land had been photographed at some time or another. Many had lent their portraits to decorate the concrete corridors. It was the consummate venue for parties and had seen hundreds in its time; the Esteem Christmas Party would be one more glitzy fashion do to add to an already impressive repertoire.

For Elle Cartwrite, it was a perfect way to create further interest in the new label. Paid for by her Japanese investors, the event would promote the forthcoming make-up range with samples of lotions and potions with names like Dream, Explore and Grow being given away in beautifully crafted ceramic vessels.

Elle surveyed the throbbing mass. A colourful assemblage of invitees made merry in all manner of unrestrained positions, while the paparazzi roamed in search of a little something for the Sunday supplements. The party was in full swing. Christmas parties were usually to be avoided at all costs, being full of people she didn't know or, worse still, didn't like, babbling incoherently about meaningless concerns. To Elle, events like these were the antithesis of festive entertainment. But tonight was different. Tonight was a celebration of Elle Cartwrite's good fortune. Those around her thought this applied to the business. But the joy she felt was anchored much closer to the heart.

The Esteem crew emerged, resplendent, for the festivities. Elle had rung the changes with an ice blue trouser suit. Colour suited her and she had virtually abandoned her preference for blacks and greys. Her life seemed so much brighter now with the addition of Trish and Becks.

Trena had also undergone a transformation from sporting femme in track livery to executive stunner. She still favoured the signature dark-rimmed glasses, but wore streamlined tailoring with Cuban-heeled boots. From these she received enough lift to promote her to eye-level with people over the age of twelve. Besides, it was no fun being the same size as her micro-colleagues from Japan. They could lay some claim to maturity in terms of marketing development and production growth, but enlightenment quotas remained low. She had lost count of the times one particular businessman had propositioned her in his pidgin English and then pretended not to understand her rebuttal. 'Fuck off!' was clear enough in any language, she had thought.

Alicia, clad in claret and gold, had hennaed her hands and forehead. She looked witchy and fecund – a Celtic diva; hers was a beauty that demanded respect and attention. She chatted happily with Maddy, the quintessential transatlantic sophisticate.

'Elle,' gushed a florid associate. He had the type of ungainly facial hair that looked like it might have been transplanted from his lower torso. 'So lovely to see you! Congratulations, my dear. You've done a splendid job and you must be very proud of Esteem.' He pulled Elle to him and prepared to plant a wiry kiss upon her cheek. Trena involuntarily shuddered.

'Melvin Drummond, how lovely to see you too,' said Elle, deftly turning her head further than was necessary to avoid the impending greeting. Melvin sucked up a mouthful of hair serum and Trena stifled a laugh. 'Have you met my team?'

The pubic pucker prepared for second helpings.

'Melvin Drummond, Managing Director of Fieldings,' he said expectantly, seizing on Trena with hands the size of spades.

'Trena Golding, not interested,' replied Trena as she drew back.

Mr Drummond was puzzled. It was as if he genuinely believed his industry credentials afforded him proprietorial intimacy. 'Ha-ha, an independent young lady,' he said stiffly. 'Of course, you nineties girls do things a little differently, don't you?' He pulled a monogrammed handkerchief from his pocket and dabbed at his mouth. 'I do apologize,' he blustered, 'in the olden days, a man could be permitted to bestow a small kiss upon a woman ... But we mustn't get nostalgic, must we?'

'In the olden days a man could birch his wife and children,' countered Trena with a mischievous smile. 'But we mustn't get nostalgic, must we?'

'Yes, quite,' nodded Melvin. Women like her were such hard work. Still there might be an opening with the curvy one. She'd be a little more accommodating, no doubt.

'If you'll excuse us, Mel,' said Elle excitedly – she had seen Trish in the corner, 'we're going to join my daughter.'

'But, my dear,' exclaimed Melvin, watching Alicia sidestep him and move off. 'I haven't been properly introduced.'

'Elle, darling!' called Kevin, intercepting the sisterhood and kissing each member flamboyantly. Where women were concerned, gay men could usually ignore the rules aimed at their predatory hetero brothers. 'Come and join us here!' He hooked a glass of something from a passing tray and thrust it upon his hostess. 'Great party,' he declared, draining his own glass and exchanging it for another whilst handing round the drinks. 'You must be delighted with the success of Esteem. I meeeann, who could have known?'

Kevin's boyfriend Nathan raised his glass.

'Ah, yes. This is Nathan,' Kevin announced proudly, 'I've finally landed a giant.' Nathan was a six-foot blond with Californian colouring. He had seven inches over his partner – a measurement Kevin frequently boasted about once he had sunk a few tequilas.

'Glad to meet you, Ms Cartwrite,' said Nathan, swiftly eradicating any notions of Venice Beach origins with a thick Birmingham accent. 'This is a luverlay do.'

'Nathan has got three sisters,' explained Kevin, 'and when they heard that he was going to meet you, they were tickled pink, weren't they?'

'They were,' confirmed Nathan smiling. 'I've never met a fashion designer before.'

'Well, thank you,' said Elle gracefully. 'As you can see, we don't look very different from ordinary humans.'

'Nathan, *really*,' said Kevin. 'Honestly, what's he like?'

'Well,' said Nathan indignantly, 'you're like royalty. You know about good taste and you always look amazing. You're on the telly. I saw you on the news when they bombed your show – everyone did. You're a fighting woman, Ms Cartwrite.'

'All women are fighters,' said Elle with a wink. 'Now, will you excuse me? There's someone I want to see.'

'Treeny, darling,' cooed Kevin as Elle squeezed past. 'Look at you!' He surveyed her approvingly. 'You look fantastic, are you in love?'

'Yes,' laughed Trena, stopping to chat, 'but you've met Rowena loads of times.'

'Well, I was thinking it had to be someone new by the looks of you. You look gorgeous, pet. Which is more than I can say for some of these old bags. Look at *it* –' Kevin pointed to a woman encased in a thin layer of organza pleating. She was as gaunt as a gatepost and hunched over a glass of Kir Royale like a vampire supping bloody nourishment from a Victorian goblet. Her make-up looked as though it had been tattooed across her eyelids, and her black hair was coiled round her crown with cardboard rigidity. 'Hundreds of pounds' worth of designer label,' he said dismissively, 'and it still looks like it's been to a car boot sale! And see her over there –' Kevin singled out another miscreant, this time a girlish woman practically drowning beneath a loud psychedelic print that obliterated her body. 'You'll have to turn your dress down, pet!' he yelled above the music. The chance to perform was always too much to resist. 'I can't hear a word you're saying.'

'Kevin, you are wicked,' laughed Trena. 'Leave the guests alone. Or at least pick on your own kind. Men aren't exempt from making fashion *faux pas,* you know.'

'They're begging for it,' he laughed, unashamed. 'Now, back to me. Yes, I am deliriously happy and, yes, we're already picking out curtains together, so I know it's the real thing.'

'Charlotte, you look fantastic!' exclaimed Guy. 'It's so lovely to see you again. Did you get my postcards? I stayed longer than I said because I got such a great response to my work.' He blushed slightly. 'Well, what I mean is, I would have liked to come back sooner because I wanted to see more of you.'

Charlotte smiled. Guy had been away for three months and she had missed him, too. But she would not have chosen his company, for she had fallen in love and needed to spend her every waking minute with the most important person in her life . . . herself. Now that she loved and cared for herself, she could begin to get to know and care for another. She had regained the weight she had lost, and more. Her hair, washed and loose, had separated into twists, even haphazard curls. Her cheeks were round and pink. Her neck and shoulders strong and full.

'You look fantastic, you know,' whispered Guy, carefully watching her reaction.

'Thank you,' said Charlotte gracefully. A few months ago she would have found any kind of compliment hard to take, especially one that had been directed at a fuller waistline. 'I've been on a journey, too, while you've been away. I've travelled through history and time and learned so much about myself. I've found answers to questions I never knew I needed to ask.'

'Do you still model?' asked Guy as he dug his hand in his pocket.

'Of sorts,' replied Charlotte cryptically. 'I like to think of myself as a role model now. You see, I've been working with the borough education department. I've begun to talk in schools about my experiences in the fashion industry, and about what I've learned. I know I was an influence, I know I promoted some sort of fantasy lifestyle that doesn't exist, and I want to make amends. I'm overcoming an eating disorder, and I know that there are many others like me; plenty get by on starvation rations and impoverished dreams, maybe without even realizing that they have been conditioned from birth to exist in this shrink-to-fit culture. If I can get into the hearts and minds of teenagers . . .' Charlotte stopped, her eyes shining, her passion inflamed. 'I want every small girl, every confused adolescent, every woman, to know that it's her right to be big and strong.' She stopped herself deliberately. 'Sorry, Guy, I've become a bit of a campaign bore, haven't I?' She smiled. 'I've also been approached by a publishing house to tell all in a book, and I've had an idea accepted by a television company. They're going to make a documentary on models with

393

eating disorders.' In a voice infused with delicious irony, Charlotte added, 'It's really become quite fashionable now.'

'I found this for you while I was away,' said Guy tenderly. He pulled his balled hand from his pocket and opened it to reveal a heart-shaped stone. It was perfectly symmetrical. 'It reminded me of you as soon as I saw it because you have a beautiful heart too.' He laughed self-consciously. 'Are you horrified? Am I too awful to go out with?'

Charlotte lingered over Guy's last question. Her suitor shrugged his shoulders and waited expectantly. Here was a person who – once upon a time, not so long ago – would have failed meet her standards, based on a purely superficial physical checklist. A pleasing physique had been her main ingredient for successful coupledom, along with obvious self-confidence and sophistication. Usually at the expense of humility, spontaneity, and sensitivity. Guy stood smiling.

'I would love see more of you, Guy,' said Charlotte sincerely, 'and thankfully there's *more* of me to see!' She smiled and laughed.

'Tess, how are you doing?' yelped Becks. 'I'm so pleased to see you. Have you been away?'

Tess had been meaning to let Becks know how mad she was about the whole tabloid mess and her own undeserved brush with the law. It had just about finished her career in the fashion industry. It was bad enough being known as the lippy fat Black woman with a chip on her shoulder, but now industry people had a real excuse not to employ her: she was a suspected criminal and, after all, there was no smoke without fire, was there? But Tess knew how close Becks had come to dying back there, and in this superficial world of perfumed farts and white mock-croc slingbacks teamed with matching clutch bags, some things were more important. So she could afford a little generosity. Besides, she had begun work as a press officer for an up-and-coming hairdresser. It was an unexpected change of direction but, with all her contacts in the fashion industry, it seemed destined to be a success.

'Becks,' she said, hugging her friend with warm sincerity, 'I'm so glad it all worked out for you.'

'I heard about Simon and the police . . . I'm sorry that I made life even more complicated for you. I was a walking disaster and –' Becks looked over her shoulder to where Elle stood, deep in conversation with a group of Japanese businessmen – 'I just about ruined it for so many people.'

'Yeah – how goes it with the new grandmother?' asked Tess with a devilish smile. 'Does she lock you in your room after choir practice, or rap your hands with a wooden spoon if you eat with your mouth open?' Elle Cartwrite had always struck her as a school governess in the wrong line of business.

'No!' Becks was laughing but there was concern in her eyes. 'I can't pretend that there isn't stuff to sort out. Coming off heroin is so much harder than I thought it would be. What with one-to-one counselling sessions, family counselling and learning to live as an ex-addict, I've no time for anything else. And I still have nightmares about some of the things I let myself in for.' Becks had spent some of the day with her therapist reliving the night Dave had tried to rape her. The suppressed memories had come flooding back, triggered by the sight of his face on a billboard advertising the release of a 'hits of the eighties' collection. Revenge could not be hers, for no official would ever believe the accusations of an ex-heroin addict. Becks wondered how many rapes were committed by men who believed they were entitled to it all and women who had been conditioned to think they deserved so very little. 'Ah, well,' she said, brightening, 'I've got myself a place at college for next September. And I'm going to try and rebuild my modelling career . . . if I can . . . I'm afraid clients might be put off by my "colourful past". They're really very conventional in this line of business, aren't they?' She bit her lip and shrugged her shoulders. 'C'est la vie.'

'Ah, Ray,' beamed Tess as that gorgeous up-and-coming hairdresser joined them. 'You know Becks, don't you?' Ray handed Tess a fruit drink and kissed her lovingly on the cheek.

'Hi, Becks,' he said warmly and gave her a hug before excusing himself. 'Tess, I'm just going to bond with my man Marcus over there and talk about hairdressing innovations – you know the thing.' He smiled and was gone.

'Well, look at you!' said Becks happily. 'Things have really turned out well.'

'Yeah,' agreed Tess. Since she and Ray had begun a relationship, life had been good. Here was someone who gave her the security and freedom to risk rejection without fear. 'I'm thinking of trying to trace my dad,' she ventured.

'Fantastic,' gushed Becks. Hers was not a world where contemplation compromised spontaneity. 'That's a brilliant idea. How will you start?'

'I'll begin with the last address my mum had. He was living somewhere in Trinidad – he had an aunt out there. I'm thinking of spending a month or two in the Caribbean.' She had so many questions to ask her father, if she ever found him, and so little to ask of him. Perhaps, with Ray's support, this would put an end to a part of her life spent permanently in search of acceptance. Being a larger woman in a world full of skinnies, being Black in an industry that prioritized White ... Tess had come to terms with such superficialities long ago, and she was happy with who she was, but being a daughter in search of a father's love ... a corner of her had always yearned for paternal acceptance. Now she was ready to seek out the source of her childhood longing and strong enough to survive a rebuff. As if in silent communication from the other side of the room, Ray turned from his conversation and locked eyes with his beautiful Ebony Woman. He placed his right hand on his heart, in a gesture that had come to speak much more than words to Tess, and smiled.

'You two are so lovely together,' cooed Becks as she turned to kiss her friend. 'I'm gonna look for my mum, she'll be hiding in a corner somewhere nursing a lemonade. Good luck finding your dad. I'll see ya.'

Patricia Cotton stood rooted to the spot. She had found herself an alcove where the relentless techno din could not pierce her eardrums and, at last, able to converse without shouting her head off, she had begun to relax. It was like being in some surreal theme park.

'Becks,' she squealed, 'that woman with the ring through her nose has *yellow* eyes!'

'They're coloured contact lenses, Mum.'

'And what has that boy done to his mouth?'

Becks turned to witness the now de rigueur metallic grimace of a youth with a complete set of gold dentures. 'It's just gold teeth,' she said nonchalantly. 'Dentists do that now.'

'Yes, but the results are horrid,' Patricia sniffed.

'It's all the rage, Mum.'

'These people are not quite right in the head,' announced her mother. Fashion for her was a smart pair of shoes and a matching handbag bought from the department store when the old ones wore out. Admittedly, she looked more up to date now than she had done for years. A gift from Elle of a trouser suit took pride of place in her wardrobe. She was wearing it tonight, teamed with a jersey T-shirt, and looked decidedly youthful. 'I'm not staying long – I told Elle I'd just pop in. This might be her world and yours, but it's not mine.'

'Mum,' said Becks defensively, 'look around – they aren't all degenerate drug addicts.'

Two women swept by and planted themselves inches away from Becks and her mother. Clearly theirs was the only site for tranquil repose. One, bedecked in expensive tailoring, lifted a perfectly manicured hand to her hair and fished for her sunglasses, perched on top of her head. Oblivious to her audience, she crowed, 'He hates women anyway. I really don't know why I stay.'

'Because he pays you well and because you like being his PR,' replied the other. She too appeared to enjoy the attention of a manicurist and top hairdresser. Like matching book ends they posed stiffly; there were photographers about and each wanted her best side documented for the *Tatler* diary.

'Well, it's not as easy as that,' retorted the other. 'Do you know, last season I had to make do with only six suits. The rest I had to buy at cost.' She raised her eyebrows; a dreadful infringement of her sartorial privileges had clearly been committed. 'And every time I set up a good piece of press, he upsets the interviewer or, worse still, locks himself in a cupboard and refuses to come out until they've gone. Honestly,' she rolled her eyes, 'I've had to pay a fortune in florist's bills just to keep them from tearing him to pieces. And last week I found him weeping – *weeping*,' she emphasized the word with ridiculous Swiss finishing-school enunciation.

'What did you do?' asked her friend horrified. The two of them were like Tweedledum and Tweedledee.

'I told him to pull himself together, of course. "They all hate me," he said. "They rubbish everything I do, so what's the point?" I was sorely tempted to tell him: "Stop designing for your queenie friends and start thinking about what real women want." That's what I should have said. I tell you,' she looked around and lowered her voice, 'he's going to have a nervous breakdown any day now . . .'

'Did you hear about the new bra girl?' said the other. 'You know, the one that's taking over from Eva . . .'

'No,' replied her friend. 'Oh, look out, here comes a camera. I'm wearing one of Tarquin's designs tonight, I promised him I'd get it in somewhere.' Both women self-consciously arched their backs and puffed out their bosoms. The photographer obliged with a single shot and moved on.

Book end number two resumed her report. 'Anyway,' she sniffed, 'I couldn't believe it. She's Czech and a six-foot blonde, of course. Legs over four feet long – and she's a qualified doctor, able to speak five languages.'

'No!' said book end number one.

'And she has perfect breasts . . . how dare she!'

The two of them contemplated their world and sipped

with evident dissatisfaction from fluted glasses. Another photographer would be along soon, no doubt.

'These people are all mad,' declared Patricia under her breath. A young woman, her face a shade of verdigris, cantered past in nine-inch platforms in a race to reach the ladies toilet. 'Thank God they aren't running the country.' Clutching her bag tightly to her body as if the route might be strewn with muggers and pickpockets, she set off for the toilet herself. It was another of the rituals Patricia Cotton performed when feeling threatened or anxious.

Becks decided to bide her time, knowing her mother would be in there for ages. But Elle spotted her standing alone and called her over. She was beaming from one side of her face to the other. Maddy and Tom, linked arm in arm, looked equally delighted.

Elle spoke loudly to prevent the music from drowning out her news. 'I wanted you to be the next to know, since you're my first grandchild.'

'What?' said Becks.

Elle could hardly contain herself. 'I'm going to be a grandmother again. Maddy is expecting a baby – isn't it marvellous?' She clapped her hands and watched for Becks' reaction.

Becks looked at Tom and Maddy, so blissfully happy. It was hard to know what to feel. From believing she was alone in the world, Becks had acquired a family. The music was booming and, around her, a mass of gyrating bodies celebrated the impending Christmas holidays. This was her world now. Like a carnival in full swing, brightly coloured costumes blended with grey suits. And amidst this festival atmosphere was her family – not just her mum and grandmother, but her spiritual family too. Over-sensitive and out to lunch some of them may well have been, but it was the world she knew and belonged to.

'Are you happy?' asked Elle hopefully.

'Yes,' said Becks, and she knew she was. In a far corner a boy with a girl's face – or was it a girl with boyish hips? – had climbed on to a table and was swinging her hips to the beat. Tess and Ray, oblivious to all but each other, slow-danced nearby. Charlotte, deep in animated conversation, threw back her head and laughed. Even Patricia, still hugging her bag, now seemed to be enjoying a temporary camaraderie with a handsome man in a tight Lycra bodysuit.

'Congratulations, Maddy!' Becks kissed the expectant mother. 'Congratulations, Tom,' she bellowed over the music. 'I am very happy for you both, and I'm . . .' she hesitated '. . . I'm very happy for me. I'm lucky to have such a wonderful –' she broke off, having spied her mother prancing round her handbag with gay abandon. Patricia Cotton's dancing partner was vogueing with professional flair, and the two of them consummated a spectacle of outlandish eccentricity. 'Wow!' gasped Becks, distracted from the end of her sentence. 'Way to go, Mum.'

'If any one can pull it off, you can,' said Maddy to her employer as Becks rushed off to witness the show at close quarters, leaving them to take up position in a nook well away from the blast of the amplifiers.

'Oh, Mad,' said Elle, 'I just hope I'm not underestimating the amount of emotional overtime I need to put in to make it up to Trish and Becks. They've had a rough old ride.'

'And you haven't?' replied Maddy. 'You've had the

toughest year of your life, and look at you – still standing, still smiling, and, hey, the business is more successful than you ever dreamed and you have a family to call your own.'

'It's true,' agreed Elle. The past year had been wilder than a bareback pony trek through the Andes. 'But I'm a hardy breed,' she said stoically.

'And they come from the same stock as you, remember?' Maddy laughed. 'That conversation we had in the restaurant a few months ago ... you talked about parents allowing their children to be the people they needed to be. But when you said it you had no idea you would be put to the test. You didn't have a daughter or a granddaughter then.' Maddy smiled. 'Now you do.' They turned to watch Becks, Trish, and the shiny-suited dance master shimmying the night away. Maddy patted her stomach. 'Well, I'm sure as hell gonna take your advice, and I hope you do too.'

'You're right,' conceded Elle. 'I can only support from the sidelines. I can't change anything that has already happened. We fashion types get an exaggerated sense of our own self-importance. We think fashion is all about reworking the past into a more performance-oriented future.' She looked to her trusty assistant and rolled her eyes. 'We allow ourselves to believe that we can mould the chaos of everyday confusion into an aesthetically acceptable, even aspirational, piece of life. Maybe that's why beauty is such a valuable commodity, because it masks the reality of the human condition.'

They strolled back to the heart of the revelry, and the heat and noise rushed to greet them.

'Real life is messy, isn't it?' declared Elle as she absorbed the atmosphere in a room full of exuberant partygoers. 'It's loud, unpredictable and totally uncontrollable.' She turned to Maddy for confirmation, but the PA had disappeared into a stream of dancers. Kevin, Nathan, Trena, Rowena, Alicia, were all grasping each other's waists in a conga line and laughing their heads off. Flailing limbs buffeted against moving bodies – it looked like a bumpy ride. Perhaps, thought Elle, everyone attracted to the business of human packaging was somehow trying to repress and regulate insecurities of their own. Fashion had become a force that vacuum-packed and gift-wrapped ordinary existence. It had its place. Well-made clothes were like fine wines to be enjoyed as part of an occasion. But they weren't the occasion. And beauty – a young woman, taut and wrinkle-free – was undeniably a lovely sight, but not the only lovely sight on offer.

Elle sighed. Fashion land and its gurus were an exotic lot – privileged, spoilt, and self-indulgent too. A few months ago she was one of them, caught up in the need to increase turnover, consolidate branding and expand the empire.

'Oh, stop it!' said Kevin as he rushed over to grab Esteem's creator by the shoulders and propel her towards the throbbing mass.

Elle was caught momentarily off-balance. Could he read her thoughts?

As if to confirm, her self-appointed dancing partner commanded: 'Whatever it is, it will wait.'

'Kevin,' protested Elle, but not forcefully enough, 'I'm not the dancing kind.'

'That was then and this is now,' he yelled as they joined the unchoreographed gathering. Maddy was already lodged at its epicentre. 'You designers are all the same,' he mouthed, activating his favourite dance steps and gesturing for her to do the same, 'faffing about with the past or worrying about the future.'

Elle was trapped, but life was like that. All anyone could do at a time like this was go with the flow, living the moment with energy and passion. And that's what she did. The beat shuddered insistently, encouraging all who partied to share its rhythmic intensity and move together, but as individuals. Observing the tempo, Elle began to wave her arms and twist her body. Happiness flowed through her limbs. Next to her Maddy swung her hips and hair, and Kevin twirled matador-style with Nathan. The DJ mixed from one anthem to another while across the floor dancers rejoiced in celebration of their own uniqueness and individuality.

'I am what I am,' cheered a euphoric songstress, and Elle lost herself in salute. Just as a dancer's response to any given tune would always be deliciously original, so the celebration of beauty or physical uniqueness should never be squeezed and hammered into one single ideal. People were people and beauty was all around. Elle Cartwrite lifted her eyes to take in the collective merriment and, accompanied by a synthesized piano, pirouetted unselfconsciously like a prima ballerina. It was about interpretation, after all.